Criminal Justice
Recent Scholarship

Edited by
Marilyn McShane and Frank P. Williams III

A Series from LFB Scholarly

Civil Gang Abatement
The Effectiveness and Implications of Policing by Injunction

Edward L. Allan

LFB Scholarly Publishing LLC
New York 2004

Library of Congress Cataloging-in-Publication Data

Allan, Edward L., 1948-
Civil gang abatement : the effectiveness and implications of policing by injunction / Edward L. Allan.
p. cm. -- (Criminal justice)
Includes bibliographical references and index.
ISBN 1-59332-041-8 (alk. paper)
1. Gangs--United States. 2. Organized crime--United States. 3. Injunctions--United States. 4. Nuisances--United States. I. Title. II. Series: Criminal justice (LFB Scholarly Publishing LLC)
KF9375.A94 2004
345.73'02--dc22

2004011081

ISBN 1-59332-041-8

Printed on acid-free 250-year-life paper.

Manufactured in the United States of America.

Table of Contents

Acknowledgements

This book would not be possible without the contributions of the county and city prosecutors who generously shared their experiences in seeking to acquire civil injunctions against gangs. Their dedication to the concept of civil gang abatement and their work to resurrect some of the most dangerous neighborhoods of California is to be commended.

I would also like to thank James R. Acker, Stephen L. Wasby, Robert E. Worden, Alissa P. Worden, and David E. Duffee of the State University of New York at Albany for their assistance in making this book possible.

Grant No. 2000-IJ-CX-0018, awarded by the National Institute of Justice, Office of Justice Programs, United States Department of Justice, supported the research for this book. Points of view in this document are those of the author and do not necessarily represent the official position or policies of the United States Department of Justice.

CHAPTER I

Introduction

There is something terribly wrong in Oakwood.

This charming enclave hard by the Pacific Ocean was once the spiritual embodiment of the California Dream...From the break of dawn when the first rays freckled the neighborhood with flickering promises of warmth and renewal until dusk when the glowing ember of the sun stole silently beneath the waves, sunshine blessed Oakwood with a spirit of fun and conviviality, beckoning people from their homes and into the streets, parks, playgrounds and beaches where they could bask in its radiant splendor and celebrate their lives and those of their children.

The sun no longer shines on Oakwood.

It has been blotted out by a poisonous mist of drugs and violence that has choked off the community spirit and left its residents nervous and fearful. Streets that once resonated with the laughter of children now stand vacant and eerily mute but for the occasional gunshot and the steady rumble of traffic cruising through to score rock cocaine. Neighbors who once strolled the streets now hole themselves up in their homes, afraid to venture out after dusk lest they stumble into a pack of drug dealers or fall victim to a drive-by shooting. Camaraderie and goodwill have been replaced by suspicion and fear. The Oakwood of friendly neighbors, safe streets, parks, and playgrounds – the very spirit of the community – has been dashed rudely asunder and left to shrivel and rot in the mid-day sun. The charm of their neighborhood is now but a faint memory, a memory that many still conjure as they stare silently at the melancholy walls of their barred homes. The good people of Oakwood rarely see the sun anymore, because they stay inside (*People v. Venice Shoreline Crips Gang*, Memorandum of Points and Authorities in Support of Motion for Preliminary Injunction 1999).

In this introduction to a *civil gang abatement* action against the Venice Shoreline Crips gang in the Oakwood section of Los Angeles, Deputy City Attorney Brooke White eloquently summarized the destructive effects of a gang on one neighborhood. Implicit in the summary is the essence of this innovative anti-gang strategy – helping communities regain control of gang-plagued neighborhoods, thus giving residents of those neighborhoods the opportunity to elevate their quality-of-life.

Civil gang abatement is an anti-gang strategy that combines the law of public nuisance and the civil remedy of the preventive injunction to provide law enforcement agencies with a tool to help reduce the destructive influence of gangs on vulnerable neighborhoods. Grounded in the concepts of "Broken Windows" and "community prosecution" (Wilson and Kelling 1982; American Prosecutors Research Institute 1995; Office of the District Attorney 1996; Los Angeles City Attorney Gang Prosecution Section 1995) and supported by contemporary gang theory (Spergel 1995; Bureau of Justice Assistance 1997, 1998), civil gang abatement emphasizes flexibility and community involvement in ameliorating the intimidating influence of gangs on a specified target area, giving the community an opportunity to regain control over its public and private space.

Civil gang abatement is part of the shifting focus by law enforcement agencies from a reactive to a proactive operating philosophy. This proactive philosophy is advocated by the problem-oriented perspective, which includes the innovative strategies of problem-oriented policing (Goldstein 1990) and community prosecution (American Prosecutors Research Institute 1995; Coles 1997). One result of this shift is an increasing reliance by law enforcement officials on civil remedies to address anti-social behavior when criminal remedies have proven ineffective. However, the accelerating use of civil remedies for law enforcement goals has clouded the theoretical distinction between the criminal and civil law (Wasby 1980; Cheh 1991). It has also raised concern about the increased ability of law enforcement officials to avoid the constitutional constraints of the criminal law while exposing individuals to greater restrictions on individual civil liberties than traditional law enforcement techniques (Steiker 1998).

This study explores the nature of the civil gang abatement phenomenon in the State of California to determine whether the use of injunctions to abate gang activity is a problem-oriented intervention addressing the causes of a pervasive public order problem. The intent of this study is not to delve deeply into the inner workings of any single gang injunction initiative, but to gain an understanding of the nature of the gang injunction phenomenon through the aggregate characteristics of all efforts to obtain gang injunctions. To gain this understanding, all identified gang injunction cases filed with the Superior Court of California from October 26, 1987 through June 30, 2001 are examined through an analysis of the court records and a survey of prosecutors involved in each effort to obtain a gang injunction.

California has the dubious distinction of being the most gang-plagued state in the United States of America, ranking first in the number of gangs (4,927) and gang members (254,618) reported by law enforcement agencies (Office of Juvenile Justice and Delinquency Prevention 1997). The California legislature has declared the existence of a statewide crisis caused by violent and criminally active street gangs (California Penal Code, section 186.21). Despite state and local initiatives to curb gang activity, gang membership has continued to grow (Marosi 1999). As a result, California has led the nation in the use of innovative strategies to combat gang activity, one of which is the gang injunction.

The gang injunction is a court order sought by a public prosecutor to prohibit a specific gang and/or named gang members and associates from conducting designated activities that contribute to a public nuisance in a geographically defined neighborhood claimed by the gang as its territory. Gang injunctions are distinguished from civil actions against gangs and gang members by private entities through private attorneys acting for their clients. For the purpose of this study, they are also distinguished from civil actions by public prosecutors to abate a specific activity throughout a jurisdiction or the public nuisance activities of gang members at a specific address (Castorena 1998b; Whitmer and Ancker 1996) or event[1]. The goal of the injunction is the elimination of a public nuisance within a specified target area comprised of the public and private property of at least one city block within a prosecutor's jurisdiction.

The gang injunction has been employed almost exclusively in California, presenting a unique opportunity to explore the characteristics of an emerging legal strategy without the potential encumbrances of varying court procedures across states. From October 1987 through June 2001, forty-two initiatives to obtain gang injunctions in eight California counties have been identified (see Appendix A). In contrast, communities in other states, including the cities of New York (Flynn 2000); Austin, Texas (Harmon 1998; Shah

1998, Tanamachi 1998); San Antonio, Texas (Hunger 1999); Cincinnati, Ohio (Goldberg 1996); Phoenix, Arizona (Villa 2000); Albuquerque, New Mexico (*Albuquerque Tribune* 1997); and Houston, Texas (Jacobius 1996), have conducted only a limited exploration of this anti-gang strategy.[2]

Although employed to address gang problems in California over the past fourteen years, civil gang abatement has received little attention from policy researchers. Research on the strategy has been limited to constitutional analyses in law review journals (Allen 1998; Boga 1994; Destro 1993 1994; Herd 1998; McClellan 1998; Stewart 1998; Werdegar 1999; Yeager 1998; Yoo 1994), evaluations of two selected injunctions (ACLU 1997; Maxson and Allen 1997), and a study of the short-term impact of thirteen injunctions in Los Angeles County on reported crime (Grogger 2000). There has been no research into whether the strategy is true to its theoretical foundation in the problem-oriented perspective (Goldstein 1990; Office of the District Attorney 1996; Los Angeles City Attorney Gang Prosecution Section 1995; Landsberg 2000) and the emerging field of community justice (Karp 1998). This study examines whether civil gang abatement fulfills the primary dimensions of the problem-oriented prosecution model, commonly known as "community prosecution" (American Prosecutors Research Institute 1995; Coles 1997).

This research is based on the theoretical distinction between problem-oriented interventions and suppressive social control. A problem-oriented intervention is flexible (Goldstein 1990), providing a custom response to the specific conditions and actors causing a persistent problem at a particular location within a jurisdiction. Although a problem-oriented response may include suppression, it is differentiated from suppressive social control, which is generally characterized by the stereotypical response of a criminal statute applying to all actors at all locations within a jurisdiction. Gang involvement in crime and disorder varies across both gangs and neighborhoods (Thrasher 1963; Thornberry and Burch 1997; Huff 1998; Esbensen and Huizinga 1996; Battin-Pearson, Thornberry, Hawkins, and Krohn 1998; Klein 1995, 1996). If civil gang abatement is a problem-oriented intervention, the situational characteristics and the provisions of requested relief will vary according to the specifics of the gang problem in a targeted location. Therefore, the first question addressed by this research is: *Do the requested relief and situational characteristics vary across injunction initiatives, and does this variation satisfy the dimension of flexibility implicit in the problem-oriented perspective?*

A problem-oriented intervention is also multilateral, involving a partnership between law enforcement agencies and various community entities in identifying a specific problem, analyzing the problem, and tailoring a custom response. In contrast, suppressive social control is characterized by a unilateral response by law enforcement with a limited, non-decision-making role for community entities. If civil gang abatement is a problem-oriented intervention, the injunction initiatives will involve collaborative partnerships between law enforcement agencies and community entities. Ideally, this partnership will include a decision-making role for community entities. Therefore, the second question examined by this research is: *Are injunction initiatives collaborative partnerships between law enforcement agencies and the community, with a decision-making role for community participants, or are the initiatives unilateral responses by law enforcement, with a limited role for the community?*

CONDITIONS IN A GANG INJUNCTION TARGET AREA

Before proceeding to delineate this study, let us set the stage with a report of the conditions in one gang injunction target area through the perceptions of individuals living and working in the neighborhood. The description is excerpted from civilian declarations provided to prosecutors to inform the judge about the conditions under which residents live in one neighborhood targeted for a gang injunction. Normally sealed by the court, the civilian declarations for one initiative were provided by a prosecutor after all identifying features were redacted. In this case, there were twelve civilian declarants[3] – three residents, an apartment manager, six owners of rental property, one local business owner, and one utility company supervisor – giving different perspectives on the gang problem in the neighborhood. For the security of the declarants, the identity of the gang and target area will remain anonymous.

The declarations provide a glimpse into the conditions in one gang injunction target area, using information that is generally not available to the public. The descriptions of the conditions in this case are not meant to be representative of all injunction target areas. They merely give a sense of some of the problems encountered in injunction target areas. Conditions in other target areas may be better or worse than those described in these declarations.

The residents all lived on a single street around which the gang activity was centered. The declarations gave a chilling account of the crime and intimidation caused by gang members in the neighborhood. There was constant drug dealing, discharging of firearms, and hanging out in large groups of up to thirty gang members. Street lights and lights on apartment buildings were shot out to keep the area dark to enable the street-sales of drugs. The gang had a schedule dictating who could sell drugs at various times on the street. The residents had become so used to gunshots that they no longer noticed them, although their children were constantly terrified. When the police were observed on the street, gang members hid in apartment buildings, sometimes demanding or forcing their way into apartments. Cars were constantly stripped and the empty frames pushed into the street. Because of the fear of stray bullets, children were generally kept inside and not allowed to go to the store or the playground. Children were robbed and had rocks thrown at them by younger gang members. Some residents paid for their children to be walked to school because of the violence and crime in the neighborhood.

Gang intimidation of the residents was immense. Residents were targeted for retaliation for calling the police or for refusing to open their doors to gang members fleeing from the police. In one case, a resident called an ambulance for a prospective tenant, who was beaten unconscious by gang members when he tried to view an apartment. Because the police arrived with the ambulance, gang members fired a bullet into the resident's apartment, striking the chair he usually sat in. Most residents would not call the police for fear of retaliation. Those who did call the police often found the windshield on their car broken out or their tires slashed. One resident was threatened for handing out flyers about a neighborhood meeting to discuss the gang problem. Another resident drove to the store, which was less than three hundred feet from his front door, because he was afraid to walk. Friends from outside the neighborhood refused to visit, having been harassed or attacked by gang members in the past. In one case, a woman's car was flooded by an open fire hydrant as she was leaving a friend's home. Children as young as eight-years-old dressed as gang members and intimidated other children. One resident summed up the conditions:

> Everyone on this street is fearful that they can become the victim of a crime at any time. They are afraid to walk down

> the street for fear that these gang members will come up to them and take everything from you. You are not safe in your house because the gang members will come in and take things from you. You can't even feel safe standing in front of the market talking to a friend for fear that some gang member will accost you. (Excerpt from Civilian Declaration).

The declaration of an apartment manager described his experiences with the gang. The manager was forced to change the name of a tenant/gang member on the rental agreement because the police were looking for him. When the police came to the building looking for the tenant, the manager kept silent for fear of retaliation. The manager was also forced to accept delivery of packages containing illegal drugs for the same tenant. Thus, through intimidation, the apartment manager was forced to be an accomplice to two crimes – harboring a fugitive and the delivery of illegal drugs.

On one occasion, fourteen shots were fired at the manager's building. The manager did not know the reason for this incident. Gang members also used a place of worship set up in the building to hide from police, yelled profanities to building residents about how they ruled the street, and threatened to rob residents when police crackdowns hampered drug sales. Gang members fired rifles from the roof of the building, causing the manager to lock access to the roof. On one occasion, the manager found cartons of rifle bullets on the roof, along with photographs of people with the names, addresses, and the phrase "testified against us in a robbery case" on the back, implying that witnesses were being targeted for execution. After the manager evicted one gang member, every light fixture in the building was broken as a warning for him to not seek the eviction of a gang member in the future. The manager observed parents and adults aiding gang members by acting as lookouts and harboring gang members in their apartment. He also observed street vendors robbed at gunpoint on three occasions. One victim was pistol-whipped and the others were forced to lie down while being taunted by the robbers.

In addition to the shootings, drug dealing, and other crimes described by residents, apartment building owners described the fear and financial hardships they suffered. These landlords did not live in the neighborhood, but often went there to attend to their investment properties. All had been accosted and threatened by gang members, causing some landlords to carry a firearm whenever they entered the neighborhood. One landlord was killed by a group of gang members who surrounded his car and demanded his handgun.

All the landlords described the difficulty they experienced in attracting tenants. Despite the inexpensive rents in the neighborhood, apartment buildings often had less than a 50% occupancy rate. Some of the owners were in or nearing foreclosure and bankruptcy. Most claimed that it was virtually impossible to rent on the street because of the intimidation and violence from the gang. When the street was named to prospective tenants, most failed to show up. To allay fear by the tenants, some owners erected expensive block-and-iron fences, only to have them scaled by gang members to escape from the police or to commit crimes – robbery, burglary, theft, and vandalism – on the property. Fences were torn down and battered by large trucks, destroying the owners' investments in security for tenants. Gang members constantly shot out security lights. Repairmen either refused to work in the neighborhood or worked only in pairs, increasing the expense to all property owners. Gang members made apartments unrentable by merely hanging out in front of the building. As a result, many owners could not make mortgage payments and lost their properties, and prospective tenants lost inexpensive housing.

At one point, a group of apartment owners hired a team of six armed security guards and bounty hunters to take control of the street from the gang. The team brought Guardian Angels into the neighborhood. After only two nights, the Guardian Angels refused to return. Gang members fired on the security team, hitting one with a shotgun blast from a roof. After one month, the team gave up their attempt to take back the street for landlords and tenants.

One building owner developed a telephone tree to allow his tenants to report crimes while avoiding retaliation. Tenants called him to report a crime and he called 911. This arrangement was used to avoid having the police go to the tenant's apartment, which would surely cause retaliation by the gang. Another owner refused to come into the neighborhood to collect rents, meeting his manager at a building outside the neighborhood. Most owners refused to come into the neighborhood at night. When they did come into the neighborhood, they used an entrance that was less frequented by gang members to avoid being confronted by groups of gang members sauntering into the street in front of their cars, forcing them to stop.

A business owner recounted a burglary into his establishment, in which $70,000 worth of merchandise was stolen. The next day, the owner saw gang members selling his goods on the street for pennies on the dollar. Because he feared retaliation, he did nothing to stop it. An employee of this business stole money and allowed the boyfriend, who was a gang member, to take merchandise from the premises. The owner was warned that the gang would destroy his place of business if he fired the employee. At one point, four gang members walked into the premises and told the owner they were going to take the store over, but the owner ran them off with a gun and locked up the store.

The businessman also described incidents he observed on the street. He related how gang members displayed their guns to intimidate the residents, pretending to clean the guns so that everybody would see that they had guns. They would hide the guns when the police were in the area, after being warned of the police presence by lookouts on rooftops using walkie-talkies. They used bicycles to retrieve drugs from hiding places for customers. There was a hole under one apartment building where gang members hid from the police and stashed their drugs and guns.

According to the businessman, neighborhood intimidation went beyond the mere display of guns. He recounted how the daughter of one family told her gangster boyfriend about a $1000 dividend check the family received. The boyfriend demanded the money, threatening the family with violence if they refused. In another incident, gang members stopped a car containing a man and his dog, shooting both and leaving them dead in the middle of the street. On another occasion, gang members tried to stop a car containing two women. Attempting to escape, the car hit a tree, killing one woman and seriously wounding the other occupant, who was pregnant. Police have been shot at and police cars have had windows smashed out and tires sliced. Gang members constantly stole and striped cars, selling the stolen tires, stereos, and other car parts on the street.

A utility company supervisor described how the cost of providing service had increased in the neighborhood. The street around which the target area was centered was unique, in that it was the only street in a large urban area on which the utility restricted service calls, including emergency service, for the protection of its technicians and equipment. Technicians had been robbed and threatened with death. Equipment had been stolen from service trucks, and trucks had been painted with graffiti while technicians made service calls. As a result, two trucks were always sent to the street, with one technician serving as a guard for the other truck. Technicians were warned to lock their wallets in their truck. Service calls were only made in the morning, when gang members were least active. If gang activity was apparent, technicians were told to pass by and call customers, telling them that they would try to respond the next day. No calls, not even for emergency service, were answered in the evening. Because of the gang activity, a new service was installed to allow the company to control utility service to the street from the main office, reducing the need for technicians to go onto the street. Cable damage from bullets was a common problem in the neighborhood.

These civilian declarations drive home the conditions under which people work and live on a daily basis in injunction target areas. The fact that only four declarants actually lived on the street around which the target area was centered attests to the degree of intimidation experienced by residents and to the difficulty experienced by prosecutors in obtaining civilian declarations. The conditions described in these declarations were consistent with the conditions described in the statement of facts and expert declarations in many other injunction initiatives. These conditions could only persist through a group effort by gang members to intimidate residents and other users of the target area, underscoring the importance of group processes to the strategy of intervention by injunction.

RESEARCH DESIGN

The design of the study is relatively simple. The study primarily relies on qualitative categorical data analysis to address the questions of *flexibility* and *community involvement* in the process of acquiring a gang injunction.

Boundaries of the Study

The study is limited to efforts to acquire preliminary injunctions and to the injunction provisions requested by prosecutors. In order to provide the broadest spectrum of the gang injunction phenomenon, this study focuses on the *injunction initiative*. An injunction initiative is an effort by prosecutors to acquire a preliminary injunction against a gang, including the terms of relief requested by prosecutors, regardless of the decision by the court. Injunction initiatives include actions resulting in a preliminary injunction, as well as actions in which the court denied injunctive relief, actions that were dismissed prior to a decision, and actions still in litigation.[4] Focusing on injunction initiatives, in contrast to limiting the research to cases in which injunctions were obtained, allows an examination of a broader spectrum of gang injunction actions.

The process of obtaining a preliminary injunction consists of two stages – acquisition and implementation (Fiss 1978). The acquisition stage is limited to the process of procuring the injunction from the court. The implementation stage consists of enforcing the injunction and assessing its effectiveness (Maxson and Allen 1997). Although effective implementation is recognized as important to the injunction process, this study focuses on the acquisition stage for both theoretical and practical reasons.

Theoretically, this research explores the nature of a non-traditional response by law enforcement officials to pervasive crime and disorder in a community, to determine if that response fits into the problem-oriented paradigm currently in vogue within the criminal justice community. The initial stage of any response consists of the acquisition of an appropriate mechanism to control the proximate and/or underlying causes of a defined problem. To meet the requirements of the problem-oriented approach, two conditions must be met. First, the response must be flexible, targeting characteristics of the problem that are specific to the local conditions. Flexibility implies that a response employed across different communities should vary. Second, the community must be involved in defining the problem and selecting one or more responses from the available alternatives (Goldstein 1990). Once the response mechanism is in place, implementation of the chosen response is generally in the hands of the police and prosecutors, with little involvement by the community in day-to-day enforcement decisions beyond the reporting of violations. To gain a sense of flexibility and community involvement, the most important stage in the process is the selection and acquisition of the appropriate response mechanism.

There are several practical reasons for limiting the study to the acquisition stage. First, although there have been studies on the implementation (Maxson and Allen 1997) and effectiveness (ACLU Foundation of Southern California 1997; Maxson and Allen 1997, Grogger 2000) of gang injunctions, there has been no research on the acquisition stage of the injunction process across numerous injunction initiatives. However, an awareness of the nature of a response is essential for conducting a knowledgeable study into its implementation and effectiveness. The terms of the injunction may have been copied from other cases with little concern for their fit to the local circumstances. In addition, the direction (support or opposition) and extent of community involvement during the acquisition stage of an injunction initiative may not be evident during implementation. Both of these characteristics (fit and community involvement) may have a strong effect on the ultimate success of the injunction.

On a broader note, the nature of a response may reveal difficulties in criminal justice decision-making in general and in the problem-oriented process in particular. Focusing solely on implementation and/or effectiveness while failing to inquire into the nature of a response may limit the broader usefulness of the study.

Second, the acquisition stage is completed when the preliminary injunction is granted or denied by the court, whereas the implementation stage continues as long as the injunction is in force. Focusing the research on the acquisition stage provides closure when the court decision is made. In contrast, a complete study of implementation or effectiveness would have to continue for the duration of the injunction order, possibly indefinitely.

Third, focusing on implementation and effectiveness would eliminate initiatives in which injunctive relief has been denied. If the court does not grant an injunction, there is no response to implement or effect to measure. If the study were limited to successful initiatives, an important subset of injunction initiatives that might yield important information on the nature of gang injunctions would be excluded. Focusing on the acquisition stage allows initiatives in which injunctions were denied to be included in the study.

Fourth, the acquisition stage of the identified universe of gang injunctions can be studied retrospectively and from a distance. The use of court records, surveys and interviews provides a relatively unobtrusive method of research (Maxfield and Babbie 1998). In contrast, implementation research is best conducted prospectively and through observation at the scene (Maxson, Hennigan, and Sloan 1997). Such research would be impractical in this study because most of the implementation efforts have already occurred or been initiated.

Finally, this research studied the aggregate of all injunction initiatives. Aggregate data provides a more sophisticated description of a phenomenon than is possible through a single case study (Miles and Huberman 1994) and increases the generalizability of a study. An aggregate study that focuses on both the acquisition and implementation stages would be unfeasible, as the injunctions have been implemented in different locations over a fourteen-year period and archival data of the implementation efforts probably do not exist.

There are three types of injunction orders in the acquisition process: the temporary restraining order, the preliminary injunction, and the permanent injunction. A *temporary restraining order* (TRO) is an emergency remedy of brief duration issued only under exceptional circumstances and typically granted after an *ex parte* proceeding.[5] A TRO is only appropriate when supported by sufficient evidence that an emergency exists, necessitating immediate relief from impending irreparable harm. Generally, the situation must preclude conducting a full hearing at which both sides of the controversy can present their case. For various reasons, prosecutors have not sought TRO's in all gang injunction initiatives.

A *preliminary injunction* is an interlocutory order[6] granted during the pendency of litigation to prevent irreparable injury. It is granted only after the defendants have been afforded an opportunity to present their case in a hearing on the action. Prosecutors may file for a preliminary injunction regardless of the existence of a TRO. Because all parties to the action receive notice of an impending hearing for a preliminary injunction, defendants have the opportunity to obtain an attorney, and *amicus curiae* interests have the opportunity to petition the court for permission to file a brief on behalf of one party prior to the hearing.[7]

A *permanent injunction* is a final decree by the court. It is obtained only at trial. A permanent injunction generally is not pursued where the controversy has been eliminated. Therefore, if the public nuisance caused by the gang dissipated prior to trial, a permanent injunction is usually not sought by the prosecutor. The prosecutor also may strategically delay a request for a permanent injunction to allow additional defendants to be named in the action, particularly when the membership of a gang is constantly changing.[8] Because many of the injunction initiatives have not reached final disposition or the public nuisance has been eliminated prior to final disposition, prosecutors have not filed motions for permanent injunctions in all gang injunction initiatives.

While TRO's and permanent injunctions are not always requested, the preliminary injunction is consistently sought in all injunction initiatives. Because filing for a TRO is part of the acquisition process and its issuance or denial may affect that process, whether a TRO was sought and obtained is examined as an intervening event, not as the focus of the study. On the other hand, filing for a permanent injunction is not an intervening event in the acquisition effort. The permanent injunction follows the preliminary injunction in the legal chronology, and there are no identified cases during this research period in which a permanent injunction has been granted without the prior issuance of a preliminary injunction.[9] Therefore, this study does not focus on requests for permanent injunctions. As the only consistent order found in all forty-two injunction initiatives, the process of acquiring a preliminary injunction is the focus of the study.

Requested relief refers to the terms of injunction proposed by the prosecutor. It is distinguished from the relief granted by the court, in which the judge may alter the proposed relief. The study focused on requested relief for two reasons: to include initiatives not resulting in an injunction and to control for the influence of judicial discretion.

A focus on the relief granted by the court would exclude initiatives where injunctions were denied, dismissed, or are still in litigation. Two cases have been identified in which the court denied a preliminary injunction.[10] One case was withdrawn prior to the hearing for a preliminary injunction;[11] and one case was in litigation at the time of the research.[12] If these cases were excluded from this study, the question of whether differences in requested relief, situational characteristics, and/or the degree of community involvement had any bearing on the success of the acquisition process would be ignored. Focusing on requested relief allows the total universe of identified gang injunction initiatives during the research period to be included in the study.

The focus on requested relief also eliminates the effects of judicial discretion. Under the civil law concept of equity, judges have extensive discretion in granting or denying injunctive relief. A judge may perceive the terms requested in an injunction as unconstitutionally infringing on individual liberties, believe that there is adequate relief under the criminal law, or alter the terms of relief to meet his/her conception of equity. The comparatively small number of cases in which injunctive relief has been denied raises the question of whether these cases were decided by the preferences of the judges, who may view an injunction as a draconian response to the gang problem, or by legal concerns, such as requesting inappropriate relief or the lack of sufficient evidence. The focus on requested relief avoids the potential influence of judicial discretion in denying or altering relief.

Methods

The methodology of the study is fairly simple. The study begins with an examination of the variation in injunction provisions requested by prosecutors. The requested injunction provisions, or requested relief, are the end product of the injunction initiatives. The variation in the requested relief is the basis for the classification of injunction initiatives through cluster analysis. The resulting taxonomy of injunction initiatives is extensively used in the analysis of the dimensions of flexibility and community involvement through categorical data analysis.

Categorical data analysis is a methodology that uses categorical variables and contingency tables to identify important attributes within a variable, as well as potentially meaningful relationships between variables. A categorical variable describes a concept through a logical grouping of the attributes of interest to the research.[13] Relationships between variables are analyzed through contingency tables, a descriptive technique particularly suited for analyzing categorical data. Analysis is performed on relationships that are found to be meaningful to the study, as well as expected relationships that failed to appear in the data.[14] Both meaningful relationships and expected relationships are based on the theoretical foundations of the study.

Three sources of information were used in this study: the case file for each injunction initiative,[15] a survey of prosecutors involved in each injunction initiative,[16] and newspaper articles covering injunction initiatives. The importance of the date sources mandates a detailed discussion of each source.

An effort to obtain an injunction is based on a documentary case establishing a nexus, or link, between the activities of named gang members and the specific local circumstances that comprise the public nuisance. The case files vary widely in size, from a single volume containing three documents[17] to six volumes of several hundred pages each. The information used in this study was retrieved from the following documents in the case file: 1) the *complaint* for injunctive relief, 2) the *memorandum of points and authorities* in support of injunctive relief, 3) the *order to seal* civilian declarations, 4) the *declarations* of police gang experts, 5) the *proposed preliminary injunction*, 6) the *order granting or denying* the preliminary injunction, and 7) filings by defense counsel and *amicus curiae* interests.

The *complaint* for injunctive relief is the initial pleading that commences the civil action against the gang. The complaint generally includes an introductory statement of the claim for relief, a statement of the court's jurisdiction over the claim, a specification of all parties to the action, a statement of each cause of action, and a prayer for judgment against the defendants. In other words, the complaint explains what problem the action seeks to address, who is party to the action, why the plaintiff is entitled to relief, and what relief is being requested. The complaint specifies whether the gang as an unincorporated association[18] is named as a defendant, the named individual defendants, the borders of the target area(s), a brief description of the activities of the gang that comprise the public nuisance, and the relief requested by the prosecutor. A map of the target area is often attached to the complaint as an exhibit.

The *memorandum of points and authorities* provides a more comprehensive picture of the public nuisance caused by the defendants and specifies the legal arguments in favor of injunctive relief. Of particular interest for this study are the introduction and the summary of facts, which combine to give an overview of the activities of the gang and the resulting public nuisance. Specific criminal incidents leading to and/or occurring during the injunction initiative, such as homicides and gang wars, and the number of sealed citizen declarations are also often noted in the memorandum.

The *order to seal civilian declarations* indicates whether the court has sealed the sworn affidavits of civilian witnesses, sometimes specifying the number sealed. This precludes examination by all persons except designated officials, such as the judge and the attorneys to the action, in order to protect the declarants from reprisals by gang members. In a very few cases, civilian declarations are not sealed, leaving them accessible to public viewing.

The *declaration* of the gang expert contains an overview of the targeted gang and other information relevant to the case. Although expert declarations vary widely in content, they often describe the gang by its history, racial and ethnic characteristics, membership size, hierarchical structure, rivalries, predominant criminal and nuisance-related activities, and specific events leading to or influencing the injunction initiative. The expert declaration may also state whether the gang has been documented as a criminal street gang under the Street Terrorism Enforcement and Prevention (STEP) Act (California Penal Code, section 186.20 et seq.),[19] the criteria used by the police department in documenting named defendants as gang members, and evidence of the nexus between individual defendants and the public nuisance. The expert declaration often provides the most complete description of the activities of the gang and of the conditions under which residents live within the target area. Similarly, declarations of community policing and senior lead officers[20] give expert evidence about the influence of the gang on neighborhood conditions. For the purpose of this study, they are considered expert declarations. Expert declarations are not available when the court seals the entire case, the declaration is missing from the court file or sealed from public viewing, or case file is missing from the court archives.[21]

The *proposed preliminary injunction* is the prayer for relief, enumerating the specific provisions of relief requested by the prosecutor. This document becomes the preliminary injunction order when the relief granted is identical or substantively similar to the requested relief. When used in this manner, the judge crosses out material or writes in new language, and initials any changes in the injunction provisions. Where the proposed preliminary injunction is not used as the injunction order or where the court has denied the injunction, a separate *order granting* or *order denying* the preliminary injunction is issued, specifying the relief granted by the court or explaining why relief was denied.

During the review of case files, appearances and filings by counsel for defendants and *amicus curiae* (friend of the court) briefs were noted. Defense filings and *amicus* briefs are not part of the official response to the public nuisance. They are reactions of the defendants and other legal interests to the official response. However, knowledge of impending defense representation and the nature of the efforts on behalf of the defense might influence the relief requested by prosecutors, thus serving as a proxy for the influence of gang members on the injunction initiatives. In order to account for the influence of the defendants, the presence of and efforts by defense representation are examined through documents filed by the defense and information offered by prosecutors.

The case files do not tell the whole story of the injunction initiatives. Information that is not legally relevant to the request for injunctive relief, such as whether the initiative originated as part of a larger program to improve the quality-of-life in the target area or as a response to community pressure after a high profile gang-related crime, is usually not noted in the case files. The case files also give little information on plans for implementation and assessment, or on the participation of community entities in the acquisition process. Therefore, information from the case files was complemented by data from a survey of prosecutors involved in each injunction initiative. Questions in the survey generally covered the nature of the gang problem, the entity responsible for initiating the legal action, specific events that triggered the initiative and that influenced the case during the investigation, the existence of other interventions or programs conducted in conjunction with the initiative, and the prosecutors' perceptions of the nature and impact of community involvement. Prosecutors were also requested to furnish information on community entities, both supporting and opposing the initiatives, for use in the second phase of the study.

Although the study covers a fourteen-year period, attrition was not a major factor in this study. Most of the respondents are career prosecutors, and those no longer employed by the prosecuting agencies were successfully contacted. The response rate was ninety-eight percent, with prosecutors from forty-one of the forty-two injunction initiatives voluntarily responding to the survey.

Throughout the study, excerpts of prosecutors' responses to the survey are offered to explain some point or serve as examples about the subject being discussed. Because confidentiality was guaranteed to all respondents to the survey, the identities of the prosecutors and the injunction initiatives will remain anonymous to assure that comments cannot be attributed to specific respondents. All non-attributed quotations in the study were drawn from the responses to the Prosecutor Survey.

Gang injunctions have been extensively covered in several California newspapers. The *Los Angeles Times*, *San Diego Union-Tribune*, *San Jose Mercury News*, and local newspapers are sources through which many of the injunction initiatives were identified. Articles on legal and ethical issues involving gang injunctions provide much of the background against which the general public judges the propriety of gang injunctions. These issues include constitutionality, effectiveness, and the connection with other criminal justice matters, such as the Rampart corruption scandal in the Los Angeles Police Department. Newspapers report on the court decisions of most injunction initiatives and sometimes provide background information about the neighborhood conditions under which individual initiatives originated. Because of the lack of research into the gang injunction phenomenon, newspaper articles are frequently the only source of information on the strategy. Where data were not obtainable from more reliable sources, newspaper articles were consulted to "fill in the blanks".

OVERVIEW OF THE STUDY

The following chapters proceed in a sequence from the general issues surrounding civil gang abatement to the specifics of the study. Chapter

II discusses the general theoretical perspectives supporting civil gang abatement. Chapter III examines the legal issues surrounding the use of civil remedies in general, and injunctions in particular, to address criminal behavior. Chapter IV describes the gang injunction, including its emergence as a legal tool in California, the case law spawned by appeals of injunction decisions, the process and related pitfalls in seeking a gang injunction, and the controversy over the effectiveness of the gang injunctions. Chapters V and VI examines the dimensions of flexibility and community involvement through categorical data analysis. Chapter VII draws conclusions related to the research questions, discusses the policy implications of the study, and suggests further research on civil gang abatement.

CHAPTER II

Theoretical Perspectives

Civil gang abatement is based on the conjunction of several theoretical perspectives – "Broken Windows" theory, the problem-oriented perspective, and their role in both community prosecution and community justice. These perspectives must address the common characteristics of gangs identified through gang research, particularly group dynamics and the variation in gang activities.

"BROKEN WINDOWS" THEORY

Broken windows theory (Wilson and Kelling 1982), which provides the conceptual foundation for civil gang abatement,[22] advances a developmental sequence through which an increase in the physical and social disorder in a neighborhood results in an increase in the vulnerability of that neighborhood to criminal invasion. Popularized through an *Atlantic Monthly* article entitled "Broken Windows: The Police and Neighborhood Safety" by James Q. Wilson and George Kelling (1982), broken windows theory has evolved (Taylor 2001: 110) from a psychological theory about individual-level fear of crime (Wilson 1975), through a socio-psychological perspective on the dynamics between the effects of incivilities on serious crime and fear of crime at the street-block level (Wilson and Kelling 1982), into an ecological perspective focusing on the relationship between disorder and community dynamics on the neighborhood level (Skogan 1990). In the twenty years since the publication of the article, the broken windows perspective has become "conventional wisdom in this country" and has been exported to countries around the world (Harcourt 2001: 57). The broken windows perspective has been the conceptual core for many popular criminal justice policies, including problem- and community-oriented policing, third-party policing, and zero-tolerance/order maintenance policing (Taylor 2001: 94), and community prosecution (Boland 1998, Office of the District Attorney

1996). Despite its popularity, there have been serious questions regarding the empirical and theoretical validity of the broken windows perspective (Harcourt 1998, 2001; Taylor 1999, 2001).

According to Wilson and Kelling's theory, untended physical disorder, anti-social behavior, and minor criminal activity lead to the breakdown of informal social control and an increase in crime. As residents perceive that crime is rising, they react by avoiding both public spaces and involvement in neighborhood affairs. This defensive reaction inhibits social interaction and community attachment, which decreases the community's ability to informally regulate public behavior. As levels of visible disorder increase, the fear of crime and the resulting defensive posture by residents increases until those with sufficient resources move from the neighborhood, leaving behind the residents that are most vulnerable to crime and least able to exert informal social control against disruptive behavior. The remaining residents become even less likely to interfere with or report crimes. As a result, potential offenders perceive visible physical and social disorder as a sign that they can commit serious crimes with impunity. Analogous to how one un-repaired broken window in a building leads to other windows being broken, the inability of the neighborhood to control anti-social behavior breeds further social decay until the community becomes so disorganized that it is incapable of reclaiming control of its public space without the assistance of outside resources.

In a study of the correlation between the prevalence of disorder, fear of crime, and neighborhood decay, Skogan and Maxfield (1981) found that the fear of crime is strongly related to the extent to which citizens alter their behavior to minimize the risk of victimization. Personal risk-reduction efforts, while sometimes effective in protecting the individual, are a heavy burden, causing individuals to forgo employment, recreation, and social opportunities. The aggregate consequences of individual defensive actions fragment the community and undermine the informal social control mechanisms that maintain order.

Skogan (1990) analyzed aggregated data from five separate surveys to determine if there was a connection between social disorder, crime, and neighborhood decline. Thirteen thousand residents from forty diverse residential neighborhoods in six cities were surveyed between 1977 and 1983. Two measures of the extent of neighborhood crime were used – residents' perception of crime as a problem and robbery victimization. The statistical analysis controlled for the influence of poverty, instability, and racial composition. While recognizing the difficulty in drawing causal inferences between disorder and crime based on a relatively small number of cases, the study found that a substantial proportion of the linkage between crime and the socio-economic measures disappeared when measurements of disorder were introduced into the equation. Skogan concluded:

> Neighborhood levels of disorder are closely related to crime rates, to fear of crime, and the belief that serious crime is a neighborhood problem. This relationship could reflect the fact that the link between crime and disorder is a causal one, or that both are dependent upon some third set of factors...However, the precise relationship between crime and disorder remains unclear...whatever the link between the two is, it is powerful. (Skogan 1990: 10).

Despite the cautions about causal inferences, the study has been hailed as empirically verifying the broken windows hypothesis (Kelling and Coles 1996: 24).

Although broken windows theory "stands, in essence, uncontested" (Harcourt 1998:293) in academic circles, it has recently been empirically challenged. Harcourt (1998, 2001) replicated Skogan's analysis and concluded that the data did not support the disorder-crime nexus. After correcting statistical problems involving missing values in the data, Harcourt found that, with the exception of robbery, all statistically significant relationships between individual crimes and disorder disappeared when socio-economic factors were held constant. The relationship between disorder and robbery also disintegrated when five neighborhoods in Newark were eliminated from the analysis.

Based on his repudiation of the broken windows hypothesis, Harcourt argues that the quality-of-life enforcement policies spawned by broken windows theory comes with extreme costs. The aggressive police practices spawned by the theory invests scarce resources in the suppression of minor misdemeanor offenses at the disproportionate expense of minorities and delegates power to define disorder to police officers and designated community members, which is inconsistent with established democratic and constitutional principles. Harcourt concludes that attention should be refocused from quality-of-life initiatives to the underlying and complex causes of neighborhood decline – socio-economic factors such as neighborhood poverty, stability, and race – that are "masked by the aesthetic and rhetoric of orderliness" (Harcourt 2001: 389) that define the capricious category of disorder.

In a longitudinal study, Taylor (1999, 2001) examined the impact of incivilities and physical disorder on fear, crime, and physical decline in sixty-six Baltimore neighborhoods. The study compared the physical conditions and crime rates of ninety street blocks through a 1994 replication of a 1981 study. The study found that, although the physical conditions of the neighborhoods had deteriorated significantly between 1981 and 1994, residents did not perceive local physical or social problems as being significantly worse. Despite evidence that the assessment of incivilities in the 1981 study had an independent, but inconsistent, impact on later changes in the crime rate, there was no substantial evidence that earlier incivilities contributed independently to changes in fear of crime. However, a relationship was established between the fear of crime and basic structural features of the neighborhood.

In a study of the sources and consequences of public disorder in 196 Chicago neighborhoods, Sampson and Raudenbush (1999) found little empirical support for a strong sense of the broken windows perspective – the direct causal relationship of disorder to crime. Using data from systematic social observation of disorder (videotape and audio commentary), the census, vital statistics, police records, and an independent survey of over 3,500 residents, the study examined the statistical relationships between disorder, crime, neighborhood structural constraints, and collective efficacy, which was defined as the combination of social cohesion among residents and shared expectations for the social control of public space. Although the study found a moderate correlation between disorder and predatory crime, the nexus between disorder and crime all but vanished when structural constraints and collective efficacy were added to the model. Robbery was the only crime that retained a significant, although moderate, association with disorder. The study concluded that "[t]he empirical results therefore support our contention that public disorder and most predatory crimes share similar theoretical features and are consequently explained by the same constructs at the neighborhood level, in particular the concentration of disadvantage and lower collective efficacy" (Sampson and Raudenbush 1999: 637).

However, disorder was not theoretically irrelevant to crime. The results support an indirect effect of disorder on crime through an increase in residential instability, resulting from people moving from the neighborhood, and the discouragement of efforts to build collective responses. A moderate, but significant, association between disorder and robbery also suggests a reduction of social control through the restraint of social interaction. In addition, there was evidence that potential robbery offenders respond to visual signs of social and physical disorder, creating "a complex feedback loop whereby disorder entices robbery, which in turn undermines collective efficacy, leading over time to yet to more disorder and ultimately robbery" (Sampson and Raudenbush 1999: 637).

In a review of the research on the incivilities thesis, Taylor (2001) has recently mapped the evolution of the broken windows perspective from an individual-oriented to an ecological-oriented model. The *incivilities thesis*, as Taylor referred to it, evolved from a focus by Wilson (1975) and Garofalo and Laub (1978) on the psychological effects of incivilities at the individual level, through an interest by Wilson and Kelling (1982) on the social-psychological processes between incivilities and crime at the street-block level, to a focus by Skogan (1990) on the effects of incivilities on community dynamics and outcomes at the neighborhood level (Taylor 2001: 110). Each step through this evolution expanded the outcomes of the thesis – from concerns about fear of crime, through concerns about neighborhood street-life and crime, to neighborhood structural decline. This evolution also altered the temporal perspective from a single point in time – a cross sectional perspective – to changes over time – a longitudinal perspective (Taylor 2001: 103). Wilson and Kelling's broken windows theory, a version of the incivilities thesis, provided the pivot point in this evolutionary progression.

Taylor found the strongest empirical support for the psychological model, based on cross-sectional studies of the differences between the perceptions of individuals regarding disorder, crime, and fear of crime in neighborhoods. In contrast, longitudinal studies of differences in neighborhoods over time provided only partial support for the ecological-oriented models advanced by Wilson/Kelling and Skogan. In short, Taylor's review of empirical research found strong support for differences in the perspectives of neighbors, but "essentially nonexistent" support for differences in neighborhoods, raising questions about the empirical validity of the broken windows perspective (Taylor 2001: 109).

The claim by proponents of the broken windows perspective that the results of quality-of-life initiatives by urban police departments in the 1990's, and the initiative by the New York Police Department in particular, supplied strong evidence of the broken windows effect has also been questioned. Harcourt (2001) examined these claims, pointing out that, while crime rates did decline in conjunction with these initiatives, there was a national decline in crime rates during the 1990's. A number of large cities, many of which did not implement quality-of-life initiatives, experienced drops in crime similar to or larger than the decrease in New York City (Harcourt 2001:91). Harcourt notes a number of possible factors that may have contributed to the decline in New York City's crime rate: a significant increase in police manpower, changing drug consumption from crack cocaine to heroin, a decrease in the population of young adult males, quicker police response through computerized crime tracking, favorable economic conditions, an increase in the incarceration of offenders, the breakup of several large drug gangs, and possible changes in adolescent behavior (Harcourt 2001: 94). According to Harcourt, the empirical evidence provided by police quality-of-life initiatives not only fails to withstand empirical scrutiny, but is methodologically flawed, relying on purported correlations between the initiatives and the declining crime rates while failing to address causal mechanisms (Harcourt 2001: 90).

Although these adverse findings place the theory into the realm of conventional wisdom (Harcourt 2001: 57), the set of assumptions behind *broken windows* theory has clearly generated policy responses to disorder offenses, including civil gang abatement[23] (Office of the District Attorney 1996; Los Angeles City Attorney Gang Prosecution Section 1995), and provided the framework for the community law enforcement perspective (Clear and Karp 1998: 5). According to Harcourt, the popular appeal of the broken windows perspective results from the theory's rhetorical transformation of "conduct that was once merely offensive or annoying into positively harmful conduct – conduct that causes serious crime" (Harcourt 2001: 8). Policymakers have justified community- and problem-oriented policing strategies, at least in part, by the "longitudinal, ecological version of the decline and disorder, or broken windows, thesis" (Taylor 2001: 366).

THE PROBLEM-ORIENTED PERSPECTIVE

The order maintenance function of the police, which is aimed at reducing the fear of crime and increasing the quality-of-life through the enforcement of norms against minor anti-social behavior, has been hailed as vital to reinforcing informal social control mechanisms in disorganized neighborhoods (Wilson and Kelling 1982; Bratton 1995).

However, with informal responses by the police to public disorder restricted by judicial decisions implementing individual rights, the police often must rely solely on the criminal law as a policy response to neighborhood disorder, limiting their response to the small fraction of individual offenses solvable by arrest. This limitation is particularly significant to responses to gang-related crimes because of the intimidation of potential complainants and witnesses by gang members, allowing gang associates to elude arrest and/or conviction (Finn and Healey 1996). As a result, the police need a broader range of options beyond the criminal law to effectively balance the restoration and maintenance of order in vulnerable neighborhoods (Bratton 1995) with the preservation of individual civil rights.

The problem-oriented perspective has been advocated as an appropriate model for addressing disorder and the resulting fear of crime (Kelling and Coles 1996). Under this perspective, various agencies and community entities coordinate their attention and assets toward a common goal, significantly broadening the options available to address problems associated with disorder. The problem-oriented perspective drives the strategies of problem-oriented policing and community prosecution, and is endemic to the emerging paradigm of community justice.

Problem-oriented Policing

The problem-oriented perspective is largely derived from the "problem-oriented policing" model. Developed by Herman Goldstein (1990) to guide the policing function away from its traditionally reactive, incident-driven focus toward a proactive, problem-solving mission, the model has provided a prototype for community problem-solving that can be applied by various criminal justice agencies. Flexibility and a multilateral approach in formulating responses to specific problems are the basic dimensions of the model.

Flexibility is implied by the goal of the model – to tailor the most effective response (Goldstein 1990: 44) to a specific problem in a targeted location. In contrast to the stereotypical response of the criminal law, which relies on specific and general deterrence after an offense has been committed, a tailored response emphasizes the ability to prevent future incidents and/or reduce future harm by customizing the response to the peculiar circumstances of the problem being addressed. The application of the criminal law is only one of many alternatives that may effectively address the problem. The flexibility of the model is constrained only by the availability of resources and the principle of fundamental fairness to all concerned parties.

A multilateral approach, which involves other agencies and community entities with an interest in ameliorating the underlying causes of the problem, is the other central feature of the model (Goldstein 1990: 21). In contrast to a response formulated unilaterally by law enforcement agencies, collaboration between various public agencies, private organizations, and individual stakeholders increases the likelihood of a permanent and more effective response. Collaboration also legitimizes the selected response in the eyes of the community, especially in low-income neighborhoods where both pervasive disorder and distrust of the police and of government interference prevail. The problem that emerges through collaboration among diverse community entities may be radically different from the problem identified solely by the police through official records. Alternative responses may arise that are beyond the ability and/or resources of law enforcement agencies to implement alone. Ideally, through community stakeholders, the community as a whole becomes involved in the decision-making process. Law enforcement officials become facilitators who advocate well-conceived solutions, which may go beyond the realm of the criminal law, in contrast to the unilateral, enforcement-oriented decisions typically made by law enforcement officials under suppressive social control (Goldstein 1990).

Non-criminal legal controls are a potentially more effective alternative than the criminal law (Goldstein 1990: 45; Bratton 1995: 452). A careful analysis of the problem may lead to fashioning civil and administrative controls that address the problem directly while avoiding the potential unfairness of overly broad and suppressive police responses. Because the police are generally unfamiliar with legal controls outside the realm of the criminal law, the use of civil and administrative law requires close collaboration between the police, the community, and public prosecutors.

Community Prosecution

An evolving innovation in criminal justice (Boland 1998a, 1998b), community prosecution applies the problem-oriented perspective to the prosecutorial function (American Prosecutors Research Institute 1995; Coles 1997). Rising from the escalation of crime that occurred in tandem with the crack cocaine epidemic of the 1980's and 1990's, community prosecution is a proactive, long-term process to enhance the quality-of-life in clearly defined target areas in response to the public safety demands of neighborhoods as expressed by citizens. Recognizing the inextricably intertwined relationship between disorder, criminal street crime, and violent behavior in high-crime neighborhoods (Boland 1998b), community prosecutors employ both enforcement and preventive measures against neighborhood disorder and crime. The prosecutors' institutional role in crime control is redefined by altering the relationship between prosecutors, citizens, and the police (Boland 1998a), resulting in the organizational capacity to respond to neighborhood crime problems that persist in spite of traditional case-by-case prosecutions.

Community prosecution is a radical departure from the prosecutor's suppressive role of reacting to incidents on a case-by-case basis through criminal prosecution. It involves the flexible use of various criminal and civil legal controls, in conjunction with community input into prosecutorial responses through direct interaction between prosecutors, law enforcement officers, public and private agencies, and members of the community (American Prosecutors Research Institute 1995: 18). Recognizing that strained police-citizen relations have created barriers to effective law enforcement, prosecutors become natural neutral facilitators, bringing all parties together to translate their concerns about neighborhood crime into innovative solutions through the application of the appropriate legal expertise. Interaction between prosecutors and beat officers allows prosecutors to provide the police with the appropriate legal tools to address diverse local crime and disorder problems. In turn, prosecutors are provided with the officers' extensive street intelligence and citizen contacts (Boland 1998b). Beyond the valuable street intelligence of citizens, interaction between prosecutors and the community allows prosecutors to evaluate whether prosecutorial responses to problems reflect the values and priorities of the community. Over time, community prosecution is expected to reduce the large caseload produced by the incident-driven suppression tactics traditionally employed in high-crime neighborhoods (American Prosecutors Research Institute 1995: 47-48).

Catherine Coles (1997) heralds community prosecution as the new watchword in prosecutorial innovations. Referred to as "community-based, problem-oriented prosecution" (Coles 1997:2), Coles describes the innovation as a problem-solving approach that emphasizes both crime prevention and enforcement, giving attention to both quality-of-life issues and violent crime. Acting on the authority of the community to tailor prosecution according to the priorities voiced by citizens, community prosecutors work beyond the narrow boundaries of traditional prosecution, leading efforts to build public safety coalitions involving diverse public and private agencies and community residents and providing appropriate alternatives to incarceration, while aggressively prosecuting habitual and violent offenders. Community prosecution is credited with breaking down barriers between law-abiding citizens and their government, by returning to the citizens a sense of responsibility in maintaining safety in the community. This approach represents a return to the historical roots of prosecution as a means for citizens to solve community problems through direct access to criminal justice processes (Coles 1997).

According to Barbara Boland (1998a, 1998b), there are several key themes to the evolving concept of community prosecution. First, community prosecution is a flexible process, not a program guided by stringent procedural rules. It is "a highly flexible new organizational arrangement that is not wedded to specific solutions or responses but to the task of generating them ... by providing citizens and precinct police with daily access to the legal expertise of the DA's office beyond the traditional arrest-convict track, and assigning line operatives the task of responding to their complaints" (Boland 1998b: 65). To accomplish this task, prosecutors are given wide latitude to fashion responses to crime and disorder problems in specific neighborhoods. They are also expected to establish a close day-to-day working relationship with beat officers, a necessity for fashioning an appropriate response to a problem.

Second, the community prosecutor's task in dealing with low-level street disorder is to devise legal alternatives to conventional prosecutorial litigation. This task is not innovative, but is solidly grounded in the traditional order-promoting skills of lawyers. The innovative use of the law to address disorder is "mostly a reworking of long-established legal principles – the communities' right to civilly sanction a public nuisance" (Boland 1998b: 65).

Finally, community prosecution is a grassroots response to nearly three decades of the domination of public discourse on crime by experts and scholars, which has framed issues in dichotomous terms and fashioned solutions according to "ideologically intractable positions". By defining crime issues in terms of concrete situations that affect their daily lives, citizens are demanding a response from locally elected representatives that can be delivered in the real, as opposed to the theoretical, world, thus sowing the seeds of an emerging community justice movement (Boland 1998b: 65-66).

Community prosecution has been endorsed by the United States Department of Justice. Deputy Attorney General Holder, the second highest official in the Department of Justice during the Clinton administration, has referred to community prosecution as a "promising new approach to law enforcement", which has helped reduce crime to its current low levels (Jackson 1999). Although there is little evidence to support this claim, the Department of Justice appropriated $5 million in 1999 and proposed allocating $200 million in 2000 to help local prosecutors set up community prosecution units (Meyer 1999; Skolnik 1999).

The Los Angeles County District Attorney's Office (LADA) has endorsed community prosecution as the operational policy for its civil gang abatement program, *Strategy Against Gang Environments* (SAGE). In the program's operational handbook, subtitled *A Handbook for Community Prosecution*, District Attorney Garcetti has defined the goals of the SAGE program in a manner consistent with the problem-oriented community prosecution perspective:

> (1) to create an atmosphere in a local community that leads to cooperative conduct between residents in that community and the law enforcement components that are there to protect them; (2) in conjunction with the community, to identify those gang members who are problems; and (3) to stop those targeted criminal street gang members from committing acts that degrade the quality of life in that community, thus preventing an escalating scale of events that leads to violence (Office of the District Attorney 1996: i).

The influence of the broken windows perspective is evident by the inclusion of Wilson and Kelling's (1982) seminal article as the first appendix in the SAGE manual. The SAGE program stresses flexibility, collaboration with other agencies, and community outreach in seeking alternatives for dealing with gang activity that causes the fear and intimidation that cripples communities. It relies heavily on the use of injunctions, in conjunction with other interventions, to abate gang activity.

Other prosecuting agencies have been exposed to the SAGE guidelines through training provided by the LADA. SAGE attorneys have instructed prosecutors from San Diego County and the cities of San Bernardino and Redondo Beach, and have collaborated with the Los Angeles City Attorney's Office in several gang injunction initiatives (Castorena 1998a). As a result, the problem-oriented approach implicit in the SAGE program is well represented in the gang injunction phenomenon and serves as a model for other agencies.

The Los Angeles City Attorney (LACA) Gang Prosecution Section (1995), which pioneered the use of injunctions against gangs in 1987, also claims a problem-oriented approach in its injunction initiatives. Declaring the ultimate goal as providing a vehicle for the coordination of various community based policing efforts to improve the quality-of-life in neighborhoods, the strategy is described as a coordinated effort between law enforcement agencies and local residents to reduce illegal gang activity. This approach is employed with other strategies to address neighborhood problems (Los Angeles City Attorney Gang Prosecution Section 1995: 325-327).[24]

The Emerging Paradigm of Community Justice

Problem-oriented interventions, including community prosecution, fall under the umbrella of the community justice paradigm, a developing movement reflecting the trend toward collaboration between criminal justice agencies and communities to increase public safety and pursue justice for all community members. This paradigm reflects a change in thinking about the role of the community in the pursuit of justice (Karp 1998: vii). In the standard centralized expert model of professional crime control, professional law enforcement agents merely use community members as informants to enhance formal social control mechanisms. In contrast, community justice envisions a strong participatory role for the community and community-based organizations in socializing and enforcing behavioral standards, using both formal and informal social control mechanisms. The objective is to make the criminal justice system more responsive to the needs of the community, with the ultimate goal of increasing the quality of community life for all community members, including offenders. According to Clear and Karp (1998), "the ideal of community justice is that the agents of criminal justice should tailor their work so that its main purpose is to enhance community living, especially through reducing the paralysis of fear, the indignities of disorder, and the agony of criminal victimization" (Clear and Karp 1998: 4).

Community justice operates at the neighborhood level, tying criminal justice responses to the characteristics of neighborhoods. The focus on the neighborhood level allows criminal justice agencies to adapt responses to the particular manifestations of community life within a neighborhood. It frees criminal justice agencies to operate in a context-specific manner, focusing on specific neighborhood problems by drawing on local resources and initiatives, bolstered by external resources where needed. In this sense, "community justice is explicitly concerned with a pattern of relations and institutions that effectively operate at the neighborhood level" and the potential consequences of the means employed to address neighborhood problems (Clear and Karp 1998: 16). The uniqueness of specific problems and varieties of community life in different neighborhoods suggests the need for flexibility in formulating context-specific responses.

Community justice envisions an expanded participatory role for community members in enhancing the quality of neighborhood life. The participation of local residents and institutions in the justice process shifts the priorities of criminal justice agencies from state- and city-wide concerns to the local level, as seen from the perspectives of those who live with the problems every day. Proponents of community justice recognize that each citizen assumes some responsibility for the welfare of society and is morally obligated to actively participate in the sustenance of the quality of life. The active participation of the community discards the false assumption "that the onus of public safety falls entirely on the criminal justice system", an assumption that has contributed to the past failures of the criminal justice system (Clear and Karp 1998: 21).

The involvement of the community in the criminal justice process is the heart of community justice. Community participation goes beyond ensuring that local concerns are addressed. It is also vital for building community capacity, so that informal social control mechanisms can eventually replace much of the formal justice apparatus in improving the quality of community life (Clear and Karp 1998: 15). However, in practice, there has been little evidence of a shared understanding of the community role in community justice. Ordinary citizens seldom participate in planning and implementing interventions, and the creation of community capacity to participate in community justice efforts has proven difficult (Kurki 2000).

Civil gang abatement falls squarely within the ideal of community justice. Flexibility in tailoring responses to the local circumstances of the public nuisance and collaborating with the community to identify problems and formulate the appropriate response are hallmarks of the problem-oriented perspective, community prosecution, and civil gang abatement. The improvement of the quality-of-life in gang-plagued neighborhoods is the goal advanced by the sparse literature on civil gang abatement (Office of the District Attorney 1996, Los Angeles City

Attorney Gang Prosecution Section 1995). Whether civil gang abatement as practiced lives up to the ideal of community justice has not been examined.

Lack of Research on Problem-oriented Interventions

There has been little research into the characteristics of problem-oriented interventions. Most studies have been conducted on problem-oriented policing initiatives within a single police agency (e.g.: Bazemore and Cole 1994; Buerger 1994; Capowich and Roehl 1994; Eck and Spelman 1987a; Green 1996; Hope 1994; Toch and Grant 1991). Although there have been comparative studies of problem-oriented policing across agencies (e.g.: Capowich 1995; Eck and Spelman 1987b) and of various problem-oriented interventions against a particular category of crime, particularly drug violations, by different agencies (e.g.: Bureau of Justice Assistance 1993; Weisel 1990), there has not been any comparative research into the problem-oriented dimensions of a single category of intervention implemented by different agencies to ascertain whether the intervention fulfills the promise of the problem-oriented perspective across agencies. Nor has there been any research into the problem-oriented dimensions of community prosecution.

Generally, when an innovative intervention is perceived as being successful, other agencies will mimic the initial effort (Knoke 1982; DiMaggio and Powell 1983). Mimicry may produce a response that is not appropriate to the local conditions. Mimicry is often evident in the stereotypical language found in both state statutes and local ordinances. In enacting a local ordinance, a municipality may use findings from other cities/towns as a basis for the ordinance. This may lead to the ordinance being stricken by the courts because it has no foundation in the local circumstances that it was intended to address. However, the United States Supreme Court has approved of the reliance of local governments on the experiences of other jurisdictions when drafting ordinances (*City of Erie v. Pap's A.M.* 2000). Under the problem-oriented perspective, such stereotypical responses would be avoided by tailoring a response to the local conditions. The concept of tailoring implies flexibility in problem-oriented responses; yet, there has been no research into a single intervention implemented across various agencies to determine whether the dimension of flexibility is fulfilled.

Implicit in tailoring a response to the local conditions is the community's input in formulating the response. For an agency to understand the local context of a problem, there must be input from those who live with the problem every day – the local residents, community groups, businessmen and employees who work in the neighborhood, and agencies that deal with the causes of the problem. Although there have been some studies into community input at the identification stage from the perception of criminal justice agencies (Capowich and Roehl 1994), there has been no research into the dimension of community involvement in the problem-oriented process from the perception of community entities.

This research was aimed at filling this void by studying a single category of intervention, the gang injunction, on the dimensions of flexibility and community involvement. Because the use of the gang injunction has been virtually limited to the state of California, there existed a unique opportunity to study a single intervention that claims to embrace dimensions of the problem-oriented perspective without the encumbrances of variations in court procedural rules across state jurisdictions.

THEORETICAL PERSPECTIVES ON GANGS

There is a tremendous amount of theoretical and research literature on gangs. Two broad characteristics of gangs to which any problem-oriented anti-gang intervention must respond are found throughout this literature. As a gang is, by definition, a group, *group processes* are common to all gangs and must be effectively addressed by any response. A *wide variation in criminal involvement* distinguishes the criminal activity of different gangs, posing various problems to which an effective response must be tailored.

Group Processes

Group processes refer to the influences of a group on the behavior of individuals within the group. Many of the provisions found in gang injunctions target the group processes that influence the behavior of individual gang members (Office of the District Attorney 1996). Gang injunctions often place restrictions on behavior/activities that are generally permitted in a democratic society. These 'non-criminal' activities are the sources of group cohesion, which often contribute to community intimidation and/or criminal activity. Their prohibition is vital to the effectiveness of any injunction initiative in eliminating the disorder caused by gangs. Hanging out with gang members, wearing clothing associated with gang membership, displaying gang tattoos, using gang hand signs, and applying graffiti are activities which collectively distinguish the gang as a group (Klein 1995), resulting in increased cohesion among gang members. These activities also generate fear among residents, who perceive the outward presence of the gang as an indication of its control over the community.

The group nature of gangs also facilitates the commission of crimes and delinquent acts. The organization of the gang and the protection that it affords gang members makes it a superior instrument for the execution of criminal enterprises. The individual gang member's attitude of superiority and indifference to law and order is augmented by the power and security of belonging to the group (Thrasher 1927/1963). Cooperation in criminal and delinquent activities provide a sense of mission in a common enterprise against external foes (Short and Strodtbeck 1965). Outsiders are regarded as proper prey whose personal and property rights can be disregarded, resulting in a terrorized neighborhood that seldom challenges the gang (Thrasher 1927/1963). Contemporary empirical research has consistently found a significant correlation between gang affiliation and delinquent behavior, suggesting that there are factors within the gang setting that contribute to greater involvement by gang members in criminal behavior beyond the existence of other risk factors (Thornberry and Burch 1997; Huff 1998; Esbensen and Huizinga 1996; Battin-Pearson et al. 1998).

Because gang membership independently contributes to the etiology of crime and delinquency, special attention must be given to the group dynamics of gangs by any intervention effort. Interventions at the individual level, to which the criminal law is generally restricted, have proved inadequate to stem the tide of gang activity. Gang injunctions attack the gang as a group, focusing on the public order and minor offenses that often occur in a group setting (Office of the District Attorney 1996).

Gang Variation

Gangs manifest a wide degree of variation in both behavior and structure. Gangs have been characterized as a "protean manifestation", emerging in an endless variety of forms, each having their own unique action pattern (Thrasher 1927/1963: 5). Contemporary empirical studies have found that gang members participate in a full range of crime, from status offenses to serious violent felonies (Thornberry and Burch 1997; Huff 1998; Esbensen and Huizinga 1996; Battin-Pearson et al. 1998). This cafeteria-like criminal involvement is characterized by a lack of specialization and a preponderance of non-serious offenses (Klein 1996) often associated with disorder. Structurally, there are several categories of street gangs, based on behavior patterns and structure, ranging from the traditional, age-graded subgroup clusters to entrepreneurial gangs. Despite these variations, treating all gangs in a stereotypical manner has been a common error in contemporary gang control by law enforcement agencies (Klein 1996).

Stereotyping results in two misleading assumptions. (1) all gangs are assumed to indulge in the same disruptive and criminal behavior; and, (2) individual action is confounded with group action. The police and the media often create popular perceptions of gangs in stereotypical terms, amplifying public fear and outrage about visible criminal behavior of young people acting in groups. Despite these popular perceptions, there are differences in gang activity, even within the same city, and some actions by gang members are aimed at attaining individual, rather than group, goals (Moore 1993).

Gang involvement in drug distribution and violence illustrates the problems caused by stereotyping. There is a popular misperception that all gangs are both highly organized and highly prone to violence. Because the proliferation of gangs, the escalation of violence, and the 'crack cocaine' epidemic occurred at the same time in many of the same neighborhoods, gangs are also presumed to be heavily involved in the distribution of crack and the increase in violent drug-turf wars. Although gang-related violence and drug-related violence are normally two separate phenomena (Maxson 1995), the police and the media have projected this interrelationship to the public, implying that a crisis exists on both the national and regional levels (Moore 1993; Howell and Decker 1999).

The argument against the gang-drug nexus does not imply that all drug activity by individual gang members is never gang-related, nor does it imply that there are no gangs in which drug sales are never central to the gang's mission. Vandalism, graffiti, and inter-gang conflict are generally activities intended to advance the gang's control over its territory (Moore 1993) for various reasons, including the illicit drug trade. Entrepreneurial gangs have been identified in which drug distribution is the major gang-related activity (Padilla 1992; Levitt and Vehkatesh 1999). The point is that any response that addresses the problem of gang activity across gangs and communities in a stereotypical fashion is inappropriate and likely to be ineffective. Appropriate responses must assess local gang problems and causal community factors (Klein 1996; Howell and Decker 1999), rather than common misperceptions based on spurious correlations.

Common suppression strategies against gangs are inherently stereotypical and inflexible because of their reliance on the criminal law. A criminal statute prohibits all activities falling within its scope, applies equally to all citizens and at all locations, and necessitates a showing of individual culpability. Response alternatives under criminal statutes are limited to the arrest and prosecution of a violator, allowing little flexibility for formulating the best possible response to individuated circumstances. While there may be some variation in the prosecution of the criminal law, the individual culpability requirement allows little opportunity to attack the group dynamics influencing gang activity. Locking up one gang member at a time has been recognized as "a woefully poor response to the ever-growing tide of gang violence" (Office of the District Attorney 1996: 44). In contrast, because they do not necessarily rely on the criminal law and its requirement of individual culpability, problem-oriented interventions based on the civil law can be more flexible in addressing the group dynamics that sustain the gang.

The variation in gang characteristics and activity, combined with the problem-oriented goal of formulating tailored responses to specific problems, lead*s* to the assumption that, if gang injunctions are problem-oriented interventions, provisions of relief from nuisance-related behavior will vary according to the specific circumstances of the public nuisance in each target area. A lack of variation in proposed relief will suggest that injunction initiatives are stereotypical responses associated with suppressive social control. Although there is a core group of restrictions common to all injunctions, including prohibitions on group association, harassment/intimidation, and illegal drug activity, variation in how these core concerns are addressed is anticipated, and prohibitions on other activities should vary widely. Because of the emphasis on the connection between drug sales and gangs by law enforcement entities, restrictions on drug-related activity is expected to comprise a substantial proportion of the relief sought by the injunctions.

Gang Interventions

Spergel (1995) has identified four basic strategies to address community gang problems: local community organization and mobilization, social intervention, opportunity provision, and suppression. When evaluated separately, each strategy has failed to have a significant impact on gang activity. A fifth strategy has emerged, which Spergel refers to as organizational/institutional change and development. It seeks to use new mechanisms and tactics through existing organizations and institutions, often leading to changes within those organizations and institutions. Although suppression is presently the dominant strategy against gangs, the key to this emerging gang strategy lies in the use of suppression in conjunction with the other basic strategies, through the interaction of concerned organizations and institutions. This emerging strategy is consistent with the problem-oriented perspective (Spergel 1995).

Under suppression strategies, local citizens and community groups are largely limited to the role of informants. Law enforcement officials make strategic decisions based on intelligence gathered from the community, but with little input from the community in identifying specific problem activity and developing an appropriate response. As a result, the community may not support the tactics used by the police, particularly in the low-income neighborhoods where gangs proliferate and the police experience the greatest level of mistrust and resistance. Where suppression has been especially intense, the scope and severity of the problem has often increased, suggesting that suppressive responses unrelated to community conditions may be causally related to the continued growth, spread, and development of gangs (Spergel 1995; Klein 1995). In order to have legitimacy in the eyes of the community, a problem-oriented intervention must incorporate meaningful community input beyond the traditional role of informant.

Spergel advocates a community problem-solving model that defines broader and more complex problems and responses than those identified through the law-and-order rhetoric of suppression strategies. The model emphasizes the importance of community mobilization in conjunction with social intervention, opportunity provision, and suppression, and coordinated through the collaboration of the appropriate institutions. Calling the model "Community Gang Problem Policing", Spergel promotes the strategy as "a rational social control and community solidarity, social-institution-building approach that strives for the prevention and control of the gang problem on the basis of careful analysis of community and situational factors" (Spergel 1995: 200).

The *Comprehensive Gang Initiative* of the Bureau of Justice Assistance (1997; 1998) provides a prototype model to help agencies and community groups overcome common barriers in addressing gang problems. The model emphasizes adaptability, flexibility, and a multifaceted approach that combines the elements of prevention, intervention, and enforcement. Consistent with Spergel's model, it recognizes the need for responses addressing the variation in gang problems across communities and incorporating community involvement. The use of civil remedies, including injunctions, is one option that is advocated by the model.

One prominent gang researcher has criticized problem-oriented gang interventions in general, and the *Comprehensive Gang Initiative* in particular. Malcolm Klein (1998) questions the propriety of applying problem-oriented interventions to street gang problems, arguing that targeting a particular pattern of problems in a particular location fails to provide a generic solution addressing the community-level factors that spawn gangs. Klein characterizes problem-oriented interventions as a weak, enforcement-driven version of community policing, with decisions made by law enforcement officials, as opposed to a strong version of community policing, in which the community makes resources and allocation decisions in conjunction with the police (Klein 1998: 58). Klein argues that the problem-oriented model enhances the status and reputation of gang members, increasing cohesiveness among members and making the gang more appealing to at-risk youths. Included in his criticism is the gang injunction, which Klein calls "the most recent toy" of the Los Angeles model of gang suppression (Klein 1998: 81). According to Klein, gang injunctions lack programs oriented toward improving the community conditions that lead to gang activity. These conditions include the segregation of the minority population, a lack of opportunities for a large number of young people, weak parental control, and inadequate social services (Ehrenreich 1999a). Although conceding that injunctions may have some short-term effectiveness against drug gangs in a given geographical area, Klein argues that they are not effective for street gangs and will have the long-term effect of increasing cohesion. Klein advocates a strong version of community policing, in which intervention decisions belongs to the community rather than the police, as a better solution to gang problems (Klein 1998).

In response to Klein, Weisel (1998) argues that problem-oriented interventions recognize the wide variation in gangs by inquiring into the nature of the local gang problem before a response is formulated. The range of problem-oriented responses goes beyond normal suppression programs to include situational prevention and partnerships with community agencies, which are aimed at improving community conditions. However, suppression may be an appropriate intervention in communities where the gang problem is out of control. In this sense, problem-oriented interventions are not enforcement-driven, but are preventive and responsive to community conditions.

Problem-oriented interventions are not intended to replace the suppression of crime as a policing tactic. A well conceived problem-oriented response might magnify suppression through forms of civil, social, and regulatory authority beyond the enforcement of the criminal law. Suppression is used 'instrumentally' (Bayley 1994; Toch and Grant 1991) to enhance neighborhood regeneration. When used instrumentally and in collaboration with extra-legal interventions and community input, a more suppressive response is not inconsistent with the problem-oriented perspective.

CHAPTER III

Legal Perspectives

Civil gang abatement is a legal intervention that employs the civil remedy of the preventive injunction to address public nuisances caused by gangs. The expressive function of legal interventions provides a transition from the theoretical perspectives underlying civil gang abatement into the legal issues surrounding the use of injunctions for public nuisances.

THE EXPRESSIVE FUNCTION OF LAW

Legal interventions have the potential to deter criminal behavior, beyond a direct suppressive effect, through the expression of the community's moral condemnation of offensive behavior. Consistent with *Broken Windows* theory (Wilson and Kelling 1982), the social influence perspective advocated by Kahan (1997) and Meares and Kahan (1998) surmises that social influence has a greater impact on criminal behavior than the formal sanctions of the criminal law.

Social influence is defined as the effects on an individual's conduct of his/her perception of the values, beliefs, and behavior of others. Individuals tend to conform their conduct to that of their peers in many aspects of life, including the commission of crime. According to this perspective, an individual's perception of peer attitudes toward criminal activity has a greater deterrent effect on the individual's decision to engage in criminal behavior than the threat of punishment. As a result, the prevalence of criminal activity in a neighborhood reinforces the individual's perception that such behavior is acceptable in that neighborhood, reducing the perceived likelihood of community condemnation. Observing others routinely committing violations sends an additional signal that obedience to laws and social norms is both burdensome and unnecessary, further reinforcing any propensity to engage in criminal behavior. Because social influence shapes the values that individuals attach to criminal behavior, effective anti-crime strategies must recognize the importance of social influence on an individual's rational choice to commit crimes (Kahan 1997).

Social influence theory draws support from the epidemiological perspective that anti-social behavior is contagious. Jones and Jones (2000) describe contagion as a social phenomenon, in which the prevalence of anti-social behavior in the youth's family and community has a strong influence on whether the youth becomes anti-social. Susceptibility to anti-social behavior is strongest in the second decade of life, commonly referred to as adolescence. Adolescent youths who are extensively exposed to anti-social activities, ideas, and people run an increased risk of displaying anti-social behavior. Both a lower prevalence of anti-social behavior and a lower level of the seriousness of such behavior in the community lessen the risk that an adolescent will become anti-social. The transmission of anti-social tendencies can be socially organized, such as through gangs that maintain 'peewee' or 'midget' cliques that prepare younger boys for full gang membership. Increasing pro-social forces in a community will drive the prevalence of anti-social behavior below a critical level and may reverse this contagion effect, setting a trend in motion that further lowers the level of anti-social behavior with little further commitment of social resources. According to Jones and Jones, "the contagion hypothesis is fully compatible with the known epidemiology of antisocial behavior." The tendency of delinquent youths to have other delinquent youths as friends or associates, the prevalence of delinquent acts committed by two or more youths acting in concert, and the consistent finding of inadequate supervision by parents and adults have all been identified as antecedents of anti-social behavior (Jones and Jones 2000: 26).

Public order laws and other legal interventions that regulate social norms are pro-social forces that serve, in part, to shape individual perceptions by giving social meaning to the values, beliefs, and behavior of others. Moral condemnation of visible disorderly behavior through laws designed to suppress disorder expresses the attitude of the community toward minor anti-social behavior, as well as the community's attitude toward more serious crime. Policies that increase the certainty of being held accountable for disorderly behavior inform the individual that the community will not tolerate more serious criminal behavior. Even largely symbolic laws and regulations of social norms that are not strictly enforced reinforce the moral condemnation of particular behavior. Suppression of visible signs of disorder and the accompanying expression of moral condemnation tend to direct the individual away from any propensity to commit more serious crimes (Kahan 1997).

Kahan (1997) and Meares and Kahan (1998) have applied the expressive function of law to gangs. They argue that legal interventions designed to reduce visible gang activity are more likely to reduce the social influence of gangs than are increases in the severity of punishment for serious crimes through gang enhancement statutes. The prevalence of highly visible gang activity in a neighborhood leads to the perception by area youths that gang membership is valued and expected by their peers. Gang membership is not intrinsically valued by all inner city youths, some of whom have directly experienced the violence and damage caused by gangs. However, many reluctant youths are drawn into gangs through a misperception of the value of gang membership to their peers. Furthermore, gang membership often appears more prevalent than it is because visible gang activity affects the emotional dispositions of non-gang members. Youths not involved in gangs often display the aggressive posture associated with gang members as a defense mechanism, increasing the visible evidence of gang activity and reinforcing the perceived acceptance of gangs in the neighborhood. This aggressive demeanor also increases the rate of violent crime, as individuals displaying such a demeanor find it difficult to back down from violent encounters. As a result of this increased visible evidence of gang activity, the fear of crime increases in the neighborhood, causing law-abiding citizens to take defensive measures in response to outwardly aggressive behavior and the perceived prevalence of gang activity (Kahan 1997; Meares and Kahan 1998).

In neighborhoods where the social influence of visible gang activity is strong, conventional crackdowns on serious criminal activity by law enforcement are often ineffective. Instead of deterring gang activity, severe penalties resulting from crackdowns and enhancement statutes reinforce the social influence of gangs by increasing the status of lawbreaking gang members, who project great strength and courage in the face of overwhelming odds. In contrast, legal strategies that suppress visible gang activity also inform youths that gang involvement is not a valued and acceptable norm. These strategies are potentially more effective against the social influence of gangs because they counter the perception of the high status of gang members in the neighborhood, diminishing the pressure to join gangs and to emulate gang behavior. Loitering ordinances, curfews, and civil injunctions are legal strategies that attempt to reduce visible gang activity, which, in turn, influences individual perceptions of community norms (Meares and Kahan 1998).

Legal interventions against gangs must gain the support of the community by increasing the certainty of, rather than the severity of, the resulting sanction. A low certainty of punishment for gang activity fails to have a deterrent effect or to express moral condemnation. Benefits for law-abiding citizens are reduced by the failure to diminish visible gang activity, decreasing the willingness of residents to cooperate with authorities. To maintain a deterrent effect, a low certainty intervention requires a more severe sanction, which is often imposed by authorities without any input from the affected community (Kahan 1997).

Harsher punishments may lead to a further loss of community support because of the destructive impact of severe sanctions on communities. Low-income communities, where gang activity is most prevalent, have experienced the collateral damage caused by longer terms of incarceration. The resulting atomization of families leads to increased economic and social hardship for family members remaining in the community and for the community at large. Harsher sanctions also increase the threat of retaliation by gang members against citizens who cooperate with authorities and convey the perception of the contempt of society for the predominately minority citizens who reside in these communities. Less cooperation and community support reinforces the lower certainty of sanction by decreasing the cooperation of citizens that authorities need to reduce disorder and crime (Kahan 1997).

A high certainty/low severity policy counteracts these dynamics by raising the expected benefits of cooperation, reducing the destructive effects of severe sanctions, diminishing the threat of retaliation, and avoiding the perception of social condemnation. Cooperation by the community raises the certainty of sanction while lowering the necessity of applying more severe sanctions to obtain a deterrent effect, which in turn leads to even greater cooperation by residents (Kahan 1997).

Gang loitering ordinances, curfews, and civil injunctions are legal interventions for which the severity of sanction is relatively low and the certainty of sanction is relatively high (Kahan 1997). Violations are classified as minor misdemeanors or civil contempt carrying, at most, relatively short periods of incarceration. Authorities can enforce them with relative ease when compared with the more stringent evidentiary requirements associated with serious crimes. Their use to combat gang activity may garner the necessary support of the community, particularly when the community has input into drafting the interventions. Statutes and ordinances aimed at enhancing public order over an entire jurisdiction may encounter constitutional challenges that civil remedies tailored to meet the needs of a specific neighborhood are able to avoid.

CONSTITUTIONAL PROBLEMS IN PUBLIC ORDER LAWS

One major impediment to the use of public order laws, such as gang loitering and curfew ordinances, for addressing visible gang activity is their susceptibility to constitutional challenges for vagueness and overbreadth. Originating in the due process clause of the Fourteenth Amendment, the vagueness doctrine requires a penal statute to give adequate notice to the ordinary person of the conduct or activity prohibited and to prevent arbitrary and discriminatory enforcement by providing adequate standards limiting discretionary decisions by the police (*Kolender v. Lawson* 1983; *Papachristou v. City of Jacksonville* 1972). Derived from the First Amendment, the overbreadth doctrine requires that a law be invalidated if its proscriptions are reasonably capable of restricting constitutionally protected speech or conduct (*Gooding v. Wilson* 1972; *Cohen v. California* 1971; *R.A.V. v. City of St. Paul* 1992). The vagueness and overbreadth doctrines have invalidated public order laws specifically aimed at reducing gang activity.[25] The result is that law enforcement authorities have been severely limited by constitutional constraints on public order laws.

The recent emphasis on preventive interventions to reduce neighborhood disorder requires new sources of authority allowing law enforcement officials to address the minor street misconduct that enhances neighborhood disorder and gang activity (Livingston 1997). The United States Supreme Court has recently implied that a targeted approach to gang activity might pass constitutional scrutiny. While invalidating Chicago's *Gang Congregation Ordinance*, under which over 42,000 arrests and 89,000 dispersal orders were made in three years, as void-for-vagueness, the Court left the constitutional door open to an intervention directly prohibiting the intimidating conduct presented by "'the very presence of a large collection of obviously brazen, insistent, and lawless gang members and hangers-on on the public way'" (*City of Chicago v. Morales* 1999: 1856-7).

The decision is significant to the future viability of the gang injunction. Proscriptions on the public association of gang members and on the intimidation of law-abiding citizens are central to the gang injunction. By prohibiting the gang members from congregating in public and openly displaying the gang's hold over a neighborhood, injunctions attack the group processes that enhance the social influence of the gang over the community (Meares and Kahan 1998), while reducing the availability of targets for drive-by shootings by rival gangs. Almost every gang injunction has some form of associational prohibition.[26] According to San Diego County Assistant District Attorney Susan Mazza, the non-association provision is "the most important tool" in the abatement strategy (*San Diego Union-Tribune* 1997). Prior to *Morales*, the Supreme Court had declined review of the leading California case on gang injunctions (*People v. Acuna* (Cal. 1997), cert. denied sub nom. *Gonzalez v. Gallo* (1997)), implying that this targeted legal intervention passes constitutional scrutiny.[27]

Despite the constitutional deficiencies in the use of public order laws to address gang activity, this approach has not been abandoned. For example, on the heels of the *Morales* decision, both the Los Angeles County Board and Supervisors and the Malibu City Council have passed gang loitering ordinances. The Malibu ordinance prohibits gang members from loitering, flashing gang signs, or intimidating non-gang members (*Westside Weekly* 1999). The Los Angeles County ordinance, applicable only in unincorporated county areas, prohibits gang members and anyone accompanying them from loitering in public places with the intent to display a street gang's dominance over public areas, intimidate others from entering public areas, or conceal criminal activity. It also imposes criminal liability on parents whose juvenile children are convicted under the ordinance. According to county officials, the wording of the ordinance was based on the outcome of the *Morales* decision (Riccardi 1999). One commentator claims that the ordinance would eliminate the need for obtaining gang injunctions (Melendi 1999). Challenges under *Morales* have been predicted for both ordinances.

Buena Park and San Bernardino, California, have recently adopted ordinances that merge the civil remedy of eviction with criminal sanctions for non-compliance by landlords. The ordinances require landlords to evict tenants who have been arrested on suspicion of drug- and gang-related offenses occurring in or around their buildings. The ordinances are modeled after a similar law enacted by the City of Los Angeles in 1997, which forced the eviction of 168 people without being successfully challenged in the courts. These ordinances attempt to give police and landlords a legal tool to help prevent the neighborhood decay that accompanies constant gang and drug activity. Eviction is based on arrest, not conviction, causing protests that innocent people who are mistakenly arrested will face eviction without rigorous due process safeguards.[28] When an eviction is appealed, the city manager hears the case in a civil proceeding to determine whether a legal basis for the eviction exists. The Buena Park law covers an entire apartment complex, including the alleys and areas immediately adjoining the complex. It is imposed on an entire family if one household member is arrested. Landlords who refuse to evict under the ordinance face fines and, if refusing four times in one year, misdemeanor charges, placing the onus for enforcement clearly on landlords (Frazier 1999; Gottlieb 1999; Hong 1999).

The Chicago suburb of Cicero, Illinois, has passed the first law in the country aimed at banishing gang members from its jurisdiction. Responding to sixty-four shootings and fifteen homicides in 1998, most of which were gang-related, a non-binding resolution garnered ninety-six percent of the vote in favor of the ordinance, leading the town council to unanimously pass the ordinance. Applying equally to juveniles[29] and adults, the ordinance requires identified gang members who, after an administrative hearing, have been determined to pose an active threat to the community to leave Cicero and not return, even to visit family members. Those who fail to leave or who return to the town face a $500-a-day fine (Belluck 1999; *Law Enforcement News* 1999; Slater 1999).[30]

By its very nature, the gang injunction differs from these broad ordinances. Injunctive relief is narrowly construed to directly prohibit specified harmful conduct that contributes to a public nuisance in a strictly defined locale, in contrast to the prohibition of relatively ambiguous conduct and the citywide application of an ordinance. Ordinances purposely target undefined groups, while the gang injunction targets individual members of an identified association. The application of the injunction is limited to named individuals previously identified by law enforcement officials as gang members and to associates whose conduct is linked to the public nuisance. It is enforceable only within the specified target area in which the public nuisance exists. It avoids arbitrary enforcement by being implemented through a written court order that has passed judicial scrutiny prior to enforcement, and the individuals enjoined must be notified of their status as defendants and of the provisions of the injunction prior to any enforcement action against them.

The increasing reliance on ordinances and gang injunctions to specifically address gang activity represents an accelerating swing in public sentiment from an emphasis on individual rights toward an emphasis on community safety. Cicero's gang banishment ordinance, the eviction ordinances and gang injunctions cropping up in California, and anti-gang loitering ordinances passed in spite of *Morales* are evidence of how innovative, and often draconian, criminal and civil measures are being formulated to combat the corrosive effect of gang activity on neighborhoods and to express the community condemnation of gang activity. These measures also illustrate how legal tools are evolving from an emphasis on criminal convictions toward a reliance on the civil law, causing an already unclear theoretical legal distinction to become even more ambiguous in practice.

THE CRIMINAL / CIVIL LAW DISTINCTION

In 1968, Herbert Packer exposed the limits of using the criminal law to regulate anti-social behavior. Challenging the law enforcement community to find a systematic way to adjust its singular reliance on the criminal law, Packer suggested that some anti-social conduct could be addressed more expeditiously through the civil law, which permits individualized before-the-fact regulation against carefully chosen areas of serious anti-social behavior. While recognizing the expense and burden of individualized proactive regulation, Packer saw an advantage in leaving the actor a free, participating member of society, inhibited only by the actor's predetermined threat to the community. Under this strategy, the sanctions of the criminal law become the option of last resort, rather than the first option under traditional crime-suppression strategies (Packer 1968: 253-255). Goldstein's proposal for the use of civil remedies as one option under the problem-oriented perspective (Goldstein 1990: 139) is consistent with Packer's reasoning. However, the application of civil law to address what is primarily activity related to criminal behavior may further cloud the already amorphous distinction between criminal and civil law.

According to Cheh (1991), the distinction between criminal and civil law has historically been a defining feature of the Anglo-American tradition of jurisprudence. Theoretically, criminal law emphasizes the adjudication of guilt in an adversarial proceeding that protects the accused through the strictly formulated rules of substantive and procedural law. In contrast, civil law emphasizes rights and responsibilities in interactions between private parties in an equitable proceeding based on the particular circumstances of the case. Criminal and civil proceedings are distinguished by being held in separate courts that follow different rules of procedure, burdens of proof, and modes of remedy. The distinction is important because the constitutional protections afforded to the accused in a criminal proceeding are generally not available to a defendant in a civil proceeding. Although some exceptions have been crafted by judicial fiat, the Fifth Amendment privilege against self incrimination and the rights to a speedy trial, trial by jury, confrontation of witnesses, compulsory process, and assistance of counsel of the Sixth Amendment expressly apply to criminal prosecutions; and, the requirement that guilt be proven beyond a reasonable doubt has been largely confined to criminal prosecutions by judicial precedent. Criminal law exacts a penalty expressing condemnation after an act has occurred, and its sanctions are substantially limited to incarceration, execution, and fines. In contrast, civil law attempts to prevent future harm as well as remedy a past wrong. Civil remedies encompass a much broader range of alternatives, including restitution and recompense, monetary penalties, loss of government benefits and privileges, asset forfeiture, preventive detention and civil commitment, and injunctive relief (Cheh 1991).

Presently, there is an accelerating tendency by law enforcement agencies to address anti-social behavior with civil remedies. The recognition of the inadequacy of conventional law enforcement methods in addressing some criminal activities has caused criminal justice officials to pursue multiple strategies to both punish and prevent anti-social behavior. Anti-social behavior is viewed as "a problem to be met, managed, and resolved by *whatever* tools will do the job" (Finn and Hylton 1994: 4). Other factors leading to the proliferation of the use of civil remedies include the undesirability of criminal remedies, with the attendant stigma and condemnation (Cheh 1998), as a solution for some problems; the increased societal emphasis on prevention (Steiker 1998); and the increased accessibility of civil remedies as alternatives to criminal remedies (Green Mazerolle and Roehl 1998).

Employing civil remedies to address criminal behavior is not a new response to crime. Victims have always had the option of pursuing compensation through civil actions against convicted criminals, and federal administrative agencies have pursued both criminal prosecutions and civil actions in regulatory areas, such as antitrust and security law violations. However, law enforcement agencies are employing civil remedies to prevent crime at a much higher rate than in the past (Cheh 1991: 1327). Today, "civil remedy solutions are the norm rather than the exception" (Green Mazerolle and Roehl 1998: 2). Among the increasing array of preemptive strikes on criminal problems through the civil law are the use of zoning and building codes to close drug houses (Green 1996), civil commitment to incapacitate sex offenders after their prison terms expire (*Kansas v. Hendricks* 1997), asset forfeiture to seize cash and property assets from convicted drug dealers (Moran 1997) and other criminals (Finn and Hylton 1994; *Bennis v. Michigan* 1994), and the use of injunctions to abate prostitution (Kelley 1999) and hate crimes (Finn and Hylton 1994).

Several reasons have been advanced for the increasing tendency of law enforcement agencies to turn to civil remedies to address criminal behavior. Civil remedies expand the responses available to law enforcement, reaching anti-social behavior that is beyond the scope of the criminal law or addressing criminal behavior in a more expeditious manner. The increased reach of the civil law is partially attributable to the less stringent due process safeguards of civil procedure when compared to the rigorous constitutional protections of criminal procedure. As a result, the civil process is often perceived as being more swift and certain than the criminal process; and, when the criminal behavior amounts to only a misdemeanor, civil remedies may be more severe than criminal sanctions (Cheh 1991). Swiftness, certainty, and severity comprise the triumvirate of elements that are theoretically necessary for the effective deterrence of criminal behavior (Maxson and Allen 1997). Finally, the non-criminal nature of civil litigation can generate more support from the community, helping overcome the widespread mistrust of inner-city residents for traditional suppression tactics and improving the quality of life of those who lack the resources to improve their environment (Finn and Hylton 1994).

In reality, the separation of criminal and civil law has never been clear or complete (Cheh 1991; Finn and Hylton 1994; Wasby 1980), and the recent acceleration of the use of civil remedies to prevent common street crime will further cloud the distinction. The rise of the 'preventive state' (Steiker 1998: 774) is most commonly evident in the increase of preventive measures through community- and problem-oriented policing initiatives, from which the concept of community prosecution was spawned. These initiatives allow law enforcement agencies to identify and proactively neutralize potential violators by imposing restrictions on their liberties before they commit crimes. The problem posed by these initiatives is two-fold: (1) identifying those practices and policies that, despite being labeled civil, are so punitive that they should be subjected to the constitutional constraints of the criminal sanction; and, (2) determining what constitutional and/or policy constraints should be placed on preventive practices that really are non-punitive in nature (Steiker 1998: 776-7). As crime prevention has recently become the rage in criminal justice, the distinction between civil and criminal law is likely to become more ambiguous, with relatively new remedies and new applications of old remedies being formulated to enhance the preventive role of law enforcement agencies.

PUBLIC NUISANCE LAW

The nuisance abatement authority of municipal governments has been advocated as a particularly appropriate tool to address difficult public order problems for which the criminal law has proven insufficient (Goldstein 1990). Perhaps this is due to the amorphous legal meaning of the term 'nuisance'. Originally meaning 'harm' (Spencer 1989), the scope of conduct brought under the legal concept of 'nuisance' has never been exactly defined and has broadened considerably since the term was first applied to anti-social behavior, changing as the needs of the public have changed (Spector 1999). Prosser raised the point most eloquently, stating:

> There is perhaps no more impenetrable jungle in the entire law than that which surrounds the word 'nuisance'. It has meant all things to all men, and has been applied indiscriminately to everything from an alarming advertisement to a cockroach baked in a pie. There is general agreement that it is incapable of any exact or comprehensive definition (*Farmy v. College Housing, Inc.* 1975: 175, citing Prosser, Law of Torts (4th ed. 1971), 571).

Early Development of the Public Nuisance

Spencer (1989) provides a history of the development of the common law concept of public nuisance. Under the early common law of thirteenth century England, *nuisance* referred to harm resulting from the prevention of the use of land, short of dispossession. Later courts allowed actions for nuisance for less serious forms of interference with land use that amounted to mere inconvenience. By the seventeenth century, nuisance was used in the context of private disputes between neighbors for harm caused by interference with the use of, enjoyment of, or rights over land by the occupant.

Public, or common, nuisance law developed in parallel with private nuisance law, proscribing the same type of conduct when committed against the community in general. At first, public nuisance centered on blocking highways and running trades that adversely affected the community's use of public space. Private nuisance, where the action only affected the plaintiff, was a civil action heard in the common law courts, whereas public nuisance, which affected the whole community, was generally a violation heard in the local criminal courts. Civil actions were brought for a public nuisance only where a plaintiff had suffered significantly greater damage than the rest of the community. Otherwise, public nuisance actions stemmed from the police powers of the sovereign and were prosecuted as crimes (Spencer 1989).

Through the public nuisance laws, the local criminal courts eventually gained jurisdiction over an assortment of petty offenses that interfered with public rights: blocking or impeding public rights of way, polluting water by trades, allowing animals to wander, selling unwholesome or short measures of food or ale, catching immature fish and hunting out-of-season, running bawdy-houses and disorderly ale-houses, night walking and eavesdropping, allowing a house to become overrun with the poor through subdivision, and being a common scold (a person who breaks the public peace). These activities were distinct from conduct interfering with the use and enjoyment of land that gave rise to the private nuisance; they were harmful to the community or damaging to the public welfare. In the early eighteenth century, William Hawkins further expanded the concept of public nuisance by placing all the crimes that he could not otherwise categorize into the residual category of 'common nuisance', defined as "an offense against the public, either by doing a thing which tends to the annoyance of all the King's subjects, or by neglecting to do a thing which the common good requires" (Spencer 1989: 66).

The late eighteenth and early nineteenth centuries saw the first actions seeking injunctions against public nuisances as a supplement to, not a substitute for, criminal proceedings. Temporary injunctions, which were in force prior to trial, were sought in cases where a criminal defendant threatened irreparable harm to the community before the case could be adjudicated. The use of injunctive relief expanded at the beginning of the nineteenth century in response to pollution from untreated wastewater, which was commonly dumped into rivers by private and municipal corporations and affected the health and welfare of downstream residents. Private corporations were regarded as incapable of committing a criminal offence and, therefore, beyond the reach of criminal prosecution for public nuisances. Municipal corporations that operated sewers under powers granted by Parliament were even further removed from criminal liability. Even if prosecution were possible, fines and jail sentences were viewed as ineffective against conduct that repeatedly or continuously threatened the health and welfare of the public. Because public officials had no meaningful remedy for these forms of public nuisance, the Chancery courts, which were administrative courts under the direct authority of the King, eventually began to grant permanent injunctions against such violations on the application of government officials. In time, the injunction was regarded as the only sensible remedy for any continuing public nuisance, and criminal prosecutions for health hazards virtually disappeared. Although the public nuisance was still a crime, the common method of suppressing it became an injunction issued in civil court, instead of prosecution in criminal court.

California Public Nuisance Law

Upon attaining statehood in 1850, California adopted the common law as the basis of the state's legal system. In 1872, the legislature first codified both 'nuisance' and 'public nuisance'. In 1873-74, the Civil Code was revised and nuisance was redefined, and in 1996, the illegal sale of controlled substances was added to the definition (Allen 1998). Today, nuisance is defined as:

> [A]nything which is injurious to health, including, but not limited to, the illegal sale of controlled substances, or is indecent or offensive to the senses, or an obstruction to the free use of property, so as to interfere with the comfortable enjoyment of life or property, or unlawfully obstructs the free passage or use, in the customary manner, of any navigable lake, or river, bay stream, canal, or basin, or any public park, square, street, or highway . . . (California Civil Code s. 3479).

Public nuisance is defined as a nuisance:

> [Anything] which affects at the same time an entire community or neighborhood, or any considerable number of persons, although the extent of the annoyance or damage inflicted upon individuals may be unequal (California Civil Code s. 3480).

The offending conduct must be continuous and repetitive, not an isolated act. It also must tend to cause substantial harm to the exercise of a common right of the public or to annoy a substantial portion of the community. Conduct that interferes with the use and enjoyment of land by a large number of persons is not automatically considered a public nuisance, and whether it is prohibited under the criminal law is legally irrelevant. The inquiry into whether conduct is a public nuisance turns upon the reasonableness of its interference with a public right under the peculiar circumstances of the case. The test is the character of the injury or right impinged upon and the possibility of substantial annoyance or inconvenience to the public by invasion of its rights, not the lawfulness of the conduct nor the number of persons injured.

Three remedies are available for a public nuisance: indictment/information,[31] a civil lawsuit, and abatement (California Civil Code s. 3491). The first two remedies seek reparations for past injury. In contrast, abatement is a civil action that applies to the future. It is aimed at stopping the offensive activity, turning on the question of whether the activity is so unreasonable that it must cease. Any attorney who is authorized to represent the state or an appropriate subdivision may bring an abatement action, including joint actions by both district and city attorneys.

THE PREVENTIVE INJUNCTION

Civil gang abatement employs the civil remedy of the preventive, or prohibitory, injunction (Fiss 1978) to abate gang activity as a public nuisance. A preventive injunction is a judicial order commanding defendants to perform or refrain from performing some specified acts . It is chiefly employed to prevent future irreparable injury when other legal remedies are inadequate. Preventive injunctions are well established in Anglo-American law as the primary equitable remedy for the abatement of public nuisances (Dunbar, 1898). Injunctive relief is a suitable problem-oriented intervention because it is proactive, allows a surgical response to specific neighborhood conditions, and may be fashioned to avoid the potential for unfairness to innocent parties (Goldstein 1990: 140).

In his classic work entitled *Government by Injunction*, Dunbar (1898) provides a summary of the injunction process:

> The power to issue writs of injunction is one of the chief characteristics of courts exercising chancery powers. An injunction perpetually restraining a defendant from doing specified acts may be granted after a full hearing as the final relief sought in the suit; but a preliminary injunction temporarily restraining the commission of certain acts, until the case can finally be decided, may also be issued immediately upon the filing of the bill of complaint, or at any subsequent time, and either with or without notice to the defendant. An injunction of either class is in substance an order of the court to the person named in it directing him to refrain from doing certain things. The penalty for any violation of this prohibition is a summary proceeding by attachment to punish the offender for a contempt of the court in disobeying its order...Such a proceeding is, invariably, in the absence of statutory provision to the contrary, heard by the court without the intervention of a jury, and with no right of appeal for error of law or fact. If the contempt is established, punishment may be inflicted by fine or imprisonment or both...The vigorous and summary nature of this remedy renders it exceptionally effective in affording relief, and, also, it must be conceded, exceptionably capable of abuse (Dunbar, 1898: 5-6).

The *California Code of Civil Procedure* defines an injunction as "a writ or order requiring a person to refrain from a particular act" (California Code of Civil Procedure s. 525). Among the cases where an injunction may be granted are:

> (1) When it appears by the complaint that the plaintiff is entitled to the relief demanded, and the relief, or any part thereof, consists in restraining the commission or continuance of the act complained of, either for a limited period or perpetually.

> (2) When it appears by the complaint or affidavits that the commission or continuance of some act during the litigation would produce waste, or great or irreparable injury to a party to the action...
> (4) When pecuniary compensation would not afford adequate relief.
> (5) Where it would be extremely difficult to ascertain the amount of compensation which would afford adequate relief.
> (6) Where restraint is necessary to prevent a multiplicity of judicial proceedings.
> (California Code of Civil Procedures. 526 (a)).

Although the preventive injunction has been likened to a mini-criminal code (Fiss 1978; Graham 1996), it is distinguished from the criminal statute by several characteristics. Unlike criminal statutes, which must address the actions of the general public, the preventive injunction operates *in personam*, addressing only the actions of clearly identified individuals. Prior to enforcement of an injunction, these named individual must be notified of the existence and provisions of the injunction. Because the injunction is a tailored remedy, the activities demanded or proscribed by the injunction are described with a degree of specificity not ordinarily found in criminal statutes, allowing the judge to make a surgical strike at harmful conduct. Unlike a criminal statute, the issuance of an injunction is conditional upon a showing of the likelihood of irreparable injury and the inadequacy of alternative remedies for the prevention or repair of the injury. Finally, because the injunction is an equitable remedy that allows a high degree of judicial discretion, more power is invested in the judge in issuing an injunction than in judging criminal liability (Fiss 1978).

The jurisdiction of a court sitting in equity over controversies involving criminal conduct is based on the greater adequacy of the injunction as a remedy when compared to the criminal law. Through a temporary restraining order, a court can intervene immediately to prevent the continuance or completion of an act that cannot be addressed by the criminal law until irreparable injury has occurred. The jurisdiction of a court of equity is not negated merely because the threatened act is defined as a crime. Equity jurisdiction exists for the adjudication of civil rights and, since every crime involves some infraction of civil rights, criminal acts are subject to injunctive relief (Dunbar, 1898).

Where the acts are repeated and almost certain to continue into the future, an injunction provides a more adequate remedy than separate criminal prosecutions for each violation. Where repeated convictions have failed to stop persistent violations of criminal statutes, the criminal law is obviously inadequate and injunctive relief is appropriate. Some state legislatures have passed statutory provisions empowering courts of equity to abate public nuisances created or maintained by criminal offenses, even where there is no showing of injury to property or to civil rights. Such statutes have been held valid and constitutional, falling within the state's police power to protect the public's health and morals. They are regarded as a proper extension of equity jurisdiction, furnishing a cumulative remedy in aid of the criminal law. Municipal ordinance violations may also fall under equity jurisdiction as public nuisances. In passing such provisions, legislatures perceive equitable remedies as speedier, and more certain and/or efficient, than a complaint under the criminal law. The clear intention is to use the civil process to punish persons guilty of violating injunctions, not to add to the prohibition of the criminal statutes. In this sense, injunctive relief is justified by greater efficacy in preventing a future injury, due to the higher probability of a conviction for contempt in a summary proceeding by a judge than by a jury, and without the encumbrance of the right of appeal (Dunbar, 1898).

Livingston (1997) has heralded the preventive injunction as a viable option to the criminal law for dealing with neighborhood public order problems. Civil injunctions have the advantage of allowing the trial judge to be more precise in restricting offensive conduct by tailoring the injunction to the specific circumstances of the case. Injunctions applied to community problems require specification of the problem that gives rise to the need for relief, necessitating community involvement in conducting a thorough examination of neighborhood conditions related to the problem. The resulting injunction can be carefully crafted to precisely prohibit the specified activities that contribute to the problem. Prior judicial scrutiny resulting in a written order avoids the problem of arbitrary enforcement often associated with public order statutes by limiting police enforcement authority to specified locations, persons, and prohibited conduct (Livingston 1997).

Despite the advantages, there are significant issues concerning the use of injunctions to address public order problems. Injunctions are generally granted on the basis of sworn affidavits and may be issued temporarily in *ex parte* proceedings, without notice to or challenge by the defendant, precluding the opportunity by the defendant to confront witnesses prior to a judgment. Under California civil procedure, a temporary restraining order can be issued without notice to the opposing parties when great or irreparable injury will result to the applicant before the matter can be heard by the court or when notice could not be made after a good faith effort by the applicant (California Code of Civil Procedure s. 527 (c)).

The judge is afforded wide discretion in determining whether to grant an injunction and what provisions to include in the order, heightening the risk of the discriminatory application of relief. The judge can issue an injunction in clear disregard of equitable and legal principles and not be reversed by a higher court until after the issue has been effectively disposed of, wrongfully prejudicing the defendants. The judge also has a great deal of discretion in deciding whether the facts of the case justify an injunction. To a large extent, his decision cannot be reviewed without clear evidence of abuse of his discretionary powers. The defendant is obliged to obey both a temporary and permanent injunction, even though it may be quashed in later proceedings (Powell 1928: 47). As a result of this heightened risk of discretionary abuse, the issues of the conditions under which injunctive relief is appropriate, the individuals who can be legitimately enjoined, and the appropriate scope of relief are controversial in the application of injunctive relief (Livingston 1997: 644), including the gang injunction.

The demand of advance specification of neighborhood conditions requires a close analysis of neighborhood problems, necessitating close collaboration between law enforcement authorities and the community (Livingston 1997: 645) to ensure that the provisions of the injunction are necessary and appropriate in the local context. Such collaboration has often been difficult to attain, especially in low-income communities where public order problems prevail alongside the lack of a "quasi formal social organizational structure that would facilitate access to community residents" (Maxson and Allen 1997) and the perception that the police represent a suppressive occupation force. Many of these issues have been raised regarding the use of injunctions to abate public nuisances and will be discussed in Chapter IV, which specifically addresses the gang injunction.

Preventive injunctions have been used in various contexts to prohibit patterns of conduct that precede and facilitate criminal conduct, including labor strikes (*Milkwagon Drivers Union v. Meadowmoor* 1941), abortion protests (*Madsen v. Women's Health Center* 1994), and civil rights violations (*United States v. Original*

Knights of the Ku Klux Klan 1965; *Commonwealth v. Guilfoyle* 1988). Preventive injunctions have also been used to redress public nuisances threatening anti-social or criminal behavior, including labor conflicts (*In re Debs*, 1895), doctor-assisted suicide (*People v. Kevorkian* 1995), prostitution (Tamaki 1995; Kelly 1999), and traffic violations (*State v. United-Buckingham Freight Lines* (Iowa1973)). Injunctions for labor strikes and abortion protests are analogous to the use of injunctions against gangs because of the influence of group dynamics in each of those situations.

In a labor strike, picketers often try to interfere with the ability of the employer to conduct business during the strike by intimidating individuals from entering the workplace. When routine police action fails to insure the protection of those choosing to cross the picket line and future violence is imminent, the police or the employer may request an injunction from the court by providing evidence that the strikers are creating a dangerous nuisance. The provisions of relief are usually in the form of some prohibition on the activities of the strikers, such as picketing close to the workplace entrance or carrying signs or other objects that might be used as weapons if violence erupts. The injunction applies to every striker who pickets after being formally notified of the injunction. If they choose to ignore the orders, they are subject to arrest for violating the injunction (Los Angeles City Attorney Gang Prosecution Section 1995).

Similar to the labor strike, requests for injunctions against abortion protestors are aimed at abating a pattern of conduct by groups intent on disrupting the business of the abortion clinic. The pattern of conduct includes protestors congregating in dangerously large groups close to the entrance of the abortion clinic, harassing employees and other individuals entering the clinic by picketing, displaying signs, singing, yelling, and approaching clients. These activities are intended to intimidate all individuals who wish to enter, regardless of their business in the clinic. In *Madsen v. Women's Health Center, Inc.* (1994), the United States Supreme Court upheld the use of the injunction to block abortion protesters from normally lawful behavior when it is used to harass and intimidate employees and clients. San Jose City Attorney Joan Gallo relied on *Madsen* as precedent in the city's appeal to the California Supreme Court in *People v. Acuna* (1997) (Kisliuk 1995), which is presently the highest legal authority on the propriety of the gang injunction.

CHAPTER IV

The Gang Injunction

Civil gang abatement is a strategy that merges "Broken Windows" theory and contemporary gang theory, operationalized through community prosecution, to address gang activity having such a corrosive effect on a community that it constitutes a public nuisance. The result is a civil remedy that combines the nuisance abatement authority of municipal governments with the equitable remedy of the preventive injunction to prohibit nuisance-related behavior by named gang members within a delineated geographic area. Although gangs have existed throughout history, the gang injunction is a fairly recent legal development that broadens the application of the public nuisance doctrine to address visible gang activity in areas besieged by the violence and disorder caused by criminal street gangs.

The gang injunction did not suddenly appear in the prosecutor's anti-gang arsenal. It emerged through the innovated use of injunctions of a more limited scope to combat gang-induced public nuisances. Since the gang injunction was first introduced in 1987, case law from appellate decisions has refined the gang injunction. Although addressing a variety of behavior and types of gangs, there is a standard process followed by prosecutors seeking gang injunctions, potential pitfalls in the acquisition process, and relevant questions regarding implementation, effectiveness, and possible abuse by officials.

THE EMERGENCE OF THE GANG INJUNCTION

Castorena (1998b) and Whitmer and Ancker (1996) have provided a historical perspective on the emergence of the gang injunction in California. The use of the public nuisance doctrine to address gang activity in California is relatively new, beginning in the early 1980's with building nuisance abatement actions against specific buildings where gang activity was problematic. The first reported application occurred in the city of Santa Ana in 1980 against a gang hangout, which was the source of rampant crime in the surrounding area. Although the court denied a preliminary injunction, a temporary restraining order that enjoined named gang members from gathering and drinking at the address reportedly eliminated the problem.

Between 1981 and 1986, the Los Angeles County District Attorney's Office (LADA) obtained three separate injunctions in Pomona, West Covina, and East Los Angeles. The Pomona injunction was a joint effort by the LADA and the Los Angeles City Attorney (LACA) against twelve named gang members and a homeowner who allowed the gang members to congregate on his property. The judge denied relief against the gang members, but issued an injunction against the homeowner. The West Covina and East Los Angeles injunctions targeted specific addresses and were issued as requested. In West Covina, five named members of the Alwood Street Lodies were enjoined from congregating, drinking and having loud, boisterous parties at a particular house. The East Los Angeles injunction targeted the owners of a crack house. All three injunctions reportedly eliminated the problems that were associated with the targeted locations (Castorena 1998b; Whitmer and Ancker 1996).

In 1988, an injunction was issued to the Burbank City Attorney prohibiting a Burbank minister and his wife from allowing more than two members of the North Hollywood Boyz gang, including their son, from congregating at their home. Claiming that they were trying to reform the youths, the couple allowed as many as thirty-five youths to gather at their home at one time. Although no arrests were made at the couple's home, complaints in the surrounding area included fighting, drinking, racing cars, carrying concealed weapons, vandalizing property, and applying graffiti. After a temporary restraining order was obtained by the city, no further problems were reported (Puig 1988).

During the same period, the LACA was taking similar actions against gangs. In 1982, three gangs (Dogtown, Primera Flats, and the 62nd Street East Coast Crips) and over seventy named gang members were prohibited from applying graffiti and from entering private and public property for the purpose of applying graffiti. Each defendant was also required to devote at least five hours painting over graffiti (Castorena 1998b; Whitmer and Ancker 1996). One prosecutor called the *Dogtown* injunction the first gang injunction.[32] *Dogtown* was the first injunction to name a gang as an unincorporated association and was not restricted to a specific address, but applied citywide (Castorena 1998b; Whitmer and Ancker 1996). *Dogtown* also highlights the importance of graffiti as gang-related activity, rather than the mere defacement of property:

> Gang graffiti is the means by which a gang establishes and announces its authority and control over a community. ... The graffiti represents the core of gang identity. It proclaims gang territorial control as superior to the rights of all other residents and property owners. It proclaims gang authority as above that of legitimate law enforcement. ... Gang graffiti serves as a permanent and constant reminder of the fear which grips the inhabitants (*People v. Dogtown* 1982, Application for Order to Show Cause re Preliminary Injunction).

The perceived success of the building abatement injunctions in addressing gang activity led to the first court order representing the contemporary gang injunction, obtained by the Los Angeles City Attorney in 1987 to address drug dealing and the accompanying violence in the Cadillac/Corning section of the city. The injunction request was controversial, with the judge questioning the logic of imposing civil sanctions on gang members who often fail to comply with probation conditions after being convicted of criminal offenses (Feldman 1987). The judge also found many of the proposed provisions – including congregating in public in groups of two or more, remaining in public streets for longer than five minutes, and having visitors in their residences for less than ten minutes – in violation of basic constitutional liberties. After eighteen proposed provisions were stricken by the judge, twenty-three named members and all other known members of the Playboy Gangster Crips were prohibited from trespassing, vandalism, blocking free ingress and egress, urinating and defecating in public, littering, and annoying, harassing, intimidating, threatening, or molesting citizens – conduct already proscribed under the criminal law. The order had no geographical limitations within the city of Los Angeles (Castorena 1998b; *People v. Playboy Gangster Crips* 1987, Statement of Decision).

The gang injunction was not used again until 1992, when the Burbank City Attorney's Office obtained an injunction against thirty-four members of the Barrio Elmwood Rifa gang in a target area comprising an entire city block. Among the incidents that triggered the injunction initiative was the shooting of a female, whose car had broken down on a freeway adjacent to a cul-de-sac where the gang congregated. Thinking that the female and her male passengers were from a rival gang, gang members opened fire on the vehicle, seriously injuring the driver. The injunction was the first to include the controversial non-association clause, which prohibited defendants from appearing in public view with any other defendant within the target area (Castorena 1998b; Whitmer and Ancker 1996; *People v. Acosta* 1992).

The Burbank injunction marks the beginning of a steady and accelerating stream of annual injunction initiatives. Following the 1992 Burbank injunction, three cases were filed with the California Superior Court in both 1993 and 1994, two in 1995, six in both 1996 and 1997, ten in 1998, six in 1999, two in 2000, and two through June of 2001 (see Appendix A).[33] During that period, the gang injunction phenomenon has spread from Los Angeles County to seven other counties: Santa Clara, Alameda, Orange, San Diego, San Bernardino, Monterey, and San Joanquin counties.

The *Strategy Against Gang Environments* (SAGE) program was initiated in 1993. SAGE was the outgrowth of the establishment of a unit in the LADA's Hardcore Gang Division to pursue injunctions in Los Angeles County in conjunction with other grass roots approaches to gang activity. SAGE is based on the concept of community-based law enforcement, encouraging the active participation of residents with the police and prosecutors to abate gang activity (Office of the District Attorney 1996). Although the program calls for the use of community outreach, gang member tracking, and various interventions attuned to the needs of the community, the centerpiece of SAGE is abatement by injunction. The first injunction procured under SAGE was in Norwalk in 1994 (Castorena 1998b; Whitmer and Ancker 1996).

The SAGE program has been involved in fourteen injunction initiatives since its inception, five in collaboration with the LACA. SAGE attorneys have trained or assisted prosecutors from other agencies in the injunction process, including prosecutors from the San Diego County, San Bernardino, Salinas, and Redondo Beach. A guide to the SAGE program – *S.A.G.E.: Strategy Against Gang Environments: A Handbook for Community Prosecution* (Office of the District Attorney 1996) – has been published by the LADA.

In spite of the claims of success and the spread of gang injunctions, not all injunction initiatives have been successful in obtaining relief. In 1993, the Orange County District Attorney's Office obtained a temporary restraining order against 59 members of the West Trece gang, which was quashed by the judge after a few weeks. Although acknowledging the incredible amount of harm being applied to the community by the gang, the judge ruled that the injunction, which banned the defendants from appearing in public view with each other within the target area, was an "impermissible invasion of privacy" under the First Amendment (Pinsky 1993; Do 1993; *People v. Amaya* 1993, Order Denying Preliminary Injunction).

In 1994, the Oakland City Attorney's Office was denied an injunction against eighteen members of the 'B' Street Boys. Ruling that there was an adequate remedy at law, the evidence of collective responsibility was constitutionally insufficient as the basis for relief, and the requested relief was unconstitutionally vague and overbroad, the judge also stated:

> The use of the civil court's equity powers to prohibit criminal behavior must be strictly circumscribed and cannot, in the pursuit of expediency, substitute for traditional criminal prosecution with its attendant constitutional safeguards (*People v. 'B' Street Boys* 1994, Order Denying Preliminary Injunction).

Attorneys from the American Civil Liberties Union intervened in both cases as *amicus curiae* (friend of the court) on behalf of the gang members. During the period of this study, there have been no other successful legal challenges to gang injunctions at the trial court level,[34] and challenges at the appellate level have had mixed results.

CASE LAW

Gang injunctions have spawned numerous constitutional controversies over the propriety of using civil injunctions to address gang activity (Allen 1998; Boga 1994; Destro 1993, 1994; Herd 1998; Livingston 1997; McClellan 1998; Moran 1997; Stewart 1998; Werdegar 1999; Yeager 1998; Yoo 1994). Implicit in these controversies is the argument that gang injunctions are an attempt by law enforcement to avoid constitutional protections through the use of the less rigorous civil law process, often imposing greater measures of social control over the gang than allowed under the criminal law. Collectively, a core group of provisions, including prohibitions on group-related non-criminal behavior and a laundry list of criminal activity, make the remedies of civil gang abatement qualitatively different from traditional law enforcement (Werdegar 1999) without comparable due process safeguards. Four cases reaching the California appellate courts have challenged the constitutionality of gang injunctions or of selected injunction provisions.

People v. Acuna (1997): Constitutionality

People v. Acuna (1997) was an appeal reaching the California Supreme Court that directly challenged the constitutionality of a preliminary injunction against two gangs – the Varrio Sureno Locos and the Varrio Sureno Treces – in the City of San Jose. The injunction was obtained by the San Jose City Attorney's Office against thirty-eight named members of the gangs in a four-square-block target area known as Rocksprings. The injunction contained twenty-four provisions prohibiting a number of criminal and non-criminal activities. The appeal was entered by eleven defendants, who claimed that the injunction was: 1) unauthorized under either the California Street Terrorism Enforcement and Prevention Act (STEP Act) (California Penal Code, s. 186.20 et seq.) or civil nuisance law, 2) an impermissible prior restraint on their First Amendment rights of speech and association, and 3) unconstitutionally vague and overbroad (*People v. Acuna* 1995: 593).

The Sixth District Court of Appeals had virtually gutted the injunction of all non-criminal provisions, concluding that only criminal conduct may be prohibited under public nuisance law by injunctive relief. Two provisions prohibiting gang signs[35] and gang clothing[36] were held to be content-related speech or expressions protected under the First Amendment. Ten provisions, including the controversial non-association clause,[37] were stricken as impermissibly vague and/or overbroad. Three provisions, including the non-intimidation clause,[38] survived only in the parts that were already defined as criminal offenses. Only nine provisions prohibiting criminal activity – drinking and using drugs, fighting, vandalism, trespassing, blocking ingress and egress, discharging firearms, demanding entry, littering, and urinating and defecating – were left intact. In effect, the court had stripped the injunction of all provisions that banned otherwise legal conduct, despite the role of that conduct in enhancing the public nuisance in Rocksprings (*People v. Acuna* 1995: 595-599).

The court also addressed the issue of who may be enjoined in an injunction. Six of the defendants claimed that they should not be named in the injunctions because they were not gang members. Although declaring that membership in a gang by itself was an inadequate foundation for civil liability, the court held that five of the six were properly named as defendants because a connection had been established between them and the prohibited conduct. All five were implicated in the sale, possession, or use of narcotics. Although the sixth defendant was identified as a gang member by her dress, claim of gang membership, and presence in the target area, the court held that she was improperly named as a defendant because there was no showing of a connection between her and the prohibited conduct (*People v. Acuna* 1995: 602).

The San Jose City Attorney's Office appealed the decision to the Supreme Court of California. In a 4-3 decision, the Supreme Court reversed the decision of the Sixth District Court of Appeals, resulting in a landmark decision on the use of injunctions to abate gang activity as a public nuisance and, by implication, on the propriety of using civil remedies to address criminal and anti-social behavior (*People v. Acuna* 1997).

The City of San Jose sought review of only two provisions rejected by the Court of Appeals – the non-association and the non-intimidation provisions. In oral arguments, which summarized the main points of the gang injunction debate, Assistant City Attorney George Rios argued that the nuisance could not be abated without prohibiting gang members from congregating in the neighborhood and that traditional law enforcement was insufficient to deter the nuisance. Attorney Amatai Schwartz, a civil rights specialist in private practice who argued the defendants' case on behalf of the ACLU of Northern California (Dolan 1996), called the injunction "a mini-Penal Code" that imposed parole conditions on people who have never been convicted of a crime. Assailing the injunction "as an unconstitutional excuse for the failure of traditional law enforcement", Justice Mosk, who eventually wrote a dissenting opinion, exclaimed that the civil action was raised because there was not enough evidence for a criminal prosecution, implied by the fact that some of the defendants had never been convicted of a crime. Justice Chin expressed concern for displacing the problem from Rocksprings to another neighborhood (Graham 1996).

The majority opinion affirmed the use of the public nuisance injunction to abate nuisance-related gang activity. The majority declared that the principal function of the centuries-old public nuisance doctrine has historically been "the maintenance of public order – tranquility, security, and protection – when the criminal law proves inadequate" (*People v. Acuna* 1997: 603). The injunction was recognized as one tool through which the public nuisance doctrine may be applied "to protect the quality of organized social life" (*People v. Acuna* 1997: 604).

In analyzing the constitutional challenges to the provisions under review, the majority embraced the concept of tailoring (Rosen 1999: 1174), by applying the constitutional standards of each challenge to the factual context of the Rocksprings neighborhood. Addressing the First Amendment challenge to the non-association provision, the majority found that the association of gang members in public was neither intimate nor instrumental, which are the only two forms of association protected by the United States Constitution. Intimate association is exemplified by personal family affiliations, and instrumental association is directly related to the "individual's freedom to speak, to worship, and to petition the government for the redress of grievances" (*People v. Acuna* 1997: 608). Instead, the gang represented "a loosely structured, elective form of social association" whose conduct within the Rocksprings neighborhood was "insufficient to command constitution protection . . . Freedom of association, in the sense protected by the First Amendment, 'does not extend to joining with others for the purpose of depriving third parties of their lawful rights'" (*People v. Acuna* 1997: 609, citing *Madsen v. Women's Health Center, Inc.* 1994: 2530).

Addressing the overbreadth challenge to the non-association provision, the majority raised the crucial point that only the defendants were subject to the terms of the injunction. Because an injunction, with its narrow and particularized focus, does not subject persons who are not before the court to its reach, the majority stated that there was less risk of the injunction deterring activities beyond the target of adjudication when compared to the general prohibition of a penal statute. Because of the narrow confinement of the association prohibition to the defendants within the target area, the overbreadth challenge was denied.

Addressing the void-for-vagueness challenge of both provisions, the majority explicitly applied the provisions to the local conditions, stating that "[a] contextual application of otherwise unqualified legal language may supply a clue to the law's meaning, giving facially standardless language a constitutionally sufficient meaning" (*People v. Acuna* 1997: 612). Although agreeing that the language in both provisions might result in the arrest of a defendant who was engaged in a prohibited act with a person that he did not know was subject to the injunction, the court ruled that this was not a classic case of constitutional vagueness. The problem could be rectified by inserting a knowledge requirement, which places the burden on the city to prove that the defendant was aware of an associate's gang membership or of an adversary's status, such as a resident, patron, visitor, or complainant. Regarding the vagueness of the non-intimidation provision, the court ruled that the wording was not constitutionally vague when read in the context of the objectives of the injunction and of the conduct reported in the declarations filed in support of the injunction.

The court also held that the two provisions fall within the statutory definition of a public nuisance and within the constitutional standard of burdening "no more speech than necessary to serve a significant government interest" (*People v. Acuna* 1997: 614, citing *Madsen v. Women's Health Center, Inc.* 1994: 2525). The activity of the defendants described in the declarations – which included threats of violence, violent crimes, and vandalism – "obstruct the free use of property and interfere with the enjoyment of life of an entire community" (*People v. Acuna* 1997: 615). Given the limited area within which the injunction was in force, the absence of constitutionally protected activity by gang members within the target area, the aggravated nature of the misconduct by the gang, and the fact that the defendants were permitted to associate out of the public view within the target area, the court held that neither provision burdened more speech than necessary to serve the significant government interest in the peace and tranquility of the neighborhood.

Finally, addressing the issue of who could be enjoined, the majority again took a contextual view. As the evidence confirmed that the gang was responsible for the conditions at Rocksprings through the actions of its individual members, individualized proof that the defendants committed specific elements of the public nuisance was not necessary. When charged with contempt, individual defendants would have the opportunity to contest any claim that they violated a specific provision of the injunction.

In sum, the court held that the conduct under review – associating with other gang members within the target area and confronting/intimidating/annoying/harassing residents and visitors – qualified as a public nuisance and was properly subjected to relief by injunction. Identification as a gang member subjected an individual to the injunction after the proper service of notice. Because the U.S. Supreme Court has denied certiorari (*Gonzalez v. Gallo* 1997), *Acuna* is currently the leading legal authority in the country on the constitutionality of the gang injunction.

Since the *Acuna* decision, California has experienced an increase in the use of gang injunctions. In the ten years prior to *Acuna*, there were fifteen injunction initiatives, of which the courts denied two and one was withdrawn without prejudice by the prosecuting agency. During the period of this study, there have been twenty-six injunctions granted, with one pending litigation and none denied,[39] in the four years since the *Acuna* decision. Thus, the gang injunction has become a well established phenomenon in California, being buttressed by the approval of the California Supreme Court.

In re David A. Englebrecht (1998): Nexus Requirement

In re Englebrecht (1998) is a Fourth District Court of Appeals ruling on a finding of contempt of court against David Englebrecht for violating a 1997 injunction (*People v. Varrio Pesole Locos* 1997) obtained by the San Diego County District Attorney's Office. Englebrecht was one of twenty-eight members of the Varrio Posole Locos gang named in the injunction, which was applicable in the one-square mile Eastside neighborhood of the city of Oceanside. The two violations underlying the contempt conviction were associating with other known gang members and possession of a pager within the target area.

Addressing the non-association provision, Englebrecht argued that his case should have been distinguished from *Acuna* because the target area of the Oceanside injunction was significantly larger than the four-block area of Rocksprings. In addition, some of the defendants either lived in or had relatives living in the target area, a condition that was not raised in the *Acuna* decision. The court ruled that the greater size of the target area was not significant without a showing by the defendant that the target area was larger than necessary to abate the nuisance. Additionally, the fact that some gang members lived in or had relatives that lived in the target area did not make the non-association clause infirm. Defendants were not enjoined from being in the target area or visiting with resident relatives. The injunction only prohibited defendants from associating with other Posole members within the target area. According to the court, the fact that there was a familial nexus did not make the gang's activities, which were often criminal and/or terrorizing, into either intimate or instrumental associational activities.

The court ruled in Englebrecht's favor on the challenge to possession of a pager within the target area, raising the importance of establishing a nexus between normally legitimate activity that is prohibited and the public nuisance. The court recognized that pagers, beepers and cellular phones were important communication devices, analogous to the telephone as an essential tool for disseminating speech, on which any restrictions must be narrowly drafted to advance a significant government interest. The potential for illegal activity through the use of these devices was also recognized. In fact, the court presumed that wireless communication devices were being employed by Posole gang members to advance illicit drug sales, communicate law enforcement movements within the target area, and aid members in eluding arrest. However, the court found that the prohibition was unconstitutional because there was no explicit attempt by prosecutors to establish a nexus, or connection, between the possession of beepers and pagers and the public nuisance; nor was there any attempt to narrowly define the provision so that it applied only to the use of these devices to aid criminal activity contributing to the public nuisance.

The ruling does not invalidate the prohibition of communicative devices in gang injunctions. The significance of the ruling for the gang injunction process is two-fold. First, the decision requires establishing a nexus between each provision of the injunction and the public nuisance. Second, the decision underscores the necessity of defining each provision as narrowly as possible, while still advancing the significant government interest in ameliorating the public nuisance.

Iraheta v. Superior Court (1999): Appointment of Counsel

In *Iraheta v. Superior Court of Los Angeles* (1999), the Second District Court of Appeals ruled on the issue of the right to appointed counsel for indigent gang members at injunction acquisition proceedings. The case arose after the Los Angeles County Public Defender's Office filed a motion with the Superior Court for appointment of counsel in the upcoming trial for a permanent injunction against ninety-two members of the 18th Street gang (*People v. 18th Street Gang* (1997)). The Public Defender's Office argued that the defendants were indigent and that the circumstances of the case were unique and extraordinary, requiring the assistance of counsel. The trial judge denied the motion, and two defendants appealed on the issue of the right to appointed counsel in gang injunction actions.

The appointment of counsel is generally not required in civil litigation. However, the petitioners argued that the case was extraordinary for four reasons: (1) the petitioners might be prosecuted for criminal contempt if they violated the injunction, (2) the petitioners' right to associate and travel freely in the target area would be restricted, (3) the state had no legitimate interest in erroneously branding the petitioners as gang members and imposing restrictions on innocent persons, and (4) the state was marshalling its enormous resources against individual defendants, increasing the risk of error. At oral arguments, Deputy Public Defender Alex Ricciardulli argued that "'the membrane between criminal and civil was so thin' that the right to counsel should apply" in gang injunction cases (*Capitol News Service* 1998).

The court rejected all of the arguments. The court found that the injunction proceedings did not directly implicate the possibility of incarceration for criminal contempt. The petitioners could not be prosecuted unless they committed a violation. If charged under criminal contempt, they would have the opportunity to challenge the lawfulness of the order, as well as whether they committed the violation, at which time they would have the right to appointed counsel. Furthermore, the court ruled that the state has a legitimate interest in avoiding the expense and the lengthy proceedings that appointed counsel might cause and in protecting the rights of residents and the public in the target area. Finally, the court ruled that risk of error did not turn on the imbalance of resources between the individual and the state. Parties were often equally unmatched in many civil suits with potentially serious legal and personal consequences. The only risk of error raised by the petitioners concerned the question of whether an individual was a gang member, which was not considered by the court to be a complex legal issue. In conclusion, the court stated "this is simply not a case where petitioner's interests are at their strongest, the People's interests are at their weakest, and the risks of error are at their peak" (*Iraheta v. Superior Court of Los Angeles* 1999: 1515).[40]

People v. Englebrecht (2001): Standard of Proof

A second appeal involving David Englebrecht was heard by the Fourth District Court of Appeals. Although Englebrecht had been released from the injunction by the trial court by the time the appeal was heard,[41] the Court of Appeals declined to dismiss the cases due to the broad public interest in the case and likely recurrence of the legal issues involved. Five issues were raised in the appeal: the right to a trial by jury on the issue of whether he was an active member of the Posole gang, the geographic scope of the injunction, the definition of active gang membership, the constitutionality of the prohibition against flashing hand signs and wearing gang clothing, and, the most significant issue, the standard of proof required to obtain injunctive relief.

On the first four issues, the court sided with the prosecutors. Because the essence of injunctive relief to abate a public nuisance is equitable, trial by jury on the issue of active gang membership is not required under either the federal or state constitutions. The court also concluded that the scope of the injunction raised no constitutional issue, but merely involved the sufficiency of the evidence of whether the target area was larger that the geographic scope of the gang's activities. Regarding the non-association provision's infringement on familial associations, the court stressed that the overriding purpose of a gang abatement action is to dispel the threat of collective conduct by gang members in a target area, a purpose that is difficult to reconcile with the effects of the non-association provision on familial relationships protected by the First Amendment. Because there was no prohibition of associations occurring out of public view or outside the target area, the court held that restrictions on contact between family members in public within the target area did not amount to a First Amendment violation. Finally, the court ruled that the prohibitions against hand signs and gang clothing were content neutral, meaning that the state's motivation for including the provision was not to interfere with the content of the communications, but to enjoin conduct that contributed to the public nuisance. Because the use of gang signs and symbols are important to the gang's ability to act collectively to maintain control of its territory though fear and intimidation, both provisions were intended "to enjoin the *conscious expression* of gang affiliation, support and allegiance" (*People v. Englebrecht* 2001: 1275), which contributed to the nuisance being enjoined. Therefore, the court concluded that the provisions were not an unconstitutionally overbroad infringement on First Amendment rights to free speech.

The most significant issue decided by the court was the standard of proof to be used in gang injunction cases. In determining whether a public nuisance existed and what provision to include in the injunctions, the trial court had used the preponderance of the evidence standard, rather than the heightened standard of clear and convincing evidence. The court explained that the standard of proof expresses the degree of confidence that society requires for the resolution of questions of fact under a particular situation, thus allocating the risk of error between the parties. The risk of error varies according to the gravity of the consequences of an erroneous resolution. Thus, a higher burden of proof is generally used only where particularly important individual interests or rights are at risk. Noting that the injunction enjoined a host of non-criminal activities that were generally considered innocuous, the court concluded that the issuance of a gang injunction must be supported by facts proven under the higher clear and convincing evidence standard. The court gave the following rationale for the decision:

> The need for a standard of proof allowing greater confidence in the decision reached arises not because the personal activities enjoined are sublime or grand but rather because they are commonplace, and ordinary. While it may be lawful to restrict such activity, it is also extraordinary. The government, in any guise, should not undertake such restrictions without good reason and without firmly establishing the facts making such restrictions necessary (*People v. Englebrecht* 2001: 1256).

The heightened standard of proof – *clear and convincing evidence* – is not expected to affect future gang injunction initiatives. Although the American Civil Liberties Union claimed that the decision was "'an important victory' to rein in overzealous prosecutors", San Diego County Deputy District Attorney Susan Mazza stated that the decision would have little effect because the higher standard is already in general use (Soto 2001). Assistant City Attorney Martin Vranicar, Jr., the supervisor of the Gang Unit of the Los Angeles City Attorney's Office stated that his unit already employs a *beyond a reasonable doubt* standard in all gang injunction cases (Los Angeles Assistant City Attorney Martin Vranicar, Jr., personal communication, January 9 2001). However, the heightened standard of proof does raise the stakes for prosecutors in future actions.

THE GANG INJUNCTION PROCESS

The injunction process consists of two phases (Fiss 1978). The acquisition, or issuance, phase involves building a case to convince a judge to grant injunctive relief. The implementation, or enforcement, phase occurs after the injunction has been issued. It involves providing notice to the gang and individual defendants and enforcing the provisions of the injunction.

The Acquisition Phase

The primary goal of the injunction acquisition process is to persuade the court that the targeted gang is responsible for creating and maintaining a public nuisance in a limited geographical area and that relief through a court order proscribing the gang's nuisance-related activity is necessary. This is accomplished through the filing of pleadings with the judge, who determines whether the public nuisance exists and what relief, if any, will be granted. Although there are sixteen steps in the acquisition process outlined in the SAGE manual (Office of the District Attorney 1996: 21-29), several are of particular importance in obtaining an injunction.[42]

The first, and perhaps most important, step is choosing an appropriate gang as the target for the injunction. The targeted gang must be responsible for causing a public nuisance in a defined geographical area. The gang should also fit the criteria of an unincorporated association, the members of which share common purposes and goals and function under a common name. The primary common purpose of the gang should be to cause or enhance the commission of criminal and other nuisance-related activity in the target area (Office of the District Attorney 1996: 29-31). Gang injunctions are generally sought against territorial gangs that claim limited geographical areas as their 'turf'. The gang may be a 'set', or clique, of a larger gang, but its claim on a specific geographic area is important, allowing prosecutors to tailor the specific terms of relief to the local circumstances comprising the public nuisance. A gang that does not claim a specific territory provides an amorphous target for the specification necessary for injunctive relief.

The next important step is collecting declarations from neighborhood residents, police officers, and other individuals who have experienced the public nuisance caused by the gang. Declarations are sworn statements, signed under the penalty of perjury, describing the activities of the targeted gang and the connection between the individual defendants, the gang, and the public nuisance. They are the primary source of facts establishing the gang as an unincorporated association, the existence of the public nuisance in the target area, and the gang's responsibility for creating and maintaining the public nuisance.

In collecting the declarations, community outreach is important to gain the trust of residents, who often are reluctant to provide written statements against a gang and individual gang members. Gangs thrive on their power to intimidate a neighborhood. Threats and acts of retribution against those who provide information cause residents to refrain from cooperating with law enforcement officials. However, for some judges, civilian declarations provide more meaningful evidence than police declarations (San Diego County Deputy District Attorney Susan Mazza, personal communication, March 13, 2000). To protect the safety of residents, citizen declarations are often submitted under seal. Sealed declarations are disclosed only to the judge or, if the defendants are represented, to their counsel after all identifying information has been redacted and counsel has been prohibited from sharing any sealed information with the defendants.

The third important step is editing the pleadings. Pleadings are the formal allegations against the gang that are to be proven at trial. They include the formal complaint for an injunction, the memorandum of points and authorities in support of the injunction, and the proposed injunction. The complaint is the charging document that initiates the lawsuit. It describes the facts giving rise to the legal action, the reasons injunctive relief is being requested, and the proposed relief. The proposed relief should be tailored to specific behavior contributing to the public nuisance. Relief should not solely target activity that is susceptible to challenge under the First Amendment, such as symbolic speech, gang clothing, or the association of gang members. The memorandum of points and authorities specifically describes the public nuisance, referring to the declarations, demonstrative evidence, and case and statutory law supporting the injunction request.[43] The proposed injunction contains the specific provisions of relief proposed by the prosecutor and may be amended as the case is litigated.

The pleadings as a whole should provide a clear nexus between each defendant and the nuisance-related activity of the gang (*In re Englebrecht 1998*). Although each defendant need not be connected to each nuisance-related activity (*People v. Acuna* 1997), it is important to show that each defendant is associated with the gang and is individually involved in at least one nuisance-related activity. In cases with a lot of evidence against the gang and individual members, a table showing a summary of the nexus between each defendant and the nuisance might be included in the pleadings.

In addition to declarations from citizens and law enforcement officials, demonstrative evidence of the nuisance is often presented. Photographs of graffiti serve to establish the territorial claim by the gang on the geographic area in question. Photographs of tattoos establish the gang membership of individual defendants and identify their monikers, or street names. Maps and diagrams are helpful in describing the scope of the nuisance to the judge and in establishing the geographic limits of the targeted area. Crime statistics, court dockets, transcripts, and judgments linking the individual defendants to past crimes help to provide the necessary nexus between the gang, the defendants, and the activity comprising the public nuisance.

When sufficient evidence of the nexus between the public nuisance and the gang has been collected, a motion for a temporary restraining order (TRO) or a preliminary injunction is filed with the court. A temporary restraining order requests immediate relief from the public nuisance for fifteen days, at which time an *order to show cause* (OSC) hearing for a preliminary injunction must take place. When an emergency exists in the target area, such as severe cases of threats, violence and intimidation against residents or law enforcement personnel, or when a danger exists that defendants will attempt to avoid the service of notice of the proceedings, a TRO may be requested. If a TRO is issued, each individual defendant must be served with the order before it can be enforced against that individual. Regardless of whether a TRO was issued, a date will be set for the OSC hearing for the preliminary injunction, and the defendants must be notified of the date of the hearing and the evidence against them.

The OSC hearing provides the defendants the opportunity to argue that the court should not issue a preliminary injunction. Defendants do not have the right to appointed counsel at any injunction proceeding, including the OSC hearing (*Iraheta v. Superior Court of Los Angeles* 1999). If the defendants do not appear at the OSC hearing, the preliminary injunction is issued by default judgment.

At the OSC hearing, the prosecutor must be able to support each provision in the proposed injunction with "clear and convincing" evidence (*People v. Englebrecht* 2001), articulating how each activity is related to the nuisance and why proscribing that activity is necessary to abate the nuisance (*In re Englebrecht* 1998). Therefore, the proposed relief must be tailored to the specific nuisance-related activities of the particular gang in the target area. The size of the target area is irrelevant as long as it is narrowly construed to meet the government's interest in abating the public nuisance (*In re Englebrecht* 1998).

If a preliminary injunction is issued, it must be served on each defendant before it can be enforced against that individual. If the gang, as an unincorporated association, is a named defendant, it must also be served. Because criminal street gangs do not have registered addresses, the court can issue an order stating that service to one or more members of the gang on behalf of the association will satisfy the notice requirement.

Unless otherwise indicated by the judge, the preliminary injunction remains in effect until the court makes a decision on a permanent injunction. A permanent injunction is issued by a judgment after trial or by default. A judgment at trial is usually not sought by prosecutors because of the reluctance of civilian witnesses to testify. If a trial is pursued, the prosecutor must prove by clear and convincing evidence (*People v. Englebrecht* 2001) that the gang can be sued as an unincorporated association, the defendants are associated with the gang, a public nuisance exists in the target area, and the gang and each individual defendant are responsible for the public nuisance. A permanent injunction is usually issued by default because the defendants often fail to respond to the complaint. All defendants must have been served and failed to answer. If one or two defendants answer, they may be dismissed from the case so that a default judgment can be entered against the others, or the case may go to trial against those who answered, while seeking a default judgment against the unresponsive defendants.

Problems in the process of acquiring a gang injunction have been documented by Maxson and Allen (1997) in their evaluation of the injunction initiative against the Crenshaw Mafia Gangsters in Inglewood. The injunction, obtained by the LADA's office under the SAGE program, was part of a broader strategy entitled the Youth Firearms Violence Initiative (YFVI). The YFVI was an eighteen-month initiative "to reduce youth firearms violence by focusing enforcement resources on local street gangs and firearms confiscation, particularly among the Crenshaw Mafia Gangsters in the Darby-Dixon neighborhood" of Inglewood (Maxson and Allen 1997: Executive Summary). The YFVI was bifurcated into enforcement and preventions components, with the gang injunction intended to be the centerpiece of the prevention component.

From the start, there were problems with the YFVI. The firearms confiscation component was implemented immediately, whereas it took over one year to obtain the preliminary injunction. This bifurcation of the enforcement and prevention components reflected a lack of integration in the initiative's design, in contrast to SAGE's emphasis on the collaboration of all actors in initiatives involving gang injunctions (Office of the District Attorney 1996).

Three problems plagued the prosecutor of the injunction component. First, the prosecutor had difficulties obtaining citizen declarations to provide evidence of the gang's impact on the community. The lack of a "quasi formal social organizational structure to facilitate access to community residents" (Maxson and Allen 1997: 23) in the Darby-Dixon neighborhood area hampered the formation of the type of partnership emphasized by the SAGE program. Without contacts through community groups, the prosecutor had problems identifying residents willing to cooperate, and citizens were fearful of coming forward on their own because of the fear of retaliation by gang members. Although community policing officers identified twenty community activists to include in a community coalition, not one activist resided in the target area. Fearing that cooperation with the injunction initiative would undermine its understanding with gang members, the neighborhood school refused to provide a location for the prosecutor to safely talk with residents. Although fifteen citizen declarations were eventually obtained through referrals from other declarants, none were submitted as evidence because the judge refused to seal the declarations. Recognizing that the communities most in need of assistance are the most impervious to efforts to rejuvenate informal social controls, the report recommends that:

> The available community infrastructure in a potential target area should be considered in the selection process... Community engagement in the injunction process likely would have been facilitated if the YFVI was integrated into a comprehensive effort to revitalize the target area... The bifurcation of prevention activities from the other components closed one avenue for fostering community social infrastructure. Alternatively, gang injunctions might be approached from a more limited deterrence-oriented perspective. The stated goal might be solely suppression of gang activity with little attention devoted to community development (Maxson and Allen 1997: 25).

The second problem encountered by the prosecutor concerned organizational collaboration in the acquisition process. The process envisioned the collaboration of the SAGE prosecutor, a county probation officer, the police department's gang unit, and a task force of selected police officers for on-going street level enforcement. The evidence needed by the prosecutor included the documentation of the criminal activities and gang associations of fifty-two hard-core gang members originally targeted as defendants. The prosecutor had difficulty acquiring the documented evidence because of conflicts between the goals of the injunction initiative and those of the probation officer and the gang unit. Although providing an outstanding declaration, the probation officer's priority was the seizure of firearms, at which he was very productive, but which "made cooperation with him somewhat tenuous" (Maxson and Allen 1997: 28).

Gang unit officers were unwilling to share intelligence on the gang, suggesting that there was a conflict of interest between the goals of gang intelligence gathering and the public exposure of intelligence information. They refused to talk to the prosecutor for fear of jeopardizing their rapport with the gang members. Their reluctance to share information was aggravated when the judge refused to seal the declarations, causing concern by the gang unit about revealing the identities of confidential informants. Although approximately twenty-five police declarations were obtained from officers outside the gang unit, many of these officers were also hesitant to have their declarations submitted unless sealed. The report recommends that future injunction initiatives establish clear guidelines on the nature of the information to be used as evidence and on the officials expected to provide that information (Maxson and Allen 1997: 27-28).

Finally, the allocation of resources impeded the injunction initiative. Because the injunction component was part of a larger program to remove guns from the street, the prosecutor lacked the support of a team dedicated solely to acquiring and implementing the injunction. The task force that was responsible for on-street enforcement of the injunction was not a team of officers assigned exclusively to the initiative; it was comprised of forty-eight officers who were rotated over an eight-month period, working in three two-man patrol units on an overtime basis. Although there was clear evidence that the task force primarily targeted gang activity, there was no evidence that it focused on the targeted gang. There was also concern regarding how productive the task force should be before the prosecutor filed for injunction. Because the evidence must establish a current on-going public nuisance, there was a concern that patrol saturation in the relatively small target area might be adverse to the acquisition of the injunction. This raises an ethical issue of whether law enforcement officials should ignore public nuisance activity in a target area in order to have enough evidence to support an injunction. However, this ethical issue was moot in the Inglewood case because, due to a funding shortfall, the task force was terminated more than three months prior to the acquisition of the preliminary injunction (Maxson and Allen 1997: 28-38).

In sum, the report recommends that future injunction initiatives recognize the potential conflicts inherent in interdisciplinary law enforcement programs. These conflicts may be addressed through clearly defined objectives for the initiative and guidelines for collaborative roles. The report also recommended that the prosecutor be designated as the leader of a multifaceted team dedicated to the injunction initiative. The report concludes that:

> Significant improvement in neighborhood environments is unlikely to be achieved unless the injunction is part of a comprehensive approach to community renewal. Barring a comprehensive effort with substantial community involvement, injunction processes should more appropriately be framed as suppression strategies than community prosecution (Maxson and Allen 1997: Executive Summary).

The potential for abuse in the acquisition of gang injunctions is highlighted by the infamous Rampart scandal in the Los Angeles Police Department (LAPD). The scandal involved the Rampart Division's Community Resources Against Street Hoodlums (CRASH) unit, a specialized unit formed to combat gang activity. Rampart Division CRASH officers had provided declarations that furnished the primary evidence supporting two injunctions against the 18th Street gang. As discussed earlier, the civil law process of using declarations as evidence for a preliminary injunction denies the defendants the opportunity to confront witnesses. With no opportunity for the defense to cross-examine the declarants, there is an increased risk of an injunction being erroneously issued based on perjured statements.

The scandal became public in a *Los Angeles Times* article on September 16, 1999 (Lait and Glover, 1999), after former CRASH officer Rafael Perez was convicted of stealing eight pounds of cocaine from the LAPD. As part of a plea bargain agreement, Perez agreed to provide LAPD investigators with information about police misconduct within the Rampart Division's CRASH unit. In one incident, Perez alleged that he and fellow CRASH Officer Nino Durden were involved in an unjustified shooting of a nineteen-year-old 18th Street gang member. The gang member, who was paralyzed from the incident, was convicted of attempted murder on a police officer and sentenced to twenty-three years in prison. The officers had originally reported that the gang member was shot four times when, brandishing an assault weapon, he burst into a room in a vacant apartment building in which the officers were conducting a stakeout. Durden described the incident in a sworn declaration in support of the 1997 Pico-Union injunction initiative against the 18th Street gang (*People v. 18th Street Gang* 1997). In a statement given to LAPD investigators as part of his plea agreement, Perez claimed that the gang member had been unarmed, shot while handcuffed, and framed for the attempted murder charge (Lait and Glover 1999). A second questionable shooting identified by Perez was described in a declaration in support of a 1998 injunction against the 18th Street gang in the MacArthur Park target area (*People v. 18th Street Gang* 1998). Perez lodged further allegations of improprieties against members of the CRASH unit, including other unjustified shootings, beatings, false arrests, theft of drugs, and planting and fabricating evidence.[44]

The enforcement of two gang injunctions in the Rampart Division was suspended as a direct result of the scandal. Both injunctions targeted the 18th Street gang, one of the most violent gangs in Los Angeles, and enjoined a total of one hundred and forty-two 18th Street gang members from nuisance-related activities in three target areas. Sixty-six of these defendants were named in the injunctions based, in part, on declarations of officers caught up in the scandal, and seven of those were among twenty defendants arrested for violating the injunctions. At the request of prosecutors, the court suspended enforcement of the injunctions until prosecutors complete an investigation into the veracity of the scandal-tainted officers' declarations. At least eight tainted officers submitted sworn statements of the activities of individual gang members, some providing declarations for both injunctions. One officer, who has been fired for allegedly beating an ex-gang member in the Rampart station, submitted two declarations that provided a lengthy overview of the activities of the 18th Street gang and evidence against twenty-four individual defendants (Lopez and Connell 1999b).

As a result of the scandal, questions have been raised about the prosecutor's role in the injunction process. In particular, critics question whether prosecutors take appropriate steps to verify the information in police declarations and whether officers prepare declarations without guidance from prosecutors. Because prosecutors often work out of police stations during the acquisition process, their independence from the officers who provide evidence of the public nuisance is questionable. Assistant City Attorney Martin Vranicar, the supervisor of the city attorney's gang unit, stated that prosecutors work from the police stations in order to gain an understanding of the scope of the gang problem in the target area. Prosecutors also work closely with community leaders in developing the legal basis for injunctions, and officers are required to submit their declarations under the penalty of perjury (Shuster 1999).

The LACA made salvaging the two injunctions a top priority (Lopez and Connell 1999b). The *Los Angeles Times* reported that open-air drug dealing and gang-related shootings in the target areas have increased sharply since the enforcement of the two injunctions was suspended (*Los Angeles Times* 1999b; Corwin 2000). According to a newspaper report, the injunctions had been effective in keeping some of the most troublesome gang members in line, even though they did not solve the gang problems in the target areas. One resident claimed that those who live in the area saw the difference when the injunctions were being enforced. A business owner claimed that the gang members believed that they were calling the shots after the enforcement of the injunctions was suspended. Calling it a mistake to suspend the injunctions, another area business owner said that gang members felt freer to act since the scandal became public. The captain in charge of the Rampart Division stated that crime statistics rose almost forty percent in the months after the injunctions were lifted (Treviot 2001). On February 21, 2002, the Pico-Union injunction was quashed at the request of prosecutors because of doubts about its validity as a result of the corruption scandal (*Los Angeles Times* 2002). On April 18, 2002, city and county prosecutors announced a new injunction initiative in the Pico-Union area (Loh 2002). There are no indications that enforcement of the MacArthur Park injunction will resume, even though the gang members are reclaiming that turf.

There is no plan by the LACA to abandon the strategy of gang injunctions (Shuster 1999). Injunctions outside the Rampart Division have not been affected by the scandal and continue to be enforced (Lopez and Connell 1999a). The new city attorney,[45] Rockard L. Delgadillo, believes that the Rampart scandal had a chilling effect on gang injunctions. However, with crime up twenty-three percent in 2001, he has vowed to expand the city's gang injunction program in conjunction with more comprehensive measures to prevent crime and provide opportunities for at-risk youths (McGreevy 2001, Rodriguez 2001, Uranga 2002). Since Delgadillo took office in July 2001, there have been eight gang injunctions issued to the LACA (*City News Service* 2003).

The Implementation Phase

After receiving notice of the temporary restraining order, preliminary injunction, or permanent injunction, individual defendants can be arrested for violating the provisions of the court order. When arrested for violating the injunction, the prosecutor must prove that the injunction was issued, the defendant was notified of the injunction, and the defendant willfully violated the court order (Office of the District Attorney 1996: 38). Copies of proof of service, which consist of a sworn affidavit signed by the law enforcement officer serving the injunction order, establishes that the defendant had been properly notified of the injunction.

If a defendant is caught violating the terms of the injunction, the prosecutor can choose to bring contempt charges in either criminal or civil court. The difference is significant. Although both criminal and civil contempt are based on the disobedience of an order lawfully issued by a court, a prosecution under criminal contempt requires proof of "willful disobedience" on the part of the accused. A civil court defendant does not have the right to a court-appointed attorney or a jury trial, convictions are based on the lower standard of preponderance of the evidence, and the judgment of the court is final, with no allowance for appeal except by extraordinary writ. In contrast, a defendant in criminal court has all the constitutional rights accorded to a criminal defendant, including the right to a court-appointed attorney, the right to appeal a conviction, and the right to trial by jury, and the violation must be proven beyond a reasonable doubt.

The most significant difference is in the sanctions. Upon a finding of civil contempt, the defendant is subject to no more than five days in jail and a $1000 fine. If convicted of a criminal violation, the defendant is subject to no more than 180 days in jail for repeat offenders, a $1000 fine, and probation. While it may seem easier to obtain a conviction under civil contempt, criminal contempt is generally preferred because the prosecutor can seek varying conditions of probation, including probation searches without probable cause by probation officers, and longer periods of incarceration for repeat offenders (Castorena 1998b: 4).

The Inglewood study by Maxson and Allen (1997) also addressed problems in the enforcement stage of the injunction process. As noted earlier, implementation of the Inglewood injunction suffered from inadequate enforcement from the start. Although the preliminary injunction was granted on January 28, 1997, as of August of that year only nineteen of the twenty-nine enjoined defendants had been served notice of the injunction, and the funds for enforcement had been exhausted. Despite these problems, four gang members were arrested and received 30-day jail sentences for contempt. The study reports that, although decreasing negligibly in the six months after the injunction was issued, crime increased substantially through the second half of the program and remained at considerably higher levels (Maxson and Allen 1997).

The report's conclusions on gang injunctions are positive despite the problems encountered by the Inglewood initiative and its disappointing impact on the crime rate. The report emphasizes the importance of community participation and enforcement in the implementation stage:

> While the community prosecution approach shows merit, implementers may be doomed to frustration and failure unless an injunction process assumes a relatively minor role in a larger effort to mobilize, enhance and capitalize on existing community resources . . . Full enforcement is critical to achieving the deterrent effect. It seems unlikely that issuing an injunction in itself would net longstanding effects in crime reduction . . . With full enforcement, it is quite possible that an injunction could produce breathing room for a community to generate or recapture the informal organizational resources that promote resilience to criminogenic features confronting many urban areas across the country. The Inglewood program could have used its prevention resources in this manner rather than bifurcating the prevention and enforcement components (Maxson and Allen 1997: 40).

Impact Studies of Gang Injunctions

Although effectiveness is not the focus of this study, it is an important issue that often represents the bottom line for policymakers considering a creative and controversial initiative. Some officials and citizens may perceive an effective intervention, which reduces crime or achieves some other goal, as justifying an abridgement of individual rights (Ehrenreich 1999a). One criticism of gang injunctions is the scarcity of empirical evidence about their impact on crime in the target areas and in adjoining neighborhoods. Based mostly on anecdotal evidence, prosecutors have claimed that gang injunctions have reduced both crime rates and fear of crime in targeted areas, without significantly displacing crime into adjoining neighborhoods. For example, the SAGE manual claims:

> In every city where an injunction has been issued, police and prosecutors report drastic reductions in gang activity and community fear. Reductions in the crime rate vary from thirty-five percent (35%) to almost eighty percent (80%). More importantly, with the reduction of gang members loitering on the street, residents feel more safe in their neighborhoods and inside their homes (Office of the District Attorney 1996: 39).

Although much anecdotal evidence has been reported in the media about the effectiveness of gang injunctions, a search of the literature revealed only two impact evaluations based on empirical evidence. Because of the importance attached to the effectiveness of any controversial intervention, the conclusions, methodology, and limitations of each study are reviewed.

The American Civil Liberties Union (ACLU), an ardent opponent of gang injunctions, sponsored the first study. Entitled *False Premise/False Promise: The Blythe Street Gang Injunction and Its Aftermath* (ACLU Foundation of Southern California 1997), the study was designed to test the impact and displacement effects of the 1993 injunction against the Blythe Street gang in the Panorama City section of Los Angeles (*People v. Blythe Street Gang* 1993). The study is important because it is often cited in support of the argument that gang injunctions have little impact on crime in the target areas and a significant displacement effect.

The study examines aggregate crime statistics of monthly totals of violent crimes (homicides, rapes/attempted rapes, robberies, and aggravated assaults), calls for service, and felony drug arrests in nineteen reporting districts of the LAPD, which are centered on the Blythe Street injunction target area. The data covers the six-year period, 1991 through 1996, although charts representing a substantially shorter period are displayed. The charts are plagued with relatively low numbers and fluctuating monthly trend lines, making them difficult to interpret visually.

The study suffers from several serious methodological deficiencies that limit its validity. First, the design fails to provide for similar control districts to which valid comparisons could be made. Control districts would have indicated whether there were influences on the reporting districts that were exogenous to the effect of the injunction. Second, there is no attempt to examine or control for competing hypotheses explaining variations in the data. Variation is attributed solely to the effect of the injunction on the reporting districts, even though there may be spurious influences. Third, there appears to be inconsistencies between some of the data offered and the conclusions drawn from that data. Finally, the study virtually ignores data from reporting districts that are inconsistent with its conclusions.

The conclusions of the study focus on the district primarily affected by the injunction (RD 925), four districts to the north of target area, aggregate data from the nineteen reporting districts, and data for the entire City of Los Angeles. Four districts north of RD 925 are identified as areas that are especially afflicted by violent crime and drug trafficking. Parts of three of these districts are included in the Blythe Street target area. Conspicuously absent is any discussion about the four districts to the east, south, and west of RD 925, even though they are also either totally or partially within the target area. In fact, the district to the immediate south of RD 925, which is partially within the injunction target area and is among the ten most crime-ridden districts in the study, is virtually ignored.

The study reports a net increase in violent crime and calls for service within RD925. When compared to the month in which the injunction was issued (April, 1993), counts of violent crime were higher in each of the six months following the issuance of the injunction and in each of the same seven months of 1994. However, there is no attempt to control for competing hypotheses that may explain these increases. A closer inspection of the data reveals the strong possibility of a seasonality effect on the counts of violent crime in RD 925, with crime counts lower in late winter/early spring and increasing into the summer months. The increase of violent crime may also be attributed to increased communication between residents and the police, resulting in an increase in the reporting of violent crime after the issuance of the injunction. The crimes of aggravated assault, rape/attempted rape, and robbery often go unreported in gang-plagued neighborhoods because of the very real fear of retaliation by gang members. This competing hypothesis is supported by the data on calls for service.

Similar to the analysis of violent crime counts, the study fails to control for a competing hypothesis regarding data on annual calls for service in RD 925:

> In all of 1992, RD 925 recorded 1,741 calls for police service. In 1993, that total *increased* to 1,853, then declined to 1,471 in 1994. But it *increased* again in 1995 to 1,516 and totaled 1,500 in 1996 (ACLU Foundation of Southern California 1997: 37 – *emphasis in the original*).

Although the study does not draw any conclusion from these data, the implication is clear: Increases in calls for service is inconsistent with the goal of the injunction to alleviate crime in the neighborhood. However, the increase in 1993 may be explained by the opening of lines of communications between residents and the police, rather than an increase in the frequency of crime. The prosecutor for the Blythe Street injunction views an increase in calls for service as indicia of the success of an injunction (Response to Prosecutor Survey). The sharp increase in 1993 and subsequent the sharp fall in 1994, followed by the sustenance of lower levels of calls for service in 1995 and 1996 may indicate an increased willingness by residents to call the police shortly after the issuance of the injunction and the decreased need for calls for service in subsequent years. Unfortunately, the study fails to examine or control for this competing hypothesis.

The study concludes that the injunction was accompanied by an increase in violent crimes in RD 925.

> The most skeptical observer of the gang injunction process might have expected that the sheer concentration of media and law enforcement resources in a confined neighborhood would result in at least a temporary reduction in crime. Instead, violent crime – four offenses likely to incite fear among the public and most often associated criminal street gang behavior – actually rose immediately after the injunction was sought and issued (ACLU Foundation of Southern California 1997: 44).

This conclusion is unwarranted considering the relatively small monthly counts of violent crime, the ambiguous data on aggravated assault, and the absence of controls on competing hypotheses regarding violent crime and calls for service.

Regarding the four reporting districts to the north of RD 925, collectively referred to as the Roscoe Boulevard Strip, the study finds a significant increase in violent crime and drug trafficking immediately after the issuance of the injunction, never dropping below the level reported in April of 1993. The study concludes:

> In the months immediately after the Blythe Street gang injunction was issued, a clear trend developed toward increased violent crime and drug trafficking activity in the Roscoe Boulevard Strip ... At the very least, the Blythe Street gang injunction had an indirect role – and may have had a direct role – in precipitating an increase in crime and drug trafficking in an immediately adjacent area far larger than the reporting district affected by the injunction itself (ACLU Foundation of Southern California 1997: 44).

This conclusion on the displacement effect of the injunctions is also unwarranted without considering or controlling for competing hypotheses. The data for violent crime in the Roscoe Boulevard Strip shows a similar seasonality effect as the data for RD 925, again suggesting the possibility of a competing hypothesis. An examination of the violent crime data for the four districts to the immediate east, south, and west of RD 925 reveals that each experienced a significant drop in violent crime in the months following the issuance of the injunction. If the Blythe Street injunction caused a significant displacement of crime into adjacent districts to the north, one would think that other adjoining districts would not be immune, particularly since one of these districts is among the ten most crime-ridden districts in the study. Furthermore, if violent crime increased in RD 925 as a result of the injunction, there would be no reason for displacement. It is more likely that any increase in an adjacent area was the result of some spurious phenomenon, not the displacement effect of the injunction.

The conclusion on the displacement of drug trafficking has similar flaws. The data is based on the reported increase in felony drug arrests in the Roscoe Boulevard Strip. However, drug arrests are dependent on police enforcement activity, and there is no indication of whether narcotics enforcement remained at a stable level or increased during this period.

Finally, the study examines aggregate data of all nineteen reporting districts chosen for the study. Collectively, the districts comprise an area of approximately 20 square miles in the Panorama City region of the San Fernando Valley, one of the most gang-plagued areas in the City of Los Angeles. The study claims that the data clearly shows a dramatic rise in violent crime in the immediate aftermath of the issuance of the injunction, particularly between February and June of 1993, when total violent crime rose 52%. However, this rise is similar to the pattern in 1994, with total violent crime again rising dramatically between February and June. In fact, the chart of violent crime data for all reporting districts displays the same seasonal effects observed in RD 925 and the Roscoe Boulevard Strip. The graphic representation of the violent crime trend in the nineteen reporting districts did show a greater rise than the trend in citywide data. Whether this effect over a 20 square mile gang-plagued area can be attributed to the influence of an injunction primarily enforced in a very small reporting district is questionable, particularly when the same seasonal pattern found in the RD925 and Roscoe Boulevard Strip data is evident, albeit to a lesser degree, in the citywide data.

The study concludes that the Blythe Street injunction failed to achieve its objectives of immediately reducing violent crime and drug trafficking and increasing community safety, calling into question the propriety of using an intervention that abridges fundamental civil liberties and highlighting the potential for the displacement of gang activity. The study offers an admonition on "the futility – and even foolhardiness – of relying on court orders to prevent crime in the absence of any other steps to address the complex factors that influence gang membership and gang violence" (ACLU Foundation of Southern California 1997: 44).

Responding to the study, Assistant City Attorney Martin Vranicar Jr., the supervisor of the Los Angeles City Attorney's Gang Unit, questioned the ACLU's motives, noting that the ACLU had mounted an unsuccessful legal challenge to the Blythe Street injunction. Believing the report to be part of a campaign to deter the LACA from obtaining a similar injunction against the 18th Street gang, Vranicar reiterated the value of the gang injunction as a tool for law enforcement (Tamaki 1997).

UCLA Professor Jeffrey Grogger conducted a competing study on the effectiveness of gang injunctions. Entitled *The Effects of the Los Angeles County Gang Injunctions on Reported Crime* (Grogger 2000), it provides the most complete analysis to date of the impact of gang injunctions on crime. Both the methodology and the conclusions of Grogger's study stand in stark contrast to the ACLU's Blythe Street study.

Grogger analyzes the impact on reported crime of thirteen gang injunctions in fourteen target areas[46] located in jurisdictions served by four Los Angeles County police departments – the Los Angeles Police

Department, the Los Angeles County Sheriff's Department, the Pasadena Police Department, and the Long Beach Police Department. The study includes all injunctions occurring in Los Angeles County between 1993 and 1998 for which suitable data for analysis were available.[47] The study examines whether gang injunctions reduced reported crime in the target areas and whether there was any significant spillover of reported crime into adjoining areas due to the displacement of gang activities. Using neighborhood-level crime from each target area,[48] areas adjoining the target areas,[49] neighboring areas,[50] and matched comparison areas,[51] the study analyzes the effects of injunctions on the seven index offenses of the FBI's Uniform Crime Reporting (UCR) system, separated into two categories: violent crime, consisting of murder, rape, robbery, and aggravated assault; and property crime, consisting of burglary, theft, and auto theft. Drug offenses and nuisance-related offenses are not included in the study because they are not uniformly reported in the UCR. Quarterly counts[52] of UCR crimes reported to the police were analyzed in a simple before-and-after/case-control design[53] using two statistical methods: difference-in-difference estimates[54] and fixed-effects regression.[55]

There are several important limitations to the study. The study does not estimate the long-term effects of the injunctions on reported crime, including whether the effects dissipate after a year. As the focus is on the average effect of the injunctions in the aggregate, the study does not attempt to estimate the effects of any individual injunction. The study does not include crimes that were not reported to the police, including drug offenses. Therefore, if the injunctions had emboldened residents to report crime more often, then the estimates might understate the effects of injunctions. In a broader sense, the study does not address the effects of the injunction on the quality-of-life and the attendant nuisance problems associated with gangs. Because it is conceivable that the injunctions reduce nuisance problems without affecting reported crime, the injunctions might have been more successful than the study indicated. Finally, the study says nothing about the civil rights issue of the police using the injunctions as a license to detain and harass people who have the general appearance of gang members. If this infringement on the rights of innocent citizens occurred, the propriety of gang injunctions is questionable regardless of their impact on reported crime (Grogger 2000: 4-6). Although the findings of the study are informative, these important limitations discount the study as a comprehensive evaluation of the success of injunctions (Grogger 2000: 43).

The study had three major findings. First, the results suggested that, in the post-injunction period (the first year after the injunctions are imposed), the injunctions had some effect on violent crimes within the target areas. Violent crime declined roughly 5 to 10 percent in the target areas. Most of the decline is attributed to reductions in aggravated assault, the most prevalent form of violent crime. There is no evidence suggesting that the injunctions reduced murders or rapes, and there is only marginal evidence that the injunctions reduced robbery.

Second, there is no evidence that the injunctions reduced property crimes in the target areas (Grogger 2000: 42-43). There are two possible explanations for the disparate effect on violent crime and property crime. First, the restrictions imposed by the injunctions, particularly the non-association clauses, may have a greater effect on the 'technology' of violent crime than on the technology of property crimes. If the injunctions are successful in breaking up the group activities that often accompany violence, the result may be a decrease in violence. Because the dynamics of property crime may be more individual in nature, successfully breaking up group activities would not necessarily affect property crimes (Grogger 2000: 42). Second, the typical restrictions of activities associated with drug dealing may successfully disrupt a gang's narcotics trafficking activities. Because drug dealing is often accompanied by violence, the violence in a target area may decrease to the extent that the injunctions reduce drug-dealing activities (Grogger 2000: 40). However, any effect of the injunctions on drug-dealing activities cannot be divorced from the effects of group activities, since drug transactions by gangs commonly involve at least three gang members acting together.[56] Thus, both these explanations suggest the importance of the non-association provisions to the effectiveness of gang injunctions.

The results of the study suggest that there is no spillover (displacement) effect on reported crime. Few of the spillover coefficients were statistically significant, and nearly as many were positive as negative (Grogger 2000: 43). This lack of displacement effect discounts the concern over pushing gang activities into adjoining areas, which is a major argument against the use of gang injunctions.

The study also analyzes several collateral issues. Because of the concern that the effects of the injunctions might be confounded with the effects of the Rampart scandal, an analysis was performed on a sample that excluded the three target areas located within the Rampart Division's patrol area. The results suggest that the Rampart scandal did not exaggerate the effects of the injunctions. To the contrary, the estimates based on the sample that excluded the Rampart injunctions were larger than those based on the full sample. In particular, robbery, the estimate of which was only marginally significant in the full sample, was significant at the 5 per cent level in the smaller sample. Grogger suggests that the Rampart injunctions may have been less effective than the average injunction because the same lax management that resulted in the scandal led to ineffective enforcement of the injunction, or because the Rampart-area gangs, all of which are cliques of the notorious 18th Street Gang, consist of more hard-core criminals (Grogger 2000: 30).

An alternative post-injunction period of six quarters was also analyzed to examine the effects of the injunctions over a slightly longer time horizon. The only differences were found in the estimates based on the matched comparison samples, which were slightly smaller than those based on the four-quarter post-injunction period. Although the full-sample estimate is insignificant and further study of the long-term effects should be conducted, the results suggest the possibility that the effects of the injunctions dissipate over time (Grogger 2000: 38).

Finally, the study analyzes whether the effects of the injunctions varied by the size of the injunctions and the jurisdiction in which the target area is located. Size of the injunction is defined as the interaction of the number of RD's in the target area and the number of defendants named in the injunction order. The size interaction did not yield significant estimates, indicating that size is not a factor in the effectiveness of the injunctions. When the jurisdiction was examined by limiting the sample to injunctions within the LAPD's jurisdiction, estimates are very close to those of the full sample, indicating that jurisdiction had no impact on the effectiveness of the injunctions (Grogger 2000: 38).

Although Grogger concedes that a 5 to 10 percent decrease in reported crime in the target areas is not a large effect, it is comparable in magnitude to the impact of many social policy interventions. He suggests that the important question is whether the injunctions are cost-effective in their reduction of crime (Grogger 2000: 43). Assistant City Attorney Martin Vranicar, Jr., the supervisor of the LACA Gang Unit addressed that issue, stating that it cost the city approximately $100,000 for the salary of a deputy city attorney dedicated full-time to one injunction per year. Because most of the police officers used in the injunctions are already involved in gang enforcement, "it only costs the citizens another $100,000 to get that kind of percentage decrease in violent crime. I'd say we come out on top of any cost-benefit analysis you can come up with" (Los Angeles Assistant City Attorney Martin Vranicar, Jr., personal communication, May 25 2001).

Grogger's study is a significant addition to the scant knowledge about the effectiveness of gang injunctions. The study was not limited to a single injunction, but looked at aggregate data from thirteen injunctions in fourteen target areas. By using neighboring and matched comparison areas, Grogger controlled for many extraneous factors that might have influenced the effectiveness of the injunctions. Although he studied only the short-term effects of the injunctions, including all injunctions for which suitable data could be obtained and using pre- and post-injunction data over an eight-year period heightened the reliability of the study. Grogger also examined alternative explanations and explicitly defined the limitations of the study in advance.

CHAPTER V

The Dimension of Flexibility

The first objective of this study is to examine the flexibility of gang injunctions. According to the problem-oriented perspective, law enforcement agencies should respond to specific crime and disorder problems in a flexible manner, by customizing official interventions to the specific circumstances of the problem being addressed within a specific locale (Goldstein 1990: 44). The concept of flexibility is implicit in the goal of injunctive relief – to tailor a surgical strike at the specific conditions contributing to the claim for relief. Flexibility in strategies addressing community problems resulting from gang activity is supported by contemporary gang theory and research, which attests to the wide variation between gangs in criminal activity and anti-social behavior (Thrasher 1927/1963; Klein 1996; Moore 1993; Thornberry and Burch 1997; Huff 1998; Esbensen and Huizinga 1996; Battin-Pearson et al. 1998), and by the wide range of activity that falls under the 'public nuisance' umbrella (Spencer 1989; *Farmy v. College Housing, Inc.* 1975: 175). When applied to the gang injunction, flexibility suggests that the relief requested of the courts and the situational characteristics across injunction initiatives will vary according to the specific nuisance-related activities and peculiar circumstances of each targeted gang and neighborhood.

In contrast, successful innovative interventions are often mimicked by other agencies with little concern for their fit to the local circumstances. Mimicry results in a stereotypical response to related, but somewhat diverse, problems. In the area of municipal reform, Knoke (1982) found that municipal reform is often the product of "some type of imitation or contagion effects" (Knoke 1982: 1337). Institutional theorists DiMaggio and Powell (1983) identify mimicry as one of three isomorphic processes through which organizations become increasingly similar while trying to be innovative.[57] In drafting municipal ordinances, the tendency of local governments to rely on the relevant experiences of other jurisdictions has been recognized by the

United States Supreme Court. In a decision on the constitutionality of a municipal ordinance banning nude dancing, Justice O'Connor writes:

> Even in cases addressing regulations that strike closer to the core of First Amendment values, we have accepted a state or local government's reasonable belief that the experience of other jurisdictions is relevant to the problem it is addressing (*City of Erie v. Pap's A.M.*, 120 S.Ct. 1382 (2000), at 1395).

Mimicry is often used in innovative legal practices to eliminate "reinventing the wheel", allowing prosecutors to decrease the expenditure of valuable resources. By copying cases that have already withstood judicial scrutiny, mimicry also protects an innovative practice against constitutional challenges. If challenged in court, over-zealous prosecutors attempting to use overbroad or inappropriate interventions, based on the experiences of other agencies, may hamper the use of that innovation in future cases.

There is evidence of mimicry in drafting gang injunctions. Prosecutors acknowledge targeting similar gang problems for injunctive relief and imitating the pleadings of previously successful gang injunctions. Prosecutors unfamiliar with gang injunctions are encouraged to model their pleadings on past successful cases and obtain assistance from experienced gang injunction prosecutors. The success of each injunction enhances the legitimacy of the strategy, increasing its future acceptance as an appropriate tool to combat the destructive effects of gangs on neighborhoods. Therefore, all agencies using the strategy have a stake in the success of initiatives in other jurisdictions. To further the success of gang injunctions, the California District Attorney's Association offers workshops for prosecutors interested in obtaining gang injunctions. Although some degree of mimicry admittedly exists, defendants are protected from unbridled imitation by the legal requirement of a nexus between each injunction provision and the public nuisance caused by the gang (*In re Englebrecht* 1998).

Whether civil gang abatement exhibits the dimension of flexibility, through variation in requested relief and situational characteristics, or represents a stereotypical response that merely imitates other injunction initiatives, with little concern into their fit to the local circumstances, has not been empirically examined. Therefore, the first question addressed by this study is: *Do the requested relief and situational characteristics vary across injunction initiatives, and does this variance satisfy the dimension of flexibility implicit in the problem-oriented perspective?*

The variables used in the analysis of the dimension of flexibility are divided into two types: descriptive variables and situational characteristics. Descriptive variables are broad attributes of the injunction initiatives. They include the provisions of requested relief, the date of the filing of the complaint, the prosecuting agency primarily responsible for conducting the injunction initiative, and the categories of associational restrictions requested by prosecutors. The situational characteristics are variables describing the local circumstances surrounding each injunction initiative. Because they are extensively used to explore the situational characteristics, this analysis begins with an examination of the descriptive variables.

ANALYSIS OF DESCRIPTIVE VARIABLES

The Provisions of Requested Relief

The provisions of requested relief are the end product of the acquisition stage of the injunction process. These provisions represent the response of prosecutors to the nuisance-related activities of the gang in the target area. They consist of the terms of the injunction as requested of the court by the prosecutors. The provisions are found in one or more of three documents in the court files – the *Complaint*, the *Proposed Preliminary Injunction*, and the *Memorandum of Points and Authorities*.[58]

The provisions of requested relief are generally contained in enumerated pleadings that often proscribe related activities. For example, the following pleading includes several activities associated with drug trafficking: "(b) Selling, possessing, or using without a prescription, any controlled substance or related paraphernalia, including but not limited to, rolling papers and pipes used for illegal drug use, or riding a bicycle to facilitate any of the foregoing activities". This provision includes three distinct activities: 1) the illegal sale, possession, or use of a controlled substance;[59] 2) the sale, possession, or use of related paraphernalia; and 3) riding a bicycle to facilitate the foregoing activities. Because of the grouping of activities, the number of enumerated pleadings is not indicative of the number of activities that prosecutors seek to prohibit.

For this study, each distinct prohibited activity has been extracted from the pleadings and represented as a binary variable indicating the presence or absence of the proscription. All of the prohibited activities form a behavioral index containing fifty-four distinct proscriptions. The behavioral index allows the variation in the total number of proscriptions of all injunction initiatives to be explored, regardless of the number of enumerated pleadings. The behavioral index is then divided into three sub-indexes according to the type of activity prohibited: (1) the drug index contains ten activities associated with the illegal possession, use, and sale of drugs; (2) the crime index contains twenty-one activities that represent non-drug-related crimes and ordinance violations; and (3) the disorder index contains twenty-three activities associated with neighborhood disorder. Only those proscriptions that are present in at least two injunctions are assigned as a variable. Proscriptions that are present in only one injunction are grouped into a miscellaneous variable in each sub-index. Appendix B describes the activities proscribed in each sub-index, along with the frequency of each proscription among all injunction initiatives.

The differences between the sub-indexes are not always distinct. Although generally associated with a particular type of activity, some non-criminal activities may be conducted for various purposes. For example, riding a bicycle in the target area is generally associated with the illegal sale of drugs, as runners often use bicycles to obtain drugs from where it is stashed for delivery to customers. However, a bicycle may also be used to escape from the police for non-drug violations or to warn other gang members of a police presence in the area. Although commonly associated with open-air drug markets, signaling and approaching passing vehicles for purposes other that drug sales may independently contribute to the public nuisance by impeding the free flow of traffic. Some of the provisions in the disorder index, such as loitering for illegal purposes and violations of juvenile curfews, may already be prohibited by local ordinances in some, but not all, jurisdictions. Although the activities in the crime index are generally illegal regardless of jurisdiction, there may be exceptions. Therefore, the choice of the provisions to place into each sub-index is somewhat subjectively based on how the activities are described in the case files and by prosecutors during the interviews.

An examination of the variation in frequencies of behavioral index provisions is a starting point for analyzing the flexibility of injunction initiatives. The amount of variation of the behavioral index can be determined by measuring the dispersion of cases relative to the average for the index. The mean, or average, number of provisions for all cases in the index is 21.8. The standard deviation represents the dispersion of cases, or the average number of provisions each individual case varies from the mean.[60] The standard deviation for the behavioral index is 6.97. The standard deviation divided by the mean indicates the amount of variation in the index (Maxfield and Babbie 1998: 357). For the behavioral index, the standard deviation is approximately 1/3 the value of the mean, suggesting that the injunctions are not stereotypical, but vary greatly in requested relief.

The number of prohibited activities ranges from four provisions to thirty-seven provisions. The highest frequency of proscriptions is five cases containing twenty-three proscriptions. One case has four proscriptions, or approximately 2 ½ standard deviations from the mean, while one has thirty-seven proscriptions, or approximately 2 standard deviations from the mean. Table 5-1 shows the frequencies of cases by number of provisions.

TABLE 5-1: Frequencies of Behavioral Index Provisions

# of Provisions	Frequency of Cases	Percent of Cases	Statistics
4	1	2.4	Mean = 21.8
5	1	2.4	Median = 23
10	2	4.8	Std. Dev. = 6.97
11	1	2.4	Min = 4
13	1	2.4	Max = 37
15	2	4.8	Range = 33
19	3	7.1	
20	4	9.5	
21	3	7.1	
22	1	2.4	
23	5	11.9	
24	3	7.1	
25	2	4.8	
26	2	4.8	
27	3	7.1	
28	3	7.1	
30	3	7.1	
31	1	2.4	
37	1	2.4	
Total	42	100.0	

The variation in the behavioral index suggests that gang injunctions are not stereotypical responses to gang activity. Although many prosecutors who were interviewed admitted that they used provisions from other injunction cases, the distribution of frequencies for the behavioral index implies that they do not blindly follow the lead of cases that preceded them. Because prosecutors must establish a nexus between the activities to be prohibited and the public nuisance caused by the specific gang being enjoined, prosecutors must attempt to fit the requested proscriptions to the local circumstances.

TABLE 5-2: Frequencies of Prohibited Activities

Provision	Category	Frequency	Provision	Category	Frequency
[illegible]	disorder	40	opencont	disorder	13
obstrpub	crime	39	useveh	disorder	13
possdw	crime	39	burgtool	crime	12
trespass	crime	39	clothing	disorder	10
drugproh	drug	36	bicycle	drug	9
harasint	disorder	35	homeintr	crime	9
garffiti	crime	34	handsign	disorder	9
pubdrink	crime	34	harbor	crime	8
intcompl	crime	33	miscrime	crime	8
graftool	crime	32	infldrug	drug	7
signalle	drug	31	exhbspd	crime	7
curfadlt	disorder	29	gambling	crime	7
paraph	drug	28	loiter	disorder	7
litter	crime	28	throwing	crime	5
vandal	crime	27	attschev	disorder	5
curfmin	disorder	26	inflalc	disorder	5
noise	disorder	25	toygun	disorder	5
prespdw	disorder	25	alcund21	crime	3
recwarn	drug	24	carrepr	disorder	3
fighting	crime	24	locrstr	disorder	3
signveh	drug	23	tarival	disorder	3
puburin	crime	23	brandwpn	crime	2
drugpres	drug	19	bannedta	disorder	2
shooting	crime	17	coopwpol	disorder	2
climbing	drug	15	dogs	disorder	2
posscomm	drug	15	noncrim	disorder	2
abandpro	disorder	14	separate	disorder	2

(See Appendix B for a description of the provisions.)

Table 5-2 further examines the issue of a stereotypical response by breaking down the frequencies of each of the prohibited activities. The frequencies range from a high of one proscription included in forty injunctions to a low of six different proscriptions found in only two injunctions.[61] No injunction initiative requests all of the prohibited activities.

The most frequent provision is the associational ban, which is part of the disorder index. Some form of associational prohibition[62] is found in forty of the forty-two injunction initiatives. Because of the importance of group conduct to gang activity, the associational ban is considered the most crucial activity to be prohibited. The street presence of gang members hanging out in groups is the greatest contributor to the gang's intimidation power over its turf. Whether it is robbery, drug dealing, or theft, gang crimes are frequently committed by groups of gang members working in concert. Furthermore, gang members congregating in groups tend to draw violence into the neighborhood, as members of rival gangs enter the neighborhood to retaliate for past incidents between the gangs, often in the form of drive-by shootings or other serious forms of violence.

The ban on harassment and intimidation[63] is the only other component of the disorder index found in more than thirty injunctions. The harassment, intimidation, and annoyance of neighborhood residents and visitors are clearly a large part of the gang problem. This activity causes law-abiding people to avoid public areas and, thus, concede that space to the control of the gang. Because harassment and intimidation by gang members is usually conducted in groups, it is closely linked to the associational ban. These related provisions – the associational and intimidation bans – were the only two provisions appealed to the California Supreme Court in *People v. Acuna* (1997), the leading legal authority on gang injunctions.

Surprisingly, the proscription on the possession, sale, and use of drugs only rank as the fifth most frequent proscription requested by prosecutors. It was expected to rank higher in the list of proscriptions because of claim by critics that gang injunctions are commonly used by prosecutors to avoid the constitutional protections of the criminal law, the common perception of the importance of drug sales as an engine of monetary gain for the gang, and the accompanying disorder that drug sales draw into the disenfranchised areas frequented by gangs. However, six injunctions do not have any provision prohibiting the sale, possession, or use of drugs, and, of the eleven proscriptions found in thirty or more injunctions, only two are related to illegal drugs. This is consistent with social science research on gangs, which attributes the sale of illegal drugs to the desires of individual gang members more than to a way of augmenting the wealth of the gang. Four injunctions do not have any drug index provisions, indicating that some prosecutors view the criminal law as a sufficient remedy for illegal drug activity.[64]

Gang experts and prosecutors stress the group nature of drug sales, claiming that at least three gang members are needed for the street sale of illegal drugs – one conducting the sale, another acting as a runner to get the drugs from where they are stashed, and a third acting as a lookout to warn about the presence of law enforcement in the area.

This group activity helps explain why eight out of the ten drug index provisions ranked in the top fifty per cent based on frequency present, the highest frequency rate of the three indexes. Sixty-four percent of the injunctions contained five or more drug index provisions, with the highest having nine of the ten provisions. Table 5-3 shows the frequency of drug index provisions.

TABLE 5-3. Frequencies of Drug Index Provisions

# of Provisions	Frequency of Cases	Percent of Cases	Statistics
2	2	4.8	Mean = 4.9
4	2	4.8	Median = 5
6	1	2.4	Std. Dev. = 2.5
7	4	9.5	Min = 0
8	5	11.9	Max = 9
9	3	7.1	Range = 9
10	2	4.8	
11	4	9.5	
12	6	14.3	
13	5	11.9	
14	5	11.9	
15	2	4.8	
16	1	2.4	
Total	42	100.0	

Seven of the eleven provisions found in more than thirty injunctions are included in the crime index. Obstructing the public, possession of dangerous weapons, and trespassing are the second most frequent proscriptions, included in thirty-nine injunction initiatives. These activities are also large contributors to the intimidation power of the gang. When gang members obstruct the public by blocking sidewalks, streets, and driveways, failing to move for vehicular and pedestrian traffic, or when they trespass on the property of others, they are in effect proclaiming the gang's ownership of the neighborhood. The possession of dangerous weapons, which are often displayed to residents, intimidates law-abiding residents and adds to the potential for violence from rival gangs.

Provisions prohibiting the application of graffiti and public drinking are found in thirty-four initiatives, while intimidating complainants/witnesses and possession of graffiti implements are found in thirty-three and thirty-two initiatives respectively. Graffiti is primarily used to proclaim the gang's ownership of a territory to both residents and rival gangs. Graffiti also serves as a news service, spreading the word of upcoming or past events to other members of the gang. The frequent and pervasive application of graffiti throughout a neighborhood is a constant reminder of the gang's presence to both residents and those who frequent the area, contributing to the intimidating effect of the gang. Public drinking is a frequent complaint by residents because it adds to the disorder in the neighborhood. Intimidation of complainants and witnesses[65] is one of the major problems associated with prosecuting gang members for criminal violations.

TABLE 5-4: Frequencies of Crime Index Provisions

# of Provisions	Frequency of Cases	Percent of Cases	Statistics
2	2	4.8	Mean = 10.2
4	2	4.8	Median = 11
6	1	2.4	Std. Dev. = 3.5
7	4	9.5	Min = 2
8	5	11.9	Max = 16
9	3	7.1	Range = 14
10	2	4.8	
11	4	9.5	
12	6	14.3	
13	5	11.9	
14	5	11.9	
15	2	4.8	
16	1	2.4	
Total	42	100.0	

The crime index is the most evenly distributed of the three indexes. Of the twenty-one provisions in the crime index, nineteen injunctions (45%) requested ten or fewer crime index provisions and twenty-three injunctions (55%) requested eleven or more provisions. The distribution ranges from two injunctions containing only two crime index provisions to one injunction containing sixteen provisions. Table 5-4 displays the frequencies of the crime index provisions.

Although the associational and harassment/intimidation provisions rank high in frequency of occurrence, the other provisions of the disorder index are under-represented in requested relief. Of twenty-three provisions in the disorder index, only four injunctions contain eleven or more, accounting for only 9.5% of all injunction initiatives. Twenty-two cases (52%) have from one to six disorder index provisions, while twenty cases (48%) have from seven to fifteen provisions. This under-representation is understandable. Because the disorder provisions effectively criminalize normally non-criminal behavior, they are the most controversial provisions and the most susceptible to constitutional challenge. The disorder index proscriptions, along with some of the non-criminal provisions in the drug index, are the provisions most frequently deleted or altered by the court. Table 5-5 displays the frequencies of the disorder index provisions

TABLE 5-5: Frequencies of Disorder Index Provisions

# of Provisions	Frequency of Cases	Percent of Cases	Statistics
1	1	2.4	Mean = 6.7
2	3	7.1	Median = 6
3	2	4.8	Std. Dev. = 2.9
4	3	7.1	Min = 1
5	4	9.5	Max = 15
6	9	21.4	Range = 14
7	3	7.1	
8	6	14.3	
9	6	14.3	
10	1	2.4	
11	3	7.1	
15	1	2.4	
Total	42	100.0	

Classification of Injunction Initiatives

One primary objective of this study is to classify the injunction initiatives. Classification organizes sets of data by patterns among one or more attributes of interest to the research. The resulting patterns are assigned class labels, forming a taxonomy that conveniently summarizes the data. The validity of the taxonomy is judged by the usefulness of the results for achieving the goals of the research, not by measures of statistical significance (Everitt 1993: 2). Classification can be accomplished subjectively, through an intuitive sense of the relative importance of certain attributes, or objectively, through numerical techniques that measure the proximities of data. Although objective techniques attempt to eliminate the traditionally subjective nature of classification, subjective decisions, such as the choice of variables and interpretation of the resulting categories, are unavoidable in any classification procedure.

This study attempts to limit the subjectivity of classification through the use of cluster analysis, a statistical procedure that is used in many fields for descriptive and exploratory purposes (Kaufman and Rousseeuw 1990). Cluster analysis discovers homogeneous groups, or clusters, in data by mathematically identifying structures in the data through the proximity of attributes on a similarity or dissimilarity coefficient. Similarity coefficients measure how alike the data are, while dissimilarity coefficients measure differences. The attributes used in this study are the presence of provisions of requested relief represented by the proscriptions in the three sub-indexes forming the behavioral index.[66]

The procedure results in three clusters, each representing a high score on one of the sub-indexes. Cluster 1 represents the high drug category. All the cases in this category scored high (above the mean) on the drug index and low (mean or below) on the crime index, with mixed results on the disorder index. Cluster 2 represents the high crime category. All cases in this category scored high on the crime index and low on the disorder index, with mixed results on the drug index. Cluster 3 represents the high disorder category, with all cases scoring high on the disorder index, with mixed results on both the crime and the drug indexes.

FIGURE 5-1

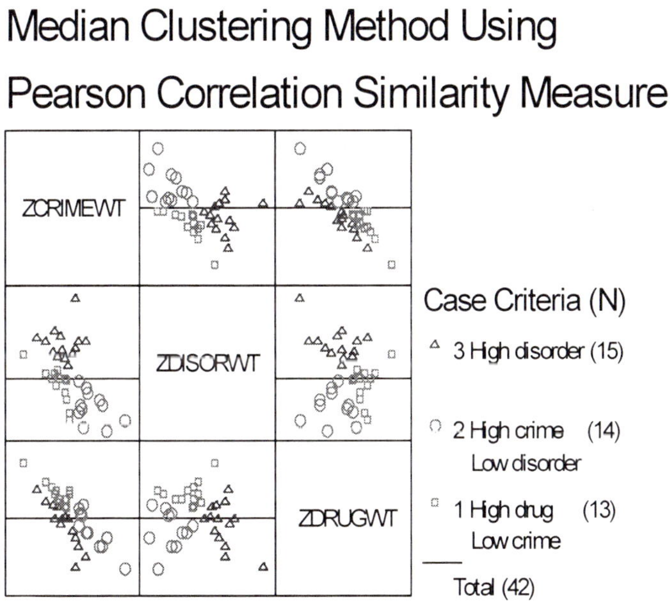

The clusters are very evenly distributed. The *high drug* category contains thirteen initiatives, the *high crime* category containing fourteen initiatives, and the *high disorder* category contains fifteen initiatives. The relationship between the clusters on each index is graphically portrayed in a scatterplot matrix (see Figure 5-1). The assignment of categories for each injunction and each injunction's score on the sub-indexes is displayed in Appendix C.

If prosecutors were merely copying requested provisions from other injunction initiatives, one would expect that at least one injunction category would contain a substantially greater percentage of injunction initiatives. However, the even distribution of the classification strongly supports the concept of flexibility in injunction initiatives when measured by the provisions of requested relief.

Date Filed

The time period in which the injunction initiative takes place is particularly relevant to the variation in requested relief. The gang injunction phenomenon can be divided into three time periods that coincide with the two appellate decisions in *People v. Acuna* (1995, 1997). Prior to April 24, 1995, there was little guidance for prosecutors and judges on the propriety and scope of gang injunctions. On that date, the Sixth District Court of Appeals released a published decision of the *Acuna* case, concluding that under public nuisance law only criminal conduct could be prohibited by injunction. The decision was the leading state authority on gang injunctions until January 30, 1997, when the California Supreme Court overturned the most important aspects of the Court of Appeals' decision. The Supreme Court affirmed the use of injunctive relief to abate gang activity as public nuisance, but overruled the Court of Appeals on two key non-criminal provisions, the non-association clause and the non-intimidation clause. The non-association clause and, to a lesser extent, the non-intimidation clause are the heart and soul of the civil gang abatement strategy. These provisions attack the group processes that are the foundation of a gang's power over a neighborhood. Since the California Supreme Court's decision, the use of the gang injunction to address gang activity has rapidly accelerated.

The variable **date filed** categorizes the injunction initiatives into three time periods related to the *Acuna* decisions: the *pre-Acuna period*, before 04/24/95; the *appellate period*, between 04/24/95 and 01/30/97; and the *post-Acuna period*, after 01/30/97. Eight injunctions were filed during the *pre-Acuna period*. Two occurrences stand out during this period. First, there were no *high drug* injunction initiatives filed during the *pre-Acuna period* (Table 5-6). Two initiatives had no drug-related proscriptions, and four did not ban the illegal possession/sale of drugs, the most frequent drug-related provision. The relative lack of drug-related provisions suggests that drug-related activity was not the priority of injunction initiatives during this period. The *pre-Acuna period* may be considered an experimental period, in which prosecutors were grappling with how to apply this innovative legal intervention. Prosecutors may have hesitated emphasizing drug-related activity for fear that the injunction would ultimately be denied as a law enforcement tool against gangs. If judges perceived that gang injunctions were primarily being used to control illegal drug sales, they might have denied injunctive relief because there was an adequate remedy under the criminal law, which also provided defendants with greater constitutional protections.

TABLE 5-6: Date Filed by Category

	CATEGORY			
DATE FILED	High Drug	High Crime	High Disorder	Row Frequency
Pre-*Acuna* Period	-	5	3	8
Appellate Period	4	1	3	8
Post-*Acuna* Period	9	8	9	26
Column Frequency	13	14	15	42

Second, the only denials of injunctive relief occurred in the *pre-Acuna period*, during which preliminary injunctions were denied for two cases.[67] Both cases fell into the *high crime* category, which is consistent with the reasoning of both courts that there was adequate remedy under the criminal law (*People v. 'B' Street Boys*, Order Denying Preliminary Injunction 1994; *People v. Amaya*, Order Denying Preliminary Injunction 1993).

Eight injunctions were filed during the *appellate period*, a two-year period after the Court of Appeals' decision and prior to the Supreme Court's decision. Despite the Court of Appeals' decision to enjoin only criminal activity, only one injunction falls into the *high crime* category during the *appellate period* (Table 5-6). Although this seems to run counter to the supposition that prosecutors would have used the appellate court decision as guidance, the decision was binding only in the Sixth District. All eight cases occurred outside the jurisdiction of the Sixth District, and it was widely known among injunction prosecutors that the Sixth District decision had been appealed to the California Supreme Court.

The earlier two denials of preliminary injunctions may also have influenced initiatives during the *appellate period*. *'B' Street Boys* and *Amaya*, both of which fell into the *high crime* category, were denied in part because the judge determined that there was an adequate remedy under the criminal law. These decisions ran counter to the Sixth District Court of Appeals' decision in *Acuna* that only criminal violations were enjoinable by injunction. Prosecutors may have reasoned that if *Acuna* were overturned, allowing non-criminal activity to be enjoined, the decisions by two different courts that there was an adequate remedy under the criminal law would stand. Several prosecutors of cases in the *appellate period* indicated a reliance on the Supreme Court to overturn *Acuna*, allowing the enjoinment of association by gang members and other non-criminal activities that enhanced the public nuisance. The fact that four cases fell into the *high drug* category and three into the *high disorder* category, both of which have a preponderance of proscriptions on non-criminal activities, supports this view.

The *post-Acuna period*, from January 30, 1997 to the present, saw a rapid acceleration of injunction initiatives, as gang injunctions became more acceptable after the California Supreme Court's decision. The twenty-six injunction initiatives filed in this period were evenly distributed over the injunction categories: nine were *high drug* injunctions, eight were *high crime* injunctions, and nine were *high disorder* injunctions (Table 5-6). During this period, the reliance on injunctions to control gang problems peaked, with ten gang injunctions being filed in 1998 and six in both 1997 and 1999.

Prosecuting Agency

Of particular interest is whether there was any variation in injunction categories and situational characteristics between prosecuting agencies and among injunction initiatives by one prosecuting agency. For this analysis, prosecuting agencies are categorized according to county, type of agency, and individual agency. These categories will be extensively used in the analysis of the situational characteristics.

The variable **county** distinguishes initiatives within *Los Angeles County* from initiatives located in *other* counties, allowing an examination of whether initiatives in Los Angeles County were different from those in other counties. Twenty-six injunction initiatives occurred in Los Angeles County. Sixteen initiatives occurred in seven other counties, resulting in relatively small numbers for each *other* county for the purpose of analysis. Therefore, the county initiatives are condensed into one category.

The discrepancy among counties is not surprising considering the enormity of the gang problem in Los Angeles County. Los Angeles County has the most extensive gang problem in the country (Office of Juvenile Justice and Delinquency Prevention 1997). Two well-known gang researchers, Cheryl Maxson and Malcolm Klein, estimate that Los Angeles County contains 1,350 named street gangs with approximately 150,000 gang members, accounting for one-quarter of the active gangs and gang members in the United States. In a 1992 survey, they found that 61 of the 74 municipalities within Los Angeles County reported that street gangs were indigenous to their communities. Los Angeles County also leads the country in gang-related homicides, with nearly 9,500 gang-related killings between 1980 and 1998. For the last several years, approximately forty percent of all homicides in the county were gang-related, and, of over 2,000 gang-related killings in the nation in 1991, one-third of them occurred in Los Angeles County (Maxson and Klein 2001). When one considers that homicides account for a miniscule amount of the crimes committed by gang members, the enormity of the gang problem in Los Angeles is apparent.

When **county** is examined by **category** (Table 5-7), *Los Angeles County* initiatives are distinguished from initiatives in *other* counties by the *high drug* category. All thirteen initiatives in the *high drug* category occurred in Los Angeles County. This may be the result of the hand-in-hand relationship between illegal drug sales and violent crime, especially homicide. Injunctions occurring outside Los Angeles County are predominately *high crime* initiatives, with eleven *other* county initiatives falling into that category, compared to three *Los Angeles County* initiatives. The proportions in the *high disorder* category are in line with the total frequencies.

TABLE 5-7: County by Category

	CATEGORY			
COUNTY	High Drug	High Crime	High Disorder	Row Frequency
Other	-	11	5	16
Los Angeles	13	3	10	26
Column Frequency	13	14	15	42

The type of prosecuting agency is examined to determine whether different types of agencies approach injunction initiatives in distinct ways. In the criminal arena, district attorney offices generally handle more serious felony crimes, while city attorney offices focus on misdemeanors and municipal ordinances. However, in some counties, the district attorney handles both felony and misdemeanor cases. Both are responsible for various civil litigations, including the abatement of public nuisances, and are authorized to prosecute civil actions jointly. Occasionally, a city government will appoint a private law firm to litigate a particular civil action, especially in smaller jurisdictions that lack the resources to accomplish the task or where the city attorney retains his affiliation with a law firm.

The variable **agency** distinguishes *district attorney*, *city attorney*, *joint* action by district and city attorney, and *private* law firm acting as city attorney. *District attorney* refers to cases in which a district attorney office is the primary prosecutorial agency, either as the sole prosecutorial agency or under contract with an incorporated municipality. When an injunction initiative is conducted under contract, the municipality pays the salary of a deputy district attorney who is assigned to the municipality to conduct the initiative, often under the auspices of the municipality's attorney.[68] For the purpose of analysis, these cases are considered district attorney initiatives, even though city attorneys are involved in the initiative to some extent.

City attorney refers to cases where the city attorney's office is the primary prosecutorial agency. In these cases, the initiative is conducted either without the assistance or with peripheral assistance of the district attorney's office. One example of such peripheral assistance is a promise by the district attorney's office to prosecute injunction violations as criminal contempt, without being involved in acquiring the injunction.

Joint refers to cases in which the initiative is jointly conducted by a city attorney's office and a district attorney's office, with relatively equal responsibilities in the initiative. *Private* refers to cases in which a private law firm is retained to conduct the initiative as the city attorney.

Twenty-one cases were filed by ten different city attorney agencies. Thirteen cases were filed by district attorneys acting without assistance or with limited support from city attorney agencies. The San Diego District Attorney's Office filed four of those cases, and nine were filed by the Los Angeles District Attorney's Office. Six cases were joint actions by city and district attorneys, five of which occurred in Los Angeles County and one in Orange County. Two cases were initiatives by private firms acting as the city attorney.

City attorney offices were involved in injunction initiatives more often than district attorney offices. City attorney offices were the sole initiators of one-half of the initiatives and were involved in all the joint initiatives. When these two categories are combined, city attorney offices have been involved in sixty-four percent of the injunctions, compared to the involvement of district attorney offices in forty-five percent of the initiatives. However, this discrepancy is deceiving because only three county district attorney offices were directly involved in injunction initiatives, implying that city attorneys in California have more fully embraced the concept of public nuisance injunctions as an anti-gang tool than district attorneys. Although state law empowers both city and district attorneys to bring civil actions against public nuisances, only two county district attorney offices, in Los Angeles County and San Diego County, have become involved in injunction initiatives to a significant degree, with Orange County being involved only in one joint initiative.[69] A possible explanation is that city attorney offices are more extensively versed in civil law, whereas district attorney offices generally concentrate more on criminal violations. According to a deputy district attorney interviewed for this study, in at least one case the city attorney's office was asked for assistance because of its greater experience with civil law and procedures.

TABLE 5-8: Agency by Category

	CATEGORY			
AGENCY	High Drug	High Crime	High Disorder	Row Frequency
District Attorney	6	1	6	13
City Attorney	3	11	7	21
Joint Action	4	1	1	6
Private Firm	-	1	1	2
Column Frequency	13	14	15	42

Another possible explanation is the empowerment of city attorney offices in some jurisdictions to prosecute misdemeanors and ordinance violations, which account for most of the nuisance-related activities, while district attorney offices generally prosecute felonies.[70] When the type of agency is examined by category (Table 5-8), city attorney offices dominate the *high crime* category, conducting eleven of the fourteen *high crime* initiatives, while district attorney offices were responsible for only one *high crime* initiative. Many of the crimes making up the high crime index are relatively low level misdemeanors and ordinance violations, which are often prosecuted by city attorneys. In Los Angeles County, where the majority of the injunction initiatives have taken place, city attorneys are generally responsible for prosecuting misdemeanors and ordinance violations, possibly making them more conscious of the aggregate effects of low-level criminal behavior on neighborhoods. In contrast, initiatives by district attorney offices and joint initiatives tend to fall into the *high drug* category, which is consistent with the notion that district attorney offices are more focused on felony violations.

Identifying individual prosecutorial agencies involved in injunction initiatives allows an examination of the variation of the initiatives across and within agencies. Six prosecutors' offices have conducted two or more initiatives, while ten have limited their initiatives to one. Unless the injunction activity occurs within an unincorporated portion of the county, the county district attorney may conduct an initiative in conjunction with the prosecutor of the city in which the target area is located. For the purpose of analysis, these cases are considered district attorney initiatives. Because of the relatively large number of joint initiatives between the Los Angeles City Attorney's Office and the Los Angeles District Attorney's Office, those initiatives comprise a separate category.

The categories of the variable prosecutor's **office** are Los Angeles District Attorney (*LADA*), Los Angeles City Attorney (*LACA*), joint initiative of *LADA/LACA*, San Jose City Attorney (*SJCA*), San Diego District Attorney (*SDDA*), San Bernardino City Attorney (*SBCA*), and *other*, representing the ten offices conducting single injunction initiatives (Table 5-9).

The LACA and the LADA were involved in over half the injunction initiatives in California. The LACA was involved in fourteen initiatives, one less than the number of initiatives by all other city attorney offices combined. Similarly, the LADA was involved in fourteen initiatives, far more than the next closest district attorney office, SDDA, which conducted four. This imbalance is consistent with the magnitude of the gang problem in Los Angeles County.

When examined by category of injunction (Table 5-9), the LACA and the LADA have conducted all of thirteen in the *high drug* category, with six being conducted by the LADA has conducted six, three by the LACA, and four conducted jointly. Drug activity was targeted in two-thirds of the LADA's initiatives and in eighty percent of the joint initiatives. Its involvement in the other categories – four in the *high disorder* category and none in the *high crime* category – suggests that the LADA's focus in acquiring gang injunctions was on reducing drug activity, which is consistent with the agency's general responsibility of prosecuting felonies. However, the tendency of the San Diego District Attorney's Office to seek *high disorder* injunctions refutes the inference that all initiatives by district attorney offices targeted felony activity. In contrast to the district attorney initiatives, the LACA's individual involvement was not focused on the *high drug* category, but was evenly spread among all three categories.

TABLE 5-9: Office by Category

	CATEGORY			
OFFICE	High Drug	High Crime	High Disorder	Row Frequency
Other	-	6	4	10
LADA	6	-	3	9
LACA	3	2	4	9
LADA/LACA	4	-	1	5
SJCA	-	3	-	3
SDDA	-	1	3	4
SBCA	-	2	-	2
Column Frequency	13	14	15	42

Office:
Other = prosecutor's offices conducting a single injunction initiative.
LADA = Los Angeles District Attorney's Office
LACA = Los Angeles City Attorney's Office
LADA/LACA = Joint initiative between the LADA and the LACA
SDDA = San Diego District Attorney's Office
SJCA = San Jose City Attorney's Office
SBCA = San Bernardino City Attorney's Office

When **office** is examined by the **date filed** (Table 5-10), the LACA was noticeably absent during the appellate period, when the constitutionality of associational bans was questionable. According to one prosecutor, this absence occurred because the LACA was awaiting the *Acuna* decision by the Supreme Court, suggesting the importance of the associational ban to the LACA. In contrast, the LADA's SAGE (Strategy Against Gang Environments) began to gather steam during the appellate period, with the filing of five cases. After the *Acuna* decision, the LACA strongly re-entered the gang injunction arena, filing for seven injunctions individually and five injunctions jointly with the LADA. The LADA's individual initiatives slowed down to three filings in the *post-Acuna period*, although it did collaborate in five joint initiatives with the LACA.

TABLE 5-10: Office by Date Filed

	DATE FILED			
OFFICE	Pre-*Acuna* Period	Appellate Period	Post-*Acuna* Period	Row Frequency
Other	3	3	4	10
LADA	1	5	3	9
LACA	2	-	7	9
LADA/LACA	-	-	5	5
SJCA	2	-	1	3
SDDA	-	-	4	4
SBCA	-	-	2	2
Column Frequency	8	8	26	42

Associational Restrictions

Associational restrictions refer to provisions that restrict named defendants from publicly associating with other members of the gang within the target area. By far the most controversial provision of gang injunctions, associational restrictions are also the most crucial provision for decreasing the gang's hold on the neighborhood. Associational restrictions address one proximate cause of gang problems by attacking the group processes that provide the gang with its power over a neighborhood. Although this provision is sometimes misinterpreted as prohibiting the association of all gang members regardless of location, the restrictions apply only within a clearly defined target area and only to named defendants, not to the entire gang.[71]

Associational restrictions address three common problems. Much of a gang's power over a neighborhood stems from large numbers of gang members 'hanging out' in public, blocking streets, sidewalks and driveways, and impeding the free movement of residents and patrons of the neighborhood. Although this behavior may seem relatively innocuous on the surface, it is probably the most insidious activity of the gang. 'Hanging out' in groups on public thoroughfares enhances the perception that the gang controls the neighborhood. By prohibiting this activity, associational restrictions attack the group dynamics that are at the root of the intimidating power of the gang.

Associational restrictions also address gang-related crime in two ways. First, gang-related crime, especially violent crime and drug dealing, which is often accompanied by violent crime, is a group phenomenon. The *modus operandi* of gang members committing street robberies and assaults generally involves two or more assailants. According to one prosecutor, one of the biggest problems resulting in gang violence is the "Where you from?" challenge, in which a person not known to the gang is confronted in the gang's turf by a group of gang members. The gang members ask "Where you from?" meaning "What gang do you claim?" Because there is no right answer, the group assaults the stranger, often with knives, ground-down screwdrivers, and/or firearms. This challenge enhances the gang's hold on the neighborhood.

Drug dealing by gang members is usually a group enterprise involving at least three gang members – a seller to initiate the transaction, a runner to get the drugs, which are usually stored at another location, and a lookout to signal the others when law enforcement officers are observed in the area. Sometimes six or more gang members are involved in a single drug transaction. By restricting the association among hard-core gang members, who are generally the most persistent perpetrators of violent and drug-related crime, and between the hard-core members and the rest of the gang, associational restrictions help reduce the frequency of violent and drug-related crime in a neighborhood.

Finally, associational restrictions obstruct "the activity of the inciting and the inviting." According to one prosecutor, the practice of gang members claiming a neighborhood as its 'turf' and 'hanging out' at certain well-known locations within that turf is the most insidious gang-related activity. This practice "incites and invites" rival gangs into the neighborhood to conduct retaliatory strikes by offering an easy target to rivals, especially when there is an active conflict between the gangs. The common areas where the gang members hang out are generally well known, permitting rivals to commit drive-by shootings to extract retribution for some past event or to enhance their standing among their own gang. Because there is often no specific gang member targeted, assailants sometimes spray gunfire into the group in the hope of hitting a member of the opposing gang. This practice not only endangers gang members; it places innocent victims at risk of being shot and killed. In some cases, bullets have penetrated walls and windows, striking innocent victims in the sanctity of their homes, or non-gang youths are mistakenly identified as gang members, resulting in injury or death to an innocent person.[72] By reducing the availability of easy targets for rivals, associational restrictions help eliminate "the activity of the inciting and the inviting", protecting both gang members and innocent bystanders from serious injury and death.

TABLE 5-11: Associational Restrictions by Date Filed

	DATE FILED			
ASSOCIATIONAL RESTRICTIONS	Pre-*Acuna* Period: Before 04/24/95	Appellate Period: 04/24/95 to 01/30/97	Post-*Acuna* Period: After 01/30/97	Row Frequency
No associational restrictions	-	1	-	1
Associating or congregating at a specific location	-	1	-	1
Congregating with intent	1	6	3	10
Associating in public (with exceptions)	-	-	9	9
Association in public (with no exceptions)	5	-	14	19
Total ban from target area	2	-	-	2
Column Frequency	8	8	26	42

Six categories of **associational restrictions** have been teased from the case files.[73] The restrictions range in degree from no associational prohibitions, the least restrictive, to a total ban from the target area, the most restrictive.[74] Table 5-11 displays both the frequency of associational restrictions (row frequency) and the correlation with the period in which the case was filed (**date filed**). As expected, the degree of associational restriction generally correlates with the periods of the *Acuna* decision. The less restrictive associational provisions tend to occur in the *appellate period*, when the Court of Appeals' decision served as legal precedent. The most restrictive association provisions occur in injunctions filed in the *pre-Acuna period*, when prosecutors were experimenting with this new strategy and had little guidance from the court. Initiatives in the *post-Acuna period*, after the California

Supreme Court upheld the constitutionality of the non-association clause, generally contained more moderate associational restrictions.

No associational prohibition refers to initiatives in which there were no provisions restricting the public association of the defendants with other gang members within the target area. The absence of associational restrictions was limited to one case occurring in the *appellate period*. The prosecutor for this case cited the Sixth District Court of Appeals' *Acuna* decision as the reason for the absence of an associational ban. The prosecutor did not want to risk a denial of the entire injunction by including an associational ban of questionable constitutionality.

One case contained a provision prohibiting *associating or congregating at a specific location* within the target area. The specified area was a park located in the center of the target area that provided where gang members gathered. The park was crucial to the gang because many defendants did not drive and could easily walk to it. As a result, many of the gang's activities were conducted in the park and as gang members walked to and from the park. When the injunction was granted, the defendants thought that the associational prohibition applied to the whole city, not just the area surrounding the park or the target area. Neither the prosecutor nor the police tried to correct this misinterpretation of the associational prohibition, since the gang claimed the entire city as its turf. The limited associational ban is consistent with the fact that the case was filed during the *appellate period*.

A prohibition on *congregating with intent* to violate the injunction or law was found in ten cases. This provision contains an intent requirement, meaning that the intent to violate the law or the other terms of the injunction must be proven to sustain a violation for congregating. This is the weakest associational restriction used by more than one injunction initiative. Six cases containing this provision occurred in the *appellate period*, suggesting that prosecutors were searching for some form of associational restriction that would withstand judicial scrutiny. One case filed in the *pre-Acuna period* and three filed in the *post-Acuna period* contained this provision. Two of the *post-Acuna* cases were filed shortly after the Supreme Court decision. The third case, which was filed after the *Acuna* decision was well established, also contained a provision requiring all defendants on probation to abide by all terms of their probation, which customarily included a prohibition on associating with other gang members. Because all but one defendant were on probation, the prosecutor used this provision as an indirect way to impose a stringent associational restriction without drawing the criticism that an outright associational ban might elicit from civil rights activists.[75] Because the injunction also contained a *congregating with intent* provision, it was included in this category, rather than in the full associational restriction category.

The next most restrictive associational ban is *association in public with exceptions*. This provision prohibits the association of defendants with other gang members in public, except at designated locations and under certain conditions. These exceptions are commonly called 'carve-outs',[76] because locations where gang members can associate under certain circumstances are carved out of the target area. The exempt locations and the circumstances under which the exemption is valid vary between injunctions and target areas. Carve-outs have been designated at: social service agencies, youth centers, and community centers, for defendants who are enrolled in a program and attending that program; hospitals, when present for a legitimate purpose; schools, for defendants who are enrolled in and attending school; places of employment, when defendants are working; vehicles, when all occupants are commuting to employment; the presence of immediate family members; church, while attending services; and public buildings, such as city halls and public libraries, when present for a legitimate purpose. Exempt locations and validating circumstances are specified in the proposed preliminary injunction, and, with the exception of commuting to employment, defendants are generally not allowed to go to and from these locations in a group. There were nine injunctions with carve-outs, all occurring in the *post-Acuna period.*

The most restrictive non-association provision that has passed judicial scrutiny is *associating in public with no exceptions*. This provision imposes a total prohibition on the association with other gang members, with no intent requirement or exceptions, other than within a dwelling unit. Nineteen injunctions (45%) contained this provision, five filed in the *pre-Acuna period* and fourteen filed in the *post-Acuna period.* As expected, this provision was not found in any initiative during the *appellate period.* The *pre- Acuna period* may be thought of as an experimental period in which prosecutors, acting with little judicial guidance, were testing the provisions that would be acceptable to judges. This provision was widely used in the *post- Acuna period* because a total prohibition was one of the two provisions approved by the California Supreme Court's *Acuna* decision.

A final category, a *total ban from the target area* without proof of a legitimate reason for being present, such as residency or employment, was included in two early injunction initiatives, both occurring in the *pre-Acuna period.* In the first gang injunction, *People v. Playboy Gangster Crips*, in which prosecutors were admittedly experimenting with this innovative tool, the total ban provision was stricken by the court along with all other non-criminal activities. In *People v. 'B' Street Boys*, this provision may have been largely responsible for the denial of the injunction.[77] However, because this research is based on requested relief, rather than relief granted by the court, the total ban from the target area is considered the most restrictive category of associational restriction requested by prosecutors.

The judicial rejection of a total ban from the target area is not surprising. Defendants often have social and family ties in the target area. A total ban would effectively prohibit a defendant from traveling in or through the target area or from associating with people who are not in the gang, including members of his/her family. A provision that totally prohibits familial association is a violation of the 1st Amendment protections afforded to associations with an intimate value (*People v. Acuna* 1997: 608). In contrast, the less drastic ban or *association in public without exceptions* merely prohibits gang members from associating with other gang members in public within the target area. There is no restriction on defendants entering the target area, associating in public with individuals not identified as members of the targeted gang, or associating out of the public eye with relatives who are members of the targeted gang.

It was previously suggested that the Los Angeles City Attorney's Office (LACA) did not file any injunction cases during the *appellate period* because of the importance of a stringent associational restriction to its cases. When associational restrictions are examined by office, the less stringent associational provisions are not included in the LACA cases. The LACA has consistently sought more severe restrictions on association, even though the LACA is also responsible for the 'carve-outs', or location exceptions. Although the San Jose City Attorney's Office (SJCA) also sought more stringent associational restrictions and did not file any cases during the *appellate period*, this may be due to the SJCA's direct involvement with the *Acuna* appeal, which was a SJCA case.[78]

ANALYSIS OF SITUATIONAL CHARACTERISTICS

Situational characteristics are variables representing the circumstances surrounding the injunction initiatives. The categories of the individual variables are the result of the information obtained from the data sources. The situational characteristics are explored through their interaction with the descriptive variables and other situational characteristics to identify relationships that are meaningful to the concept of flexibility.

For the purpose of discussion, the situational characteristics are organized into five sections. The first four sections mirror the steps of the problem-solving methodology generally used in problem-oriented interventions – problem identification, analysis, response, and assessment. This format is convenient because the problem-oriented philosophy is one of the theoretical foundations of civil gang abatement. The fifth section examines the circumstances under which gang injunctions have been considered but not pursued, allowing the identification of circumstances under which injunctions may be considered an inappropriate response to gang activity.

Problem Identification

Problem identification is a process that goes beyond a preliminary inquiry into the immediate problem to be addressed. The conditions under which a problem is identified and the entity that identifies the problem may have a strong influence on the ultimate definition of the problem and on the response chosen to address it. The identification process includes redefining the problem after a thorough analysis of information gathered from all sources. Theoretically, the process should produce a more accurate understanding of the precise problem to be addressed, allowing the prosecutor to prioritize among different facets of the problem (Goldstein 1990: 76-77). Ideally, the result will be in the most effective response to the problem.

<u>Catalyst</u>

Prosecuting agencies generally react to crimes and offenses that have already been committed.[79] When combined with the relative scarcity of gang injunctions,[80] the reactive nature of prosecuting agencies suggests that some catalyst attracts the attention of the prosecutor's office to gang activity in a particular neighborhood. Even where a protocol exists to identify areas that might be suitable for injunctive relief, such as in the City of Los Angeles,[81] it is anticipated that in most cases some unusual gang-related activity, or **catalyst**, brought the gang to the attention of prosecutors. Six categories of catalysts have been identified from the data: (1) *high profile incident(s)*, (2) *high rates of gang-related crimes*, (3) a preponderance of *disorder offenses*, (4) *news media event*, (5) *public facilities* taken over by the gang, and (6) *not specified* (Table 5-12).

TABLE 5-12: Catalyst

Catalyst	Frequency	Percent
Not specified	3	7.1
High profile violent incident(s)	15	35.7
High rates of gang-related crimes	9	21.4
Disorder offenses	5	11.9
News media event	4	9.5
Public facility	6	14.3
Total	42	100.0

A *high profile incident* or group of incidents, such as a drive-by shooting that victimizes an innocent party, is the most frequent catalyst for injunction initiatives. High profile incidents raise the consciousness of the community to the gang problem and receive much publicity in the news media, often resulting in an outcry from the community, politicians, and/or law enforcement officials for an extraordinary response, such as a gang injunction. Some prosecutors stated that gang injunctions are often a response to high profile shooting incidents, particularly in the City of Los Angeles. According to one prosecutor, "invariably it is some horrific event that captures media attention and people are scrambling 'Oh my God, what do we do', leading somebody to suggest obtaining an injunction." A *high profile incident* or group of incidents was identified as the catalyst in 35% of the initiatives.

The second most frequent catalyst is *high rates of gang-related crime*. Gang-related crimes include illegal drug trafficking and felony victimizations, both of which are responsible for many problems in gang-plagued neighborhoods. Drug trafficking draws other crimes and disorder to a neighborhood. Felony victimization, such as aggravated assault and robbery, adds to the intimidation effect of gangs by increasing the sense that gang members, rather than the police, control the neighborhood. Because these crimes seldom attract the same degree of attention from the news media as do high profile incidents, often only residents and those familiar with the neighborhood, such as the police and prosecutors dedicated to gang-related crimes, are aware of the gang problem in the neighborhood. *High rates of gang-related crime* are the catalyst for 21% of the initiatives.

Public facilities taken over by the gang is the third most frequent catalyst identified by the research. Gang members often use public facilities, especially parks and recreation areas, as convenient gathering places and staging areas for their gang activities. As these areas are often the only large 'green' tracts in urban neighborhoods, unfettered access for local residents to parks and recreation facilities is an important part of community life, providing a place where children can play, adult residents can associate freely, and sports can be pursued by residents of all ages. When a gang takes over a park or recreation area, the attendant drug dealing, violence and disorder limits access to the area. The area becomes dangerous for non-gang members, eliminating an important source of community cohesion. Domination of *public facilities* by the gang is identified as the catalyst for 14% of the initiatives.

Disorder offenses refer to the preponderance of relatively minor crimes committed by gang members and disorderly conditions resulting from the presence of the gang in a neighborhood. Although relatively innocuous on the surface, the aggregate of minor offenses and disorder reduces the quality-of-life for the residents of the neighborhood. Although some of this activity is not considered criminal, *disorder offenses* are a nuisance *per se* when prohibited by municipal ordinance. For example, the Oceanside municipal code states:

> Any condition caused, maintained, existing or permitting to exist in violation of any article, section or provision of this code or of any other ordinance of the city...is hereby declared to be public nuisance and may, in addition to imposition of the penalties by this section, be abated as such…(Oceanside City Code section 1.7(g)).[82]

Although the most frequent activity of gang members (Maxson and Klein 2001), *disorder offenses* are identified as the catalyst for only 12% of the initiatives.

The direct influence of a *news media event* refers to a major article or a series of articles about the targeted gang and/or the target area in the print and broadcast news media. News stories about gangs and gang-infested neighborhoods give unwanted publicity to gang activity, sometimes forcing law enforcement authorities to respond to local gang problems. *News media events* are identified as the catalyst for 10% of the initiatives.

The category *not specified* includes initiatives where there is little evidence of a specific catalyst. Although the relative scarcity of gang injunctions leads to a presumption that some catalyst will be present for each injunction initiative, some prosecutors viewed the gang injunction as a tool to control a locally persistent gang problem without the need for a specific catalyst. A catalyst could not be clearly identified for 7% of the injunction initiatives.

An examination of the interaction between **catalyst** and **county** reveals that the Los Angeles County initiatives were triggered by *high profile events* in ten of the twenty-six initiatives, while initiatives in other counties were attributed to *high profile events* in five of the sixteen initiatives. *Disorder offenses* sparked three injunction initiatives in *other* counties, compared to only two initiatives in *Los Angeles County*. The largest discrepancy is in *new media events*, which sparked four initiatives in *Los Angeles County* and none in *other* counties.

All four initiatives triggered by *news media events* occurred in the City of Los Angeles. Three of these initiatives were at least partially in response to a 1996 series of articles in the Los Angeles Times on the 18th Street Gang, the largest and most violent gang in Los Angeles. The series sparked a demand from the Mayor of Los Angeles for a joint injunction project by both the city and the district attorneys. The result was three separate injunctions against five cliques of the 18th Street gang, one by the LACA in the LAPD's Southwest Division and two joint initiatives in the LAPD's Rampart Division. A fourth injunction was triggered by a separate series of articles in the Los Angeles Times, after a reporter and a photographer took up residence in the Langdon Street area. The series documented the influence of the Langdon Street Gang, which was primarily involved in selling drugs in this small neighborhood in the San Fernando Valley.[83] The LACA conducted this initiative.

Examining the interaction between **catalyst** and the type of prosecuting **agency** (Table 5-13) indicates that initiatives by city attorneys and joint initiatives were largely driven by high profile events. Nine of the twenty-one initiatives by city attorneys and three of six joint initiatives were the results of *high profile incidents*.

The interaction between **catalyst** and the prosecutor's **office** shows that the reliance by city attorney offices on *high profile incidents* as a catalyst is largely due to the disproportionate influence of the LACA.

Five of the nine LACA individual initiatives and two of the five joint LACA/LADA initiatives were preceded by *high profile incidents*, suggesting that LACA injunctions were more strongly influenced by *high profile incidents* than other agencies. This relationship is probably due to the large number of high profile incidents that occur in Los Angeles. The *Los Angeles Times* is riddled with stories of particularly horrific gang-related crimes, including gang-related murders and drive-by shootings victimizing innocent persons not affiliated with gangs.[84]

TABLE 5-13: Office by Catalyst

CATALYST

OFFICE	Not specified	High-profile	Gang-related crimes	Disorder offenses	News media event	Public facilities	Row Frequency
Other	1	3	1	3	-	2	10
LADA	1	2	3	2	-	1	9
LACA	1	5	1	-	2	-	9
LADA/LACA	-	2	1	-	2	-	5
SJCA	-	1	2	-	-	-	3
SDDA	-	1	-	-	-	3	4
SBCA	-	1	1	-	-	-	2
Column Frequency	3	15	9	5	4	6	42

TABLE 5-14: Date Filed by Catalyst

CATALYST

Count
Row Percent

DATE FILED	Not specified	High-profile	Gang-related crimes	Disorder offenses	News media event	Public facilities	Row Frequency Percent
Pre-Acuna Period	-	3 37.5	4 50.0	1 12.5	-	-	8 19.0%
Appellate Period	1 12.5	2 25.0	2 25.0	-	-	3 37.5	8 19.0%
Post-Acuna Period	2 7.7	10 38.5	3 11.5	4 15.4	4 15.4	3 11.5	26 61.9%
Column Frequency Percent	3 7.1%	15 35.7%	9 21.4%	5 11.9%	4 9.5%	6 14.3%	42 100%

The catalyst that triggered the highest proportion of initiatives for one office was gang domination of *public facilities*. This category accounts for three of the four initiatives by the San Diego District Attorney's Office (SDDA). A prosecutor explained that similar activities were usually targeted by the SDDA in its injunction initiatives. When **catalyst** was examined by **date filed** (Table 5-14), the *pre-Acuna period* is prominent, with one-half of the injunction initiatives triggered by high rates of gang-related crimes. This rate is at least twice that of the two subsequent periods, 25% in the *appellate period* and 11.5% in the *post-Acuna period.* The drop in frequency in the *appellate period* was most likely due to the denial of preliminary injunctions in two cases, *People v. Amaya* and *People v. B Street Boys*, both of which occurred in the *pre-Acuna period.* The reasoning by the judges in both cases was, in part, that there was an adequate remedy for the public nuisance activities under the criminal law. These decisions may have caused prosecutors to refrain from basing their initiatives on criminal activity during the appellate period, despite the appellate ruling that struck all non-criminal provisions in the *Acuna* case. After the state Supreme Court overruled the appellate *Acuna* decision, the door was opened for prosecutors to rely even less on criminal activity as the basis for the public nuisance.

TABLE 5-15: Category by Catalyst

CATALYST

Count
Row Percent

CATEGORY	Not specified	High-profile	Gang-related crimes	Disorder offenses	News media event	Public facilities	Row Freq. Percent
High Drug	1 7.7	5 38.5	3 23.1	1 7.7	2 15.4	1 7.7	13 31.0%
High Crime	2 14.3	7 50.0	4 28.6	1 7.1	-	-	14 33.3%
High Disorder	-	3 20.0	2 13.3	3 20.0	2 13.3	5 33.3	15 35.7%
Col. Freq. Total	3 7.1%	15 35.7%	9 21.5%	5 11.9%	4 9.5%	6 14.3%	42 100%

When **catalyst** is examined by **category** (Table 5-15), *high profile incidents* dominate the *high drug* and *high crime* categories, accounting for 38.5% and 50% respectively. This is consistent with the theory that high profile incidents raise the consciousness of the community to other gang activities. Drug dealing draws anti-social activity into a neighborhood, and criminal behavior enhances the intimidating influence of a gang on a neighborhood. The *high disorder* category is dominated by gang domination of *public facilities*, which accounted for one-third of the *high disorder* injunctions. This is consistent with the disorder caused by gangs in public parks and recreation centers.

It is apparent from these data that gang injunctions are initiated in response to various catalysts. Although the response to high profile violent incidents is over represented, this finding is not unexpected considering the often violent nature of gang activity and its destructive effect on the community. What is surprising is that the response to high profile incidents reaches 50% in only one contingency, that between catalyst and high crime initiatives.

Initiator

The reactive nature of prosecutorial agencies, coupled with the relative scarcity of injunction initiatives, suggests that most injunctions initiatives are requested by a non-prosecutorial entity. Although prosecutors may be knowledgeable about gang-related crimes that are prosecuted, their duties may not allow them to remain in touch with neighborhood residents and conditions outside of their normal reactive role. Local government authorities (city council or city manager), elected officials (councilpersons, mayors),[85] representatives of community organizations, individual citizens or groups of citizens,[86] and the police are likely to be more knowledgeable about neighborhood conditions and to request gang injunctions from prosecutorial agencies. Under certain circumstances, an injunction initiative may be self-initiated by a city or district attorney's office without a request from non-prosecutorial entities. For example, a prosecutor of misdemeanor offenses took a proactive stance when members of a gang were constantly being prosecuted for nuisance-related violations. An in-house prosecutor for a task force assembled to deal with gang problems started another initiative.

One prosecutor, who was involved in multiple initiatives, pointed out that the community is ultimately behind the decision to pursue an injunction, regardless of the entity initiating an initiative. According to this prosecutor's perception, municipal authorities seek injunctions in areas where the community expresses frustration over numerous problems in their neighborhood. This frustration may be expressed directly to officials or indirectly through the media after some high profile incident. Because the initiators, whether they are the police, politicians, or prosecutors, are responding to the needs of the people in the neighborhood, the citizen component is always significant, even though it is not always explicit. While recognizing the significance of the citizen component, this research focuses on the role of the prosecutor and the community entities that interact directly with the prosecutor. Therefore, this study is limited to the entities that directly encouraged prosecutors to seek gang injunctions.

The variable **initiator** contains seven categories of entities responsible for initiating intervention by the prosecutor's office: *self initiated* by the prosecutor's office, *local governing authority* (city council, county board of supervisors), *elected official*[87] (excluding city/district attorney), *representative of a community organization*, *individual citizen(s)* (including town hall-type meeting between prosecutors and citizens), and the *police*. A final category is a *combination* of initiators, in which the primary initiator cannot be identified because the police, elected officials, and the general community are part of a general outcry for a response (Table 5-16).

TABLE 5-16: Initiator

INITIATOR	Frequency	Percent
No request – self-initiated by city/district attorney's office	3	7.3
Local governing authority	7	17.1
Elected official, excluding city/district attorney	7	17.1
Representative of a community organization	2	4.9
Individual citizen or citizens, including town hall-type meeting	3	7.3
Police	17	41.5
Combination of police, elected officials, and community outcry	2	4.9
Total	4	100.0
Missing Cases: 1		

Prosecutors identified the *police* as the initiator in seventeen initiatives. *Local governing authorities* and *elected officials* each initiated seven cases. When combined, non-prosecutorial government sources were responsible for starting over three-quarters of the initiatives, while only three were self-initiated by prosecutorial agencies. This imbalance is consistent with the generally reactionary role of prosecutorial agencies.

Of particular interest are injunction initiatives originated by requests made directly to prosecutorial agencies by community entities. Community entities directly requested only five initiatives, two by *representatives of community organizations* and three by either *individual citizens* or unorganized groups of citizens, usually at a community meeting. Two initiatives resulted from a general community outcry by a *combination* of the community, the police, and elected officials. Thus, the community was directly involved in some degree of initiation in less than 20% of the injunction initiatives. Although this is far less than expected for a problem-oriented intervention, it is consistent with the perception of one prosecutor that the influence of the community on injunction initiatives is often masked by the police and government officials acting as an intermediary between community entities and prosecutorial agencies. Another prosecutor supported this perception, noting the difficulty of determining the influence on elected officials who request injunction initiatives. This intermediary role is further supported by indications from prosecutors that many injunction initiatives requested by the police are offshoots of community- and problem-oriented policing programs, in which community entities theoretically play a significant role.

One criticism often raised against gang injunctions is that law enforcement officials use them to avoid the constitutional protections of the accused, especially in the enforcement of narcotics laws. Critics claim that the injunctions effectively criminalize normally non-criminal activities at a lower standard of proof than required under the criminal law, allowing law enforcement officials to use injunctions as an 'end-run' around the more stringent constitutional protections of the criminal law. If this criticism is valid, the injunction initiatives requested by the police and prosecutors, who are directly responsible for narcotics enforcement, should tend to target illegal drug activity. To explore this issue, Table 5-17 examines the interaction of initiator and category.

Only three of the twenty initiatives requested by law enforcement officials (*police* and *self-initiated*) fall into the *high drug* category, all initiated by the *police*. Prosecutors, who are involved in narcotics enforcement in their normal prosecutorial duties, did not self-initiate any *high drug* initiatives. Non-law enforcement government officials requested most of the initiatives in the *high drug* category. A local governing authority requested three *high drug* initiatives, and an elected official requested four *high drug* initiatives. Three were requested by community entities as the sole initiator or as part of a community outcry. Thus, of thirteen initiatives in the *high drug* category, three-quarters were requested by non-law enforcement entities.

Law enforcement entities were more significant in initiating *high crime* initiatives. Twelve initiatives by law enforcement officials fall into the *high crime* category, ten requested by the police and two self-initiated by prosecutors. An elected official requested only one *high crime* initiative, and local governing authorities or community entities requested none.

TABLE 5-17: Initiator by Category

	CATEGORY			
INITIATOR	High Drug	High Crime	High Disorder	Row Frequency
No request - self-initiated	-	2	1	3
Local governing authority	3	-	4	7
Elected official	4	1	2	7
Representative of community organization	1	-	1	2
Individual citizen(s)	1	-	2	3
Police	3	10	4	17
Combination	1	-	1	2
Column Frequency	13	13	15	41

Missing: 1 case

High crime initiatives are not as controversial as *high drug* initiatives. State law and municipal ordinance already prohibit all the provisions in the *high crime* index, and many are declared public nuisances *per se* under the jurisdiction's municipal code. Although prosecution as civil contempt raises the concern about conviction under a lower standard of proof, most violations of gang injunctions are prosecuted as criminal contempt due to the relatively light penalties for civil contempt. When prosecuted as criminal contempt, the heightened standard of proof under the criminal law – beyond a reasonable doubt – is required. Because injunction provisions prohibiting criminal and ordinance violations do not criminalize non-criminal behavior and are generally prosecuted as criminal contempt, they have not been the focus of criticism.

According to this analysis, law enforcement officials initiated few injunctions focusing on illegal drug activity. Instead, law enforcement officials are more focused on relieving other criminal activity. Although drug-related provisions are included in *high crime* initiatives, the focus of these initiatives is on non-drug-related activity already declared illegal by legislation, which is not the focus of critics. One-half of the *high drug* initiatives were requested by local governing authorities and elected officials, suggesting that, because of the high visibility of street sales of drugs, illegal drug activity may be more of a political issue than a law enforcement issue in the initiation of gang injunctions.

TABLE 5-18: Initiator by Catalyst

	CATALYST						
INITIATOR	Not Specified	High Profile	Gang-related Crimes	Disorder offenses	News Media	Public Facilities Taken Over	Row Frequency
No request – self-initiated	-	1	1	1	-	-	3
Local governing authority	1	1	2	1	-	2	7
Elected official	-	2	1	-	4	-	7
Representative of community organization	-	2	-	-	-	-	2
Individual citizen(s)	-	-	-	2	-	1	3
Police	1	7	5	1	-	3	17
Combination	-	2	-	-	-	-	2
Column Frequency	2	15	9	5	4	6	41

Missing: 1 case

When the interaction between initiator and catalyst is examined (Table 5-18), several trends are evident. First, both of the requests from a *combination* of entities (police, elected officials, and community outcry) were triggered by a *high profile incident*. This is not surprising since a general outcry is often the result of some horrific event that raises the conscience of the entire community to the local gang problem. Second, all the injunctions triggered by *news media events* were initiated by *elected officials*, suggesting political motivation caused by a series of news articles about a gang or gang-plagued area. All these initiatives occurred within the City of Los Angeles. Furthermore, when examined by prosecutor's office, all initiatives requested by elected officials involved the LACA, three as solo initiatives and four as joint initiatives with the LADA. One prosecutor from another jurisdiction raised concern about the effect of political influence in gang injunction initiatives:

> Once (gang injunctions) became known and people could see that it was successful, all the politicians jumped on it. Then the city attorneys were getting on it. Los Angeles has an elected city attorney and an elected district attorney. All of a sudden it's 'get re-elected' time, publicity time. So they were going about it quite imprudently, not spending the time ... and they started rushing to do it. They didn't know all the names (of the gang members). They had old intelligence information. I was thinking they were going to blow it for everybody ... I think it was because of the publicity.

Finally, of particular interest to this study is the involvement of community entities in the injunction process. *Representatives of community organizations* requested two initiatives. The catalyst for both was a *high profile incident*, suggesting that community organizations tend to be more responsive to high profile incidents. In contrast, *individual citizens* requested three initiatives, two triggered by *disorder offenses* and the third by *public facilities* taken over by the gang, which also affects the quality-of-life in a neighborhood. These results suggest that individual citizens are more disturbed by the reduction in the quality-of-life in their neighborhoods. According to one prosecutor:

> What residents would really find disturbing is the drinking of alcohol in public and urination in public. It decreases the quality-of-life to have to look at all this stuff.

Although the low number of initiatives commenced by community entities severely limits any conclusions, these results suggest that community organizations and individual citizens requested gang injunction for different reasons. Community organizations appear to be more concerned with high profile incidents, while individual citizens appear more interested in the reduction of the quality-of-life in their neighborhoods.

Action requested

Action requested refers to the type of prosecutorial action requested by the initiator. Initiators who are aware of gang injunctions, either through past experience, knowledge of the experience of others, or the news media, might specifically request an injunction. However, when an initiator approaches the prosecutor's office with a request to solve an identified problem, there may be no specific remedy sought, leaving the specific action up to the prosecutor. Initiators might also request other actions to resolve the problem, such as stricter enforcement of disorder violations or vertical prosecution.[88] Regardless of whether an injunction or some other action is requested, the decision to pursue an injunction is generally made by the prosecutor, based on the legalities of the facts and the available evidence. The variable **action requested** is divided into three categories: unspecified assistance, injunction, and other.

Initiators overwhelmingly request gang injunctions. Initiators for thirty-four initiatives requested injunctions, while initiators for four initiatives did not request any specific remedy. Significantly, initiators for only two initiatives requested assistance other than an injunction. One of these initiatives stemmed from a crack house abatement program, which was broadened to a gang abatement initiative when law enforcement officials realized that they were dealing with a criminal street gang. The second was a request to a district attorney's office for a dedicated prosecutor to vertically prosecute gang-related offenses. Because an existing contract between the district attorney's office and the municipality prohibited such an arrangement, a gang injunction employing resources outside the bounds of the existing contract was suggested to deal with the gang problem.

Table 5-19 illustrates that only two of the five requests by citizens and community organizations were specifically for an injunction, with the remaining three seeking unspecified assistance. In contrast, local governing authorities, elected officials, and the police overwhelmingly requested injunctions. This suggests that citizens and community organizations are either not as likely to accept gang injunctions as a legitimate intervention or not as familiar with gang injunctions as are government and law enforcement officials. The fact that all initiatives requested by elected officials within the City of Los Angeles were requests for an injunction supports the previous suggestion of the political importance of gang injunctions in Los Angeles.

TABLE 5-19: Initiator by Action Requested

INITIATOR

ACTION REQUESTED	No request – self initiated	Local government authority	Elected official	Community Organization	Individual citizen(s)	Police	Combination	Row Frequency
Unspecified action	-	-	-	1	2	1	-	4
Injunction	2	6	7	1	1	15	2	34
Other	-	1	-	-	-	1	-	2
Column Frequency	2	7	7	2	3	17	2	40

Missing: 2 cases

Problem identified by initiator

As previously indicated, initiators overwhelmingly request injunctions in response to a catalyst. However, the process of problem identification goes beyond identifying a catalyst. To justify a request for an extraordinary intervention like an injunction, it is assumed that initiators identify gang-related problems of substantive concern for the community (Goldstein 1990: 66). While a catalyst triggers a call for action, the problem identified by the initiator represents the underlying problem in the area from the initiator's perception. This problem should rise above the concerns brought to light by the catalyst.

Violence is a major community problem related to street gangs. Violence may be sparked by gang wars, illegal drug transactions 'gone bad', or the protection of the gang's turf. Gangs often employ violence to intimidate residents from cooperating with the police and to maintain control of the neighborhood. Violence can occur at any time or location without warning, placing both gang members and innocent persons at risk of serious bodily harm or death. Rival gang members commit violence in retaliation for past incidents and as a display of bravado to impress peers. Many incidents that incite violence are seemingly quite innocent, such as crossing out graffiti. However, such acts are interpreted in gangland as an act of disrespect calling for retaliatory action. As a result of such acts, innocent persons have been shot and killed, some through the wall of their own homes, in drive-by shootings in which rival gang members spray bullets into an area with the intent to hit a member of the targeted gang.

The *illegal sale of drugs* and *felony victimizations* are crimes frequently conducted by gangs for economic gain. Illegal drug sales are sometimes the financial engine driving a gang. Felony victimizations generally target vulnerable people in the neighborhood, such as illegal immigrants who fear deportation if they complain to the police. Gang members sometimes extort money from small business proprietors by charging 'rent' to conduct business in the neighborhood. Unlicensed street vendors and drug dealers not affiliated with the gang are often victimized because they will not complain to the police.

All the foregoing gang activities amount to serious crimes. However, many complaints by residents are for minor infractions and activities that add to neighborhood disorder and intimidation. Gang members hanging out in large groups tend to attract violence by providing targets for rival gangs. Drinking and urinating in public, blocking the sidewalk and impeding street traffic, loud noise and partying, and speeding in vehicles all decrease the quality-of-life for residents and have a chilling effect on community cohesion. The aggregation of these relatively innocuous minor infractions and activities are often more annoying to residents, who have to live with these activities on a daily basis, than the gang-related crimes that attract most of the attention of outsiders and the news media.

The variable **problem identified by initiator** contains six categories emphasized by prosecutors: *violence*, consisting of assaults and homicides not directly related to illegal drug sales; *illegal drug activity*, consisting of non-violent activity directly related to the illegal sale and use of drugs; *violence resulting from drug trafficking*, which is distinguished from the category *violence* by the direct relationship to illegal drug activity; *felony victimizations for monetary gain*, including robberies, extortion, burglary, and larceny; *offenses/activities related to disorder and intimidation*, consisting of relatively minor offenses and activities and the possession, display, and firing of weapons; and *not specified*, which covers initiatives in which the problem was not identified by the initiator. Because the violence in a neighborhood often cannot be separated from the sale of illegal drugs, violence specifically resulting from illegal drug sales was considered a separate category. Although neighborhoods controlled by gangs are usually subject to all these problems to some degree, it is assumed that one will arise as the primary problem identified by the initiator.

TABLE 5-20: Primary Problem Identified by Initiator

Primary Problem/Initiator	Frequency	Percent
Not specified	5	12.5
Violence (assaults and homicides)	9	22.5
Illegal drug activity (sales and use)	4	10.0
Violence resulting from illegal drug trafficking	9	22.5
Felony victimizations for monetary gain.	5	12.5
Offenses/activities related to disorder and intimidation (including possession and firing of firearms)	8	20.0
Total	40	100.0
Missing Cases: 2		

Initiators identified either *violence* or *violence resulting from illegal narcotics trafficking* as the primary problem in almost half of the injunction initiatives (Table 5-20). This is consistent with the identification of *high profile incidents*, which are usually violent, as the catalyst in fifteen initiatives. Violent high profile incidents are often a symptom of the violent tendencies of street gangs, whether these tendencies stem from a propensity for general violence or violence related to illegal drug trafficking.

Closely following the two violence categories are *offenses and activities related to disorder and intimidation*, which were identified in eight initiatives. *Felony victimization* accounted for five initiatives. Surprisingly, initiators identified *illegal drug activity* as the primary problem in only four initiatives. The relatively low frequencies of both *felony victimizations* and *illegal drug activity* again raise questions about the claim that injunctions are an end-run around the constitutional protections under the criminal law. The emphasis on violence and disorder suggests that gang injunctions are perceived as preventive interventions by initiators, rather than an alternative means of enforcing the criminal law, as suggested by critics.

To explore the relationship between the **problem identified by initiators** and injunction **category**, initiator identified problems are condensed into three categories: *drug-related*, combining illegal drug activity and violence resulting from illegal drug trafficking; *crime-related*, combining violence and felony victimization for monetary gain; and *disorder related*, consisting of offenses/activities related to disorder and intimidation. The *not-specified* cases are dropped from consideration, resulting in an analysis based on thirty-five initiatives.

TABLE 5-21: Problems Identified By Initiators by Category

Count Row Percent PROBLEMS	CATEGORY High Drug	High Crime	High Disorder	Row Frequency Percent
Drug-related	5 38.5	4 30.8	4 30.8	13 37.1%
Crime-related	4 28.6	6 42.9	4 28.6	14 40.0%
Disorder-related	2 25.0	2 25.0	4 50.0	8 22.9%
Column Frequency Missing: 7 Cases	11 31.4%	12 34.3%	12 34.3%	35 100%

There appears to be little association between the problems identified by initiators and the injunction categories (Table 5-21). Only five of thirteen initiatives (38.5%) in which initiators identified drug-related activity as the primary activity fall into the *high drug* category. Similarly, six of fourteen initiatives (42.9%) identified by primarily crime-related problems and four of eight initiatives (50%) identified by primarily disorder-related problems fall into the *high crime* and *high disorder* categories. No combination of initiator identified problems and injunction category rises above 50%, suggesting that, in formulating the proposed relief, prosecutors analyzed the gang problem and activities independent of the problems identified by initiators.

Primary problem identified by prosecutor

The primary problem identified by the prosecutor refers to the underlying gang problems that the prosecutor identified after investigating the circumstances in the neighborhood. The categories in this variable differ somewhat from those in the problem identified by the initiator, which is more representative of symptoms than of underlying problems. For example, violence is a common symptomatic gang activity which can have several root causes, including conflict between rival gangs, illegal drug sales, protection of gang territory, and economic gain unrelated to drug sales (robbery, extortion). Unless the prosecutor identifies the root cause of the violence and includes provisions to specifically address that cause, the injunction will probably have little effect against the violence. For example, if the violence is primarily caused by illegal drug sales 'gone bad', provisions designed to reduce violence caused by gang conflict will probably be ineffective. Therefore, for the injunction to be effective, the prosecutor must dig deeper into the gang's activities to determine the root cause of the problem. The problem must then be redefined, so that the injunction provisions can be tailored to address the underlying source, rather than the symptoms, of the problem (Goldstein 1990: 76).

The variable **primary problem/prosecutor** consists of four root causes identified by prosecutors: *gang war*, *illegal drug trafficking*, *gang war/illegal drug trafficking*, and *dominance* of the gang over the target area. *Gang war* refers to a conflict between rival gangs that is not principally attributed to illegal drug trafficking. Rival gangs may claim the target area as their turf, or a rival may enter the territory of another to commit acts of violence and disrespect against the other gang, such as crossing out graffiti. *Illegal drug trafficking* refers to cases in which the illegal sale of drug is identified as the underlying problem. Illegal drug trafficking draws many other criminal and disorderly activities into a neighborhood, putting residents at risk of random violence and reducing the quality-of-life in the neighborhood. Illegal drug trafficking may also introduce a high level of violence in response to conflicts over drug-selling turf, or the 'right' to illegally sell drugs within a territory. *Gang wars/illegal drug trafficking* is a separate category because of the unique nature of the interaction between gang warfare and illegal drug trafficking. Finally, *dominance* of the gang over the target area refers to the control of a gang over a neighborhood, resulting in the intimidation of residents. Gang dominance over a neighborhood allows gang members to commit felony street crimes, including turf-related assaults and murders, robberies, extortion, and car theft, with impunity. Intimidation also permits various minor violations and offensive conduct to thrive. Perhaps more than drug sales and violence, the aggregate of these relatively minor infractions and disorder-related activities substantially reduce the quality-of-life of residents.

Although all these categories are present to some extent in most areas heavily impacted by gangs, prosecutors emphasized certain activities in the survey responses and in court documents. In addition, the declarations of police gang experts, who may be versed in the methods of problem-oriented policing, often emphasized the underlying cause of the identified problems. In some cases, newspaper articles shed some light on the underlying causes, as prosecutors often described the gang problems in the area to the media.

TABLE 5-22: Problems Identified by Prosecutors

Primary Problem/Prosecutor	Frequency	Percent
Gang War	[illegible]	11.9
Illegal drug trafficking	6	14.3
Gang war/illegal drug trafficking	8	19.0
Dominance	23	54.8
Total	42	100.0

Prosecutors overwhelmingly identify *dominance* of the gang over the target area as the underlying problem (Table 5-22). This concern for dominance underscores the importance of gang turf to prosecutors seeking injunctions. A distant second was *gang war/illegal drug trafficking*, identified as the underlying problem in eight initiatives. *Illegal drug trafficking* accounted for six initiatives and *gang war* for five initiatives.

Gang warfare is often territorial in nature, conducted to maintain a gang's dominance over its turf. Conflict between gangs may start because rival gang members showed disrespect by crossing out another gang's graffiti, which serves as a sign of the gang's dominance over its turf. Gang conflict may also occur over drug sales territory, with the underlying problem being illegal drug sales. To determine whether the problem identified by the prosecutor is associated with the injunction categories, prosecutor identified problems are collapsed into two categories: *dominance-related* activity, the controlling characteristics of non-drug gang conflict and turf dominance, and *drug-related* activity, the controlling characteristic of illegal drug trafficking and gang war resulting from illegal drug sales.

Dominance-related activity accounts for two-thirds of the identified problems, while *drug-related* activity accounts for only one-third (Table 5-23), indicating that prosecutors identify turf-related dominance as the primary gang problem twice as often as drug-related activity. Dominance over turf is a well-known characteristic of predominately Hispanic gangs. While gang researchers have questioned the predominance of gangs in the illegal drug trade (Moore 1993, Maxson 1995, Howell and Decker 1999), the 'varrio effect', as one prosecutor calls it, is central to the gang phenomenon in California because of the large number of Hispanic gangs. In some parts of California, particularly in urban area such as the City of Los Angeles, gangs are hemmed into a particular turf by surrounding rivals, making it dangerous for a gang member to leave his/her turf. Gang warfare is often conducted to protect the turf from interlopers. Turf-based Hispanic gangs use defense of their neighborhood as a basis for existence, although they are also protecting a territory in which they can victimize residents with impunity.

TABLE 5-23: Collapsed Primary Problems/Prosecutors by Category

Count Row Percent PROBLEMS	CATEGORY High Drug	High Crime	High Disorder	Row Frequency Percent
Dominance	8 28.6	10 35.7	10 35.7	28 66.7%
Drug related	5 35.7	4 28.6	5 35.7	14 33.3%
Column Frequency Percent	13 31.0	14 33.3	15 35.7	42 100%

Dominance over turf, or territoriality, is also central to the specificity of the gang injunction. Prosecutors are encouraged to target a limited geographical area within which the gang is responsible for a public nuisance (Office of the District Attorney 1996: 29). An injunction extending over too large an area, such as an entire city, is likely to be ineffective or may fail to pass judicial and constitutional scrutiny. According to one prosecutor, public nuisance theory, upon which the gang injunction is based, is grounded in the land. The loss of the right to enjoy one's property is a basic characteristic of the public nuisance. The domination of turf by the gang is a vital part of the prosecutors' legal argument in virtually all gang injunction cases. Because of the importance of the gang's dominance over the target area to both the gang and the legal theory behind injunctive relief, it is not surprising that many prosecutors emphasize problems related to dominance over those related to illegal drug trafficking.

There are no identifiable pattern of association present between the collapsed **primary problems/prosecutor** and **category.** This lack of association suggests that the injunction provisions are not necessarily related to the primary underlying problem identified by the prosecutor, but rather are related to the symptoms of the problem. Focusing on the proximate cause of the problem allows prosecutors to target the specific activities of the defendants that directly enhance the public nuisance, which may in turn indirectly affect the underlying problem in the area. For example, the problem might be a series of gang-related murders in the target area. However, there is no injunction that includes a provision prohibiting murder (or other serious crimes, such as rape and robbery), and no prosecutor interviewed in this study expressed an opinion that an injunction would directly reduce gang-related murders. However, prosecutors have determined that gang members hanging out in large groups provide easy targets for rival gangs. Restrictions on public association in groups decrease the availability of targets, potentially reducing the instances of gang-related murders of both gang members and innocent by-standers. Therefore, while the problem identified by the prosecutor may be the broad underlying gang problem leading to the public nuisance, it may not be significantly or directly associated with the injunction category, which represents the provisions of requested relief.

Another issue meriting examination is the relationship between the problems identified by prosecutors and by the initiators. Using the collapsed categories, Table 5-24 reveals a strong relationship between the two sources of problem identification. In eleven of thirteen cases, prosecutors and initiators agreed that drug-related activity is the primary problem. In twenty-one of the twenty-two cases in which initiators identified crime- and disorder-related activity, prosecutors identified dominance as the primary problem. As noted earlier, crime- and disorder-related activity are more representative of dominance over the neighborhood than of drug-related problems.

The general agreement between problem identifiers suggests two things. First, initiators have a good handle on the underlying characteristics of gang problems in their neighborhoods. Assuming that prosecutors identify problems only after some degree of analysis, the strong agreement by prosecutors with the initiators' definition of the gang problem indicates that their analysis supports the initiators' definition. Second, prosecutors seriously consider the complaints of initiators about the nature of the gang problems. A further examination of problem identification, controlling for the type of initiator, exposed only three instances of disagreement between prosecutors and initiators, one each for elected officials, the police, and individual citizens, suggesting that prosecutors gave equal weight to the complaints of all entities that are identified as initiators.

TABLE 5-24: Collapsed Primary Problems/Prosecutors by Collapsed Problems/ Initiator

	INITIATOR-IDENTIFIED PROBLEMS			
PROSECUTOR-INDENTIFIED PROBLEMS	Drug-related	Crime-related	Disorder-related	Row Frequency
Dominance	2	14	7	23
Drug related	11	-	1	12
Column Frequency	13	14	15	35
Missing: 7 cases				

Method of identification

The preceding discussion begs the question of how prosecutors identify the underlying gang problems in a neighborhood. An important part of the problem identification process, **method of identification** examines the sources used by the prosecutor to analyze gang activity for the purpose of identifying the underlying problem. Sources of problem identification for prosecutors are *law enforcement*, *citizens*, and *news media reports*. *Law enforcement* refers to official police records, law enforcement officer (police and probation/parole) observations, and prosecutor observations gained while working with law enforcement officers. The category *citizens* refers to information reported to prosecutors by citizens, regardless of whether the citizen submitted a declaration. Included in this category is information gained from groups of citizens at community meetings and from door-to-door solicitation of information.[89] The category *news media reports* refers to the use of the news media as a source of information. Some prosecutors stated that their analysis began with a historical perspective on the gang problem by searching for news articles over a certain number of years on the *Lexis-Nexis* news database. Because one source is seldom relied upon to get a total picture of the gang problem in a neighborhood, two categories – *combination of police and citizen* and *combination of all* – allow multiple responses. Responses from the Prosecutor Survey are the sole source for this information.

Prosecutors did not report using citizen observations/complaints and news media reports as the sole sources of information in any initiative (Table 5-25). These sources were used in combination with law enforcement sources. The combination of law enforcement and citizen observations/complaints accounted for problem identification by the majority of prosecutors (57.5%), followed by law enforcement as a sole source (34.1%).

TABLE 5-25: Method of Identification

Primary Source	Frequency	Percent
Law enforcement	14	34.1
Citizen observations/complaints	0	0
Combination of law enforcement and citizens observations/complaints	23	57.5
News media reports	0	0
Combination of all sources	4	10.0
Total	41	100.0
Missing cases: 1		

Although not used by all prosecutors, many consider information from citizens as vital to the acquisition of a gang injunction. When **method of identification** is examined by **agency**, initiatives involving district attorney offices, including joint initiatives, rely heavily on information from citizens to identify underlying problems. Initiatives by city attorneys tend to rely on law enforcement as the sole source. This tendency by city attorneys is likely due to the strong influence of the LACA, which has, as a matter of policy, ceased using citizens in the acquisition process because of strong concerns about both retaliation and operational security.[90] Seven of the thirteen city attorney cases in which prosecutors did not rely on citizen information for problem identification, were LACA initiatives. Only two LACA initiatives included citizen information, along with news media reports, in the problem identification process.

Four initiatives (10%) used a combination of all sources, including news media reports. Because news media events are also a catalyst in four initiatives, **method of identification** is examined by **catalyst**. Surprisingly, the four initiatives in which prosecutors use the news media as a source for problem identification are not the same four initiatives in which news media events are identified as a catalyst. The information in the news series may not have pertained to the identification of the underlying gang problem, or prosecutors may not have wanted to appear to be reacting to the news media in seeking injunctions.

Summary of Problem Identification Variables

On the whole, the problem identification variables display a high level of variation. High profile violent incidents, the most frequent category of catalysts, triggered gang injunctions in less than half of the initiatives, with the remainder dispersed over five categories of catalysts. Prosecutors identified the police, the most frequent category of initiators, as the entity initiating less than half of the initiatives. The problem identified by the initiators is also well distributed among several categories. The distributions of these variables are far greater than would be expected if gang injunctions were stereotypical responses to gang activity.

The lack of variation in the other problem identification variables – the problem identified by the prosecutors, the action requested by the initiators, and the method of problem identification – is consistent with other data gathered in the study and the goal of the problem identification stage. Prosecutors' identification of dominance over the target area as the primary problem in two-thirds of the initiatives is consistent with the importance of territoriality to the legal concept of public nuisance, which is "grounded in the land." The low variation in action requested by initiator is consistent with the status of the gang injunction as a response of last resort, generally considered only after other methods to control gang activity have proven ineffective. The strong reliance by prosecutors on information from both law enforcement and citizen sources to identify problems is consistent with the problem-oriented goal of a comprehensive identification of the problem.

Analysis

Analysis, the second step in the problem-solving process, refers to an in-depth inquiry into all the characteristics of and factors contributing to the substantive problem. There is no bright line differentiating analysis from the stages of problem identification and selecting an appropriate response. As a result, analysis is a rather amorphous stage that actually begins during problem identification. However, an in-depth analysis goes beyond identifying the underlying problem. It involves objectively collecting precise information about the problem and accurately portraying the current responses to the problem (Goldstein 1990). By applying information on the experiences of other jurisdictions with the same general problem to the local situation, analysis merges with the response stage in a quest for alternative responses. Perhaps because of its amorphous character, analysis has been a weak stage in problem-oriented policing, with officials often jumping directly from problem identification to response with little analysis of the problem (Capowich and Roehl 1994, Skogan et al. 1999: 23). Three general categories of variables are particularly relevant to analysis: 1) the number of gangs in the target area and the reason the targeted gang(s) was chosen over the others; 2) characteristics of the gang(s), including those that lead prosecutors to believe that an injunction would be effective; and 3) characteristics of the target area(s), including those that lead prosecutors to believe that an injunction would be effective.

Gangs in the target area

Neighborhoods are not always subjected to the public nuisance activities of a single gang. In some case, several gangs claim the neighborhood as turf, and the activity of these gangs may vary in nature and degree. The two variables **number of gangs** active in the target area and **chosen** examine whether more than one gang actively claims a target area as turf and, if so, why one particular gang was targeted by the injunction initiative.

For the purpose of this study, a gang includes a distinct clique of a larger gang when that clique claims a discrete territory as its turf, such as the cliques of the 18th Street gang, the largest gang in California. Therefore, two or more cliques that share a turf are not considered separately in this analysis. In addition, gangs that are active in a target area without claiming the area as turf are not included in this research, even though they may significantly add to the public nuisance in a neighborhood.

The target area was claimed by one active gang in twenty-six initiatives, while more than one active gang claimed the target areas of fifteen initiatives. The **number of gangs** ranges from one to four gangs. Thirty-seven initiatives targeted one gang, four initiatives targeted two gangs, and one initiative targeted four gangs. This data indicates that prosecutors have a distinct preference for actions against a single gang claiming a discrete turf.

With fifteen initiatives occurring in an area claimed by more than one gang, one might ask why one particular gang was chosen as the subject of the injunction over the other gangs claiming the same turf. In two of these initiatives, both gangs claiming the target area were selected, leaving thirteen initiatives in which prosecutors selected one gang over others. The variable **chosen** examines the reasons for the selection. *Propensity toward violence*, which refers to selecting the gang because the level of violence attributed to it is significantly higher than that of the other gangs, was the reason for the selection in two initiatives. The *size of the gang*, meaning prosecutors selected the largest gang in the area, was reported as the selection criteria for four initiatives. *Control over the target area*, which refers to gang's dominance over the area despite the existence of other gangs, was the criteria used for three initiatives. The category *other*, a miscellaneous category, includes four initiatives: one initiative in which the gang was empowered by an injunction against another gang in the target area; two initiatives in which the targeted gang was the most active gang in the area; and one initiative in which the targeted gang was confined, with no place to move its activities.

Gang characteristics

Although California has the most extensive gang problem in the nation, only about one per cent of the identified gangs in the state have been targeted by injunction initiatives over the fourteen-year period of this study. The relatively scarce use of gang injunctions suggests that some characteristics of the targeted gangs cause prosecutors to believe that an injunction would be effective. Ideally, the analysis stage of the problem-solving process seeks to identify characteristics that make a gang particularly amenable to intervention by injunction. To explore this issue, the variable **gang characteristic** is divided into four categories: *structure of the gang*, *activities amenable to injunction*, *territoriality*, and *other* (Table 5-26). Although all these categories were evident to some extent in each gang, prosecutors' responses to the survey and the case file documents often emphasize one characteristic of the gang over others.

Territoriality refers to a gang's strong attachment to a claimed territory, or turf. Territoriality is significant because gang members will often defend their turf with violence. There are two general types of gang territories. The territory of the traditional 'turf-oriented' gang is often the neighborhood in which the gang members reside. Often referred to as a varrio (or barrio) by Hispanic gangs, the turf is generally defined by the geographic boundaries of the neighborhood. Members of the traditional 'turf-oriented' gang view themselves as soldiers defending their 'varrio' from incursions by outsiders. Somewhat different is a sales territory claimed by an entrepreneurial gang involved in illegal narcotics trafficking or some other criminal enterprise, such as extortion. Although many members of an entrepreneurial gang may not reside in the territory, they will defend it with violence to maintain their share of an illegal enterprise.

TABLE 5-26: Gang Characteristics

Gang Characteristics	Frequency	Percent
Structure of gang	1	2.4
Activities amenable to injunction	16	39
Territoriality	22	53.7
Other	2	4.8
Total	41	100.0
Missing cases: 1		

Territoriality is also very important to the prosecutor. A territorial gang establishes clear boundaries for a target area. Gang territories are often clearly marked by graffiti so that rivals and residents are aware of the gang's claim on the area. As the legal theory of public nuisance is grounded in "the land", the concept of territoriality provides a legal basis for injunctive relief. It is also important for prosecutors to limit the physical reach of the injunction to pass the scrutiny of the courts and to enhance the potential impact of the injunction on the gang's activities. The significance of *territoriality* to the gang injunction is obvious, as it is the gang characteristic emphasized in over one-half of the injunction initiatives.

The category *activities amenable to injunction* is the next most salient gang characteristic, emphasized in over one-third of the initiatives. Activities particularly amenable to injunctive relief include a strong daily street presence, group activity, open-air drug sales, and constant low-level nuisance activity. As one prosecutor stated, "the necessary characteristic is that they are out there in the public eye," so a strong daily street presence is vital. The daily street presence is generally accomplished in groups by hanging out – "the thugs on the street corner" type of activity. Group activity is the primary means through which gang members create a menacing presence, intimidating residents and others who frequent the neighborhood. Felonious crimes, such as street robberies and assaults, are often conducted in groups to intimidate potential victims. Open-air drug sales, usually conducted by teams of three or more gang members, is the most emphasized serious criminal activity because the injunction can disrupt the business of drug dealing, hitting gang members where it hurts – in the pocketbook.

Finally, constant low-level nuisance activity is important because the prosecutor must show evidence of an ongoing public nuisance. Low-level nuisance activity makes up the bulk of the gang's activity that contributes to the public nuisance. An injunction limited to serious crimes would likely be denied because the activity is not continuous, a necessary element of the public nuisance, and there are adequate remedies at law. When combined with constant nuisance activity, serious crime merely makes the case for an injunction more compelling. One prosecutor summed it up:

> There has to be some kind of street-level activity, but it varies. The beauty of the injunction is that you can address the lower level nuisance activities and, not so much drive-by shootings because it's hard to predict where a drive-by is going to happen, but you can address more violent activity, drug dealing, and kind of felonious activity as well through an injunction.

Structure of the gang refers to the existence of a hierarchical organizational structure. Although most gangs are very loosely organized groups, some gangs show indications of a hierarchical structure, usually based on age. An expert declaration attested to the variation in the organizational structure of gangs:

> Many of the cliques of the 18th Street Gang are highly organized with leadership roles clearly defined, while some of the cliques exist with no structure or definitive leadership (*People v. 18th Street Gang*, BC190334, 1998, Declaration of Officer Montoya, p. 6).

The declaration goes on to describe the leadership roles of two Mexican Mafia[91] 'shot callers'. Despite the importance of structure to some gangs, the prosecutor for only one initiative chose *structure of the gang* as the characteristic on which potential effectiveness turned, possibly because gang injunctions generally target the most hard-core members who would be near the top of any hierarchical structure.

The category *other* contains two initiatives. One initiative did not identify any characteristics, stating that the injunction was a last resort in the hope that it would be effective. The other initiative emphasized the age and residence of the majority of the gang members. Most gang members were young adult males who did not reside in the target area.

The purpose of the injunction was to move the gang out of their turf, knowing that the gang dynamics of the municipality, in which over forty rival gangs claimed territory, would not permit the targeted gang to simply move their activities to another location within the municipality.

Surprisingly, the longevity of the gang in the target area was not emphasized in any injunction initiative. Many of the gangs targeted by the injunction initiatives are multigenerational, having controlled their turf for many years despite efforts by law enforcement to root them out. While multigenerational longevity might suggest that an injunction would be used as a last resort to free the neighborhood of the gang, longevity may work against injunction initiatives. In multigenerational gang neighborhoods, gangs are often accepted as part of neighborhood life. Extensive family and neighborhood networks result in gang members being regarded as relatives and friends, rather than dangerous people (Horowitz 1996). Because many gang-plagued neighborhoods have a history of poor relations with the police, residents may perceive an injunction as a police tactic that further suppresses already disadvantaged neighborhood youths, rather than as a last ditch effort to rid the neighborhood of a persistent problem.

Demographic characteristics

Demographic characteristics are statistical facts about both the gang and the injunction initiative. Demographic characteristics of the gang include the predominant race/ethnicity of the gang, the longevity of the gang in the target area, and the estimated number of members of the gang. Demographic characteristics of the initiative include the number of named defendants, the gang's status as an unincorporated association, and the presence of a legal defense.

The predominant **race** of the gang is comprised of four categories: *Asian*, *Hispanic*, *Afro-American*, and *Hispanic/Afro-American* (when more than one gang is targeted). White street gangs are not included in the analysis because there are no predominately white gangs targeted by the injunction initiatives. Because of the exclusion of white gangs from the injunction universe, critics have claimed that gang injunctions are a racially biased tactic, imposing restrictions on the non-criminal activities of people of color and further stigmatizing disadvantaged minority youths (Stewart 1998). However, two related racial differences in gangs are especially salient to the racial demographics of gang injunctions: types of criminal involvement and attachment to territory.

In general, gangs tend to specialize in types of criminal involvement along racial lines. Hispanic gangs are relatively more involved in turf-related violence. Afro-American gangs tend to be more entrepreneurial through their involvement in the illegal drug trade. White and Asian gangs are more involved in property crimes (Howell 1998). This tendency toward a particular illegal activity is reflected in, and perhaps in part caused by, the attachment to territory according to race. Hispanic gangs are fiercely territorial, with a strong cultural attachment to the neighborhood. Much of the violence by Hispanic gangs is in defense of the neighborhood turf (Howell 1998, Vigil 1993). The attachment of Afro-American gangs to territory is generally related to their entrepreneurial focus on making money (Howell 1998, Klein 1995, Sanders 1994). Their territorial claims are generally larger and for the purpose of marketing illegal goods, particularly drugs. Violence by Afro-American gangs is often related to encroachment on that 'sales' territory by others players in the drug trade (Sanders 1994). White and Asian gangs are more fluid and mobile, and not spatially limited in their activities (Klein 1995, Alonso 1999). Because the gang injunction is grounded in the concept of territory for practical, theoretical, and constitutional reasons, predominately white gangs are often not amenable to injunctive relief because of their lack of attachment to a territory.

Hispanic gangs are targeted in over three quarters of the initiatives (31 of 40), while Afro-American gangs are targeted in seven initiatives and Asian gangs in only one initiative. One initiative enjoined two gangs of different races that shared a target area, a Hispanic and an Afro-American gang.

The dominance of Hispanic gangs in the injunction universe is not surprising. California has a large Hispanic population. The *1998 National Youth Gang Survey* reports that Hispanic gangs account for 60% of the gangs in the West region of the nation, while Afro-American gangs account for 22%, and Asian gangs for 8% (Office of Juvenile Justice and Delinquency Prevention 2000).[92] The racial figures for the injunction initiatives are similar to those of the national survey, especially considering the strong turf-orientation of predominately Hispanic gangs and the importance of a discrete target area to the viability of the gang injunction.

To determine whether Hispanic gangs are targeted primarily because of their turf-orientation, **race** is examined by **gang characteristics**. Of the thirty-one injunctions targeting Hispanic gangs, prosecutors for over one-half (17) emphasized *territoriality* as the primary gang characteristic on which the effectiveness of an injunction turns. Prosecutors for three of the seven initiatives targeting Afro-American gangs emphasized *territoriality*, while the remaining four emphasized *activities amenable to an injunction.* The single initiative targeting two gangs – one Hispanic and one Afro-American – emphasized *territoriality*, while the single initiative targeting an Asian gang emphasized *activities amenable to injunction.* This analysis suggests that prosecutors view *territoriality* as an important characteristic more often when enjoining Hispanic gangs than when enjoining Afro-American gangs. One prosecutor discussed the difference between Hispanic and Afro-American gangs in their attachment to turf:

> The Hispanic gangs tend to be much more territorial, the varrio thing. Black gangs' emphasis is on the financial. They don't usually have any illusions about owning any particular area. Although they're territorial in a certain sense, their activities most often focus around drugs, because it's economic.

The **longevity** of the gang in the target area is often emphasized in gang expert declarations. Although not the primary consideration by prosecutors, longevity may be an important consideration in some injunction initiatives. Initiatives against a gang that has controlled its turf for many years, despite numerous social service and suppression interventions, suggests that injunctive relief is viewed by officials as a last resort to ameliorate the gang's influence on the neighborhood. As discussed earlier, residents often accept the gang as a normal part of the environment of multigenerational gang neighborhoods. The perception of the injunction as an attempt by outsiders to further suppress the activities of disadvantaged neighborhood youths may impede the injunction initiative.

Longevity is divided into three categories: *in the first decade*, *in the second decade*, and *in the third decade or more* (Table 5-27). The use of decades is convenient because police gang experts often describe gang longevity in terms of decades, rather than years or generations. When one considers that socialization into the gang often begins in elementary school (Vigil 1993) and that, according to one prosecutor, gang members often have children before 15 years of age, a decade is roughly equivalent to a generation of gang membership. The first decade of longevity suggests that the gang is in its first generation, with no children of gang members socialized into the gang. The second decade of longevity suggests that the gang is beginning its second generation of membership, with the children of gang members from the first decade beginning their socialization into the gang lifestyle. Three decades or more of longevity suggests that the gang is well into its second generation of membership, and possibly beginning its third generation, with both children and grandchildren of original members being indoctrinated into gang life. By this time the gang is well entrenched in the target area, with many neighborhood youths claiming membership in the gang and many inhabitants accepting, or at least tolerating, the gang as part of the neighborhood environment (Horowitz 1996).

TABLE 5-27: Longevity

Longevity	Frequency	Percent
In the first decade	7	25.9
In the second decade	2	7.4
In the third decade or more	18	66.7
Total	27	100.0
Missing: 15		

Data on **longevity**, which is available for only twenty-seven initiatives, shows a clear preference for targeting gangs that are *in the third decade or more.* Although there are more gangs with shorter histories and fewer ties to neighborhood traditions (Klein 1995), gang injunctions are more often sought against multigenerational gangs that are well entrenched in the target area, suggesting that gang injunctions are, more often than not, last ditch efforts against persistent gang problems that law enforcement had been unable to control for a long period of time.

The **size** of the gang refers to the estimated number of members in the targeted gang or clique. This information, available for twenty-eight injunction initiatives, is generally found in the declarations of police gang experts. For injunction initiatives against more than one gang, size refers to the total number of members in all targeted gangs. The **size** of the gangs range from 40 to 1500 members.[93] Dividing gang size into categories, seven initiatives targeted gangs with *100 or fewer* members, eight initiatives targeted gangs ranging from *120 to 250* members, seven initiatives targeted gangs from *300 to 400* members, and six initiatives targeted gangs with *450 or more* members. When initiatives that targeted more than one gang or individual clique are eliminated from the analysis, three initiatives against individual gangs with *450 or more* remain, including the gang with the highest estimated membership.

When **size** is examined by **category**, the *high disorder* initiatives tend to target smaller gangs than either the *high drug* or *high crime* initiatives. Of twelve initiatives in the *high disorder* category, nine target smaller gangs, five with *100 or fewer* members and four with *120 to 250* members. This compares with only two *high disorder* initiatives targeting gangs in the *300 to 400*-member category and only one in the *450 or more* member category. There is little difference between the injunction initiatives in the *high drug* and *high crime* categories. This suggests that smaller gangs are targeted primarily for low-level nuisance activity, not that smaller gangs are more likely to commit low-level nuisance activity.

When **size** is examined by **date filed**, larger gangs tend to be targeted in the *post-Acuna period.* Of thirteen cases targeting gangs with over 300 members, eleven occurred in the *post-Acuna period*, six in the *300 to 400-member* category and five in the *450 or more* category. Only two larger gangs were targeted before the California Supreme Court's *Acuna* decision, one with *300 to 400* members occurring in the *pre-Acuna period* and one in the *450 or more* members occurring in the *appellate period.* This suggests that there has been a tendency for gang injunction initiatives to increasingly target larger gangs as the strategy became more accepted by the courts.

The variable **named defendants** refers to gang members who are named as defendants to the action in the pleadings. To be named as a defendant, an individual must be identified as a member or associate of the gang. Criteria used to determine whether an individual is a member of the gang generally include:

> (1) The individual admits to any peace officer, school official, probation officer, Juvenile Hall employee, or youth ranch employee, membership in a specific gang; or, under any two (2) of the following conditions:
> (2) the individual is tattooed with a gang specific logo, wears clothing which bears gang specific identification, or is observed using gang specific hand signs;
> (3) the individual is named by two (2) or more members of a gang as a member of that gang;
> (4) the individual is an active participant in a criminal street gang crime;

(5) the individual is identified as a gang member by a reliable informant;
(6) the individual is observed associating with identified gang members two (2) or more times (*People vs. Avalos* 1994, Declaration of Robert Avila, p. 16).

The number of named defendants ranges from nine to ninety-two. When categorized by number of defendants, six initiatives targeted *20 or fewer* defendants, twenty-one initiatives targeted *21 to 40* named defendants, six initiatives targeted *41 to 60* defendants, and seven initiatives targeted *more than 60* named defendants.[94]

Two early initiatives did not name individual defendants. Both named the gang as an unincorporated association as the defendant. One initiative was the first gang injunction, which was originated as an experiment. The court ordered that the method of service include personal service to five or more active gang members and the posting of copies of the Notice of Intention to seek an injunction in at least ten visible locations throughout the target area (*People v. Playboy Gangster Crips* 1989, Order re Method of Service). The other initiative was the third gang injunction conducted. Because the gang contained a large number of juveniles, prosecutors did not want to stigmatize them by placing their names on the injunction. How notice was accomplished in this case was not specified.

Of the thirteen initiatives with over 40 named defendants, nine initiatives occurred in the *post-Acuna period*, including four of the six initiatives in the *41 to 60* category and five of seven initiatives in the *61 or more* category. There was only one initiative in each of the two higher categories in both the *pre-Acuna* and *appellate* periods, suggesting that more defendants have been named as gang injunctions have gained judicial acceptance.

An **unincorporated association** is defined as:

> 1) a group whose members share a common purpose, and 2) who function under a common name under circumstances where fairness requires the group be recognized as a legal entity. Fairness includes those situations where persons dealing with the association contend that their legal rights have been violated. Formalities of quasi-corporate organization are not required (*Barr v. United Methodist Church* (1979): 266-7).

The California Code of Civil Procedure states:

> A partnership or other unincorporated association, whether organized for profit or not, may ... be sued in the name which it has assumed or by which it is known (California Code of Civil Procedure section 369.5(a)).

In a *Statement of Decision*, Judge John H. Major of the Los Angeles County Superior Court found the Blythe Street Gang to be a legal entity for the purpose of abating a public nuisance. Because members of the gang shared common purposes and goals and functioned under a common name, the judge found that the gang was properly named as an unincorporated association and, therefore, as a defendant in the lawsuit (*People v. Blythe Street Gang* 1993, Statement of Decision 7-8).

Where the public nuisance activity of a gang is conducted for a common purpose, such as the enhancement of a gang's control over its territory, that activity is committed by gang members by virtue of their gang affiliation under the associational protection of the gang. Therefore, the gang can be sued in its associational capacity as an unincorporated association, sending the message that the gang, through the actions of its individual members, is responsible for the public nuisance by allowing the conditions to occur. Although gang membership is not required to include a defendant in a gang injunction, the fact that the gang allows the nuisance activity to occur makes it easier to include gang members as defendants solely because of their gang affiliation. According to the California Supreme Court:

> Individualized proof is not a condition to the entry of preliminary relief based on a showing that it is the gang, acting through its individual members, that is responsible for the conditions" (*People v. Acuna* 1997: 618).

The *Acuna* court found that three of the defendants who contested the preliminary injunction were subject to the injunction even though there was no evidence that they committed any acts comprising specific elements of the public nuisance.

The criteria often used to prove that the gang is an unincorporated association is provided in the *Street Terrorism Enforcement and Prevention Act* (Office of the District Attorney 1996), which defines a criminal street gang as:

> ...any ongoing organization, association, or group of three or more persons, whether formal or informal, having as one of its primary activities the commission of one or more of the criminal acts enumerated . . . having a common name or common identifying sign or symbol, and whose members individually or collectively engage in or have engaged in a pattern of criminal gang activity (California Penal Code, section 186.22 (f)).

A pattern of criminal gang activity is the commission, attempted commission, solicitation, or conviction of two or more of twenty-three enumerated criminal acts occurring within three years of a prior offense and committed on separate occasions or by at least two persons (California Penal Code, section 186.22 (e)).

The prosecutor does not have to name the gang as a defendant in the suit. Where the gang is not named, both the organization and its members are still subject to the injunction. However, where the gang is named as a party to the action, gang affiliates who have received notice of the injunction are subject to its provisions under the longstanding practice of applying injunctions to persons through whom the enjoined parties may act, such as aiders and abettors (*People v. Acuna* 1997: 618-7). Unincorporated association status allows the gang to be served by serving one or more of the defendants as representatives of the gang.

According to one prosecutor, naming the gang as a defendant may be helpful under some circumstances, but it is not always necessary. When the prosecutor and the police know the individuals that they want to abate and have good documentation and evidence on the gang activity of those individuals, the gang need not be named as a defendant. On the other hand, if a gang member has not been named as an individual defendant, it has never been established in court that the individual is a member of the gang. To sustain a charge of contempt for a violation of the injunction, the prosecutor has the additional burden of proving that the individual is subject to the injunction as a member of the enjoined gang. Naming the gang as a defendant is helpful where gang membership is fluid and unnamed members continue the nuisance activity in the target area.

The variable **unincorporated association** indicates whether the gang is named as a defendant. The targeted gang(s) is a named defendant as an unincorporated association in thirty-five initiatives. Only seven initiatives do not name the gang as a defendant. A preliminary injunction was denied in only one of these seven initiatives, indicating that the failure to name the gang as a defendant has no bearing on the success of the acquisition initiative. The San Jose City Attorney's Office, which appealed the *Acuna* case, did not name the gang in any of its three initiatives.

Whether defendants have legal representation and the nature of that representation may influence a prosecutor's response to gang activity. Defendants are often subjected to an injunction through a default judgment for failing to mount a legal defense. The California courts have denied the right to appointed counsel at injunction acquisition proceedings[95] (*Iraheta v. Superior Court of Los Angeles* 1999), and the state legislature has recently defeated a bill that would have provided public defenders for indigent defendants named in injunction pleadings (*New York Times* 2000). The prevalence of a lack of defense has given prosecutors a fairly free hand in tailoring injunction provisions, with only the judge's conception of equity to inhibit inappropriate relief. However, the appearance by counsel for only one defendant can endanger the effort to obtain an injunction against all the defendants if the attorney does not agree to a stipulated judgment for the client.[96]

Where counsel represents defendants, the defense attorney often becomes involved in the case only after the complaint is filed and the defendants receive notice of the impending lawsuit. Therefore, defense actions are generally reactive, with little influence on the prosecutor's response to the public nuisance. However, there are some cases in which Afro-American groups[97] have raised legal resistance prior to or immediately after a case was filed. Similarly, briefs by *amicus curiae* (friend of the court) interests in opposition to injunctive relief are also a reactive. Although *amicus curiae* briefs are normally limited to the appellate level, the American Civil Liberties Union (ACLU), an active opponent of gang injunctions, has petitioned for permission to file briefs in several cases at the trial level.[98] Anticipation of some form of legal defense may influence injunction initiatives, including the decision of what relief to request.

The variable **defense** distinguishes between *no defense*, *defense attorney* for at least one defendant, and *amicus curiae*, which includes cases in which private counsel was also involved. Of the thirty-eight initiatives for which data are available, almost one-half (18) report no defense. There is private attorney representation for at least one defendant in thirteen initiatives. *Amicus curiae* briefs were filed in seven initiatives.

TABLE 5-28: Defense by Category

	CATEGORY			
DEFENSE	High Drug	High Crime	High Disorder	Row Frequency
None	9	3	6	18
Defense Attorney	2	5	6	13
Amicus curiae	1	3	3	7
Column Frequency	12	11	15	38

Missing: 4 cases

Defense is examined by **category** to determine whether the presence of defense representation may have an influence on the relief requested by prosecutors (Table 5-28). Seventy-five percent (9 of 12) of the *high drug* initiatives lacked any defense representation. Although far from conclusive, this suggested a tendency on the part of prosecutors to emphasize activity related to the illegal sale of drugs in cases where there was no legal defense anticipated. Where prosecutors anticipate that a legal defense might be raised, either by private attorneys or *amicus curiae* interests, there may have been a tendency to downplay drug-related activities in favor of less controversial provisions. However, prosecutors often do not know whether gang members will mount a legal defense until after the gang has been served, which may render the correlation between no defense and the *high drug* category as either a coincidence or spurious.

When the interaction of **defense** and **race** is examined, the proportion of defense representation for *Hispanic* gangs is consistent with the total proportion of *Hispanic* gangs. However, *Hispanic* gangs are under-represented by *amicus curiae* interests (57%), while *Afro-American* gangs are over-represented in this category, with 43% represented by *amicus curiae* interests compared to 19% of the total gangs targeted by injunction initiatives. This suggests that the Afro-American community is more active than the Hispanic community in garnering legal support against gang injunctions, possibly due to the greater experience of Afro-American with legal institutions through their past struggle for civil rights.

Target area

The elements of the physical environment are important characteristics in the analysis of a problem (Goldstein 1990: 36). Likewise, the physical environments in which gang injunctions occur are an important consideration for prosecutors. Because of the importance of territoriality to the potential effectiveness of an injunction, the characteristics of the target area may influence both the activities of the gang and the initiative to obtain an injunction.

The target area, referred to as the safety zone in some injunction initiatives, is the physical environment in which the gang problem occurs. Generally, one area is targeted for injunctive relief. However, if more than one gang or clique is targeted by an initiative or if the targeted gang claims two neighborhoods separated by an area in which there is insufficient public nuisance activity, such as a commercial strip of national chains, more than one target area may be designated for relief. An injunction may also have primary and secondary target areas. Incidents of violent retaliation resulting from a gang conflict may cause a gang to be enjoined within its turf and within the turf of a rival gang. Target areas also differ in size. Some are measured in blocks, while others are measured in square miles. Regardless of the number and size of the target area(s), the goal of the prosecutor is to choose a gang creating a public nuisance in a limited geographical location (Office of the District Attorney 1996: 29).

The variable **target area characteristics** identifies traits of the target areas that led prosecutors to believe that an injunction would be effective.[99] Six categories of target area characteristics stand out: *defined by the gang as its turf*, *isolated by physical barriers/rivals*, *longevity of the gang in the target area*, *physical configuration lends itself to primary gang activities*, and *centered at one location*, and *residence of defendants* (Table 5-29).

TABLE 5-29: Target Area Characteristics

Characteristic	Frequency	Percent
Defined by gang as turf	12	29.3
Isolated by physical barriers/rivals	19	46.3
Longevity of gang in the area	1	2.4
Physical configuration facilitates primary gang activity	2	4.9
Centered at one location	5	12.2
Residence of defendants	2	4.8
Total	41	100.0
Missing cases: 1		

The category *isolated by physical barriers/rivals* refers to target areas within which a gang is isolated in some manner. When considering injunction initiatives, prosecutors look for discrete areas that are separated by physical barriers, such as freeways, major thoroughfares, railroad tracks, canals, and industrial areas. Both neighborhoods and gang territories form naturally within such boundaries. Territories of neighboring rival gangs also form effective boundaries that isolate a gang. Because physical barriers and rival territories tend to contain a gang's activities to a target area, the potential for displacement of the gang's activities after the injunction takes effect is reduced. Responses for almost one-half (19) of the initiatives indicated that physical barriers, rival gangs, or a combination of both isolated the target area.

In some cases, the target area is *defined by the gang as turf* without physical barriers or neighboring rivals. According to one prosecutor, "The gang picks the area. We just have to be able to define it." A gang's turf may be defined by the area where most of the members reside or by the activity of the targeted gang, including where the members usually hang out and conduct illegal enterprises. Police contacts with gang members are sometimes mapped to determine turf boundaries. However, turf boundaries are typically marked by gang members with graffiti, which is photographed by law enforcement officials as evidence of a gang's claim on a target area. As one prosecutor stated:

> Physical characteristics of the target area might make it easier and frequently will be a dividing line. Social and ethnic makeup of the area does not matter. It all comes down to the gang activity and their presence.

Almost one-third (12) of the responses indicated that the gang defined the target area through its activities, constant presence, and graffiti.

Longevity of the gang in the target area refers to the physical and social entrenchment of the gang in its territory. Multigenerational gangs are perceived, and often accepted, by residents as part of the neighborhood environment. In the response for the single initiative in which this characteristic is cited, the prosecutor stated that the gang had been in the area for twenty to thirty years, was well known in the area, and was without doubt going to stay in the area. The intent of the injunction was to reduce the activity and street presence of the gang, not eliminate gang members from the target area.

Responses for two initiatives indicated that the *physical configuration of the target area lent itself to the primary gang activities*. The primary gang activity in both initiatives was illegal drug sales, which was facilitated by the design of the neighborhood. The layout of the neighborhood lent itself to the effective use of lookouts to warn about the approach of law enforcement officers. Carports in the back of residences facilitated stashing drugs and conducting drug sales out of view of the street.

Responses for five initiatives indicated that the gang activity was *centered at one location*, such as a house or a park. Two initiatives were centered on a single house in each target area. In one of these initiatives, the house of a gang member's grandfather was taken over by a gang originating in another town. The prosecutor was confident that the gang would leave the area if the court enjoined the gang from activity at the house and the surrounding area. The house was sold before the injunction was obtained and the gang disappeared from the area. The other initiative centered on a house owned by a leader, or shot-caller, of the gang. Gang members used the house as a base of operation to conduct illegal activities throughout the target area. One of the injunction provisions prohibited the shot-caller from allowing gang members to hang out in and around the property. Two initiatives began with parks as the center of the gangs' activities. The target areas were extended to the areas around the parks to address activity occurring as gang members traveled to and from the parks. The fifth initiative began as an abatement of a narcotics nuisance at a single residence. The abatement action expanded into a gang injunction as the investigation accumulated evidence about the gang's drug sales activities. The prosecutor formed the boundaries of the target area by drawing a perimeter around the locations where gang members sold drugs. Significantly, this initiative was against an entrepreneurial Afro-American drug gang that did not have a strong attachment to the territory, other than for the purpose of illegal drug sales. As a result, the prosecutor had difficulty keeping the size of the target area manageable as drug-selling locations were added.

Responses for two initiatives indicated that the *residence of the defendants* was a significant characteristic of the target area. Most of the defendants lived in the target areas for both initiatives. One prosecutor noted that, because the injunction tries to affect nuisance behavior on quasi-private as well as public property, the provisions of the order are often contingent on whether defendants live in the area. According to this prosecutor, "the characteristics of a target area contribute to the actual order you are going to ask for, not whether you are going to do an injunction."

The **size of the target area** may be an important factor in the decision to grant an injunction and, if granted, whether it will pass constitutional scrutiny on appeal. The SAGE manual suggests that a gang be chosen that is causing a public nuisance in a limited geographical area (Office of the District Attorney 1996). The issue of the relative size of the target area was addressed in *In Re Englebrecht* (1998), in which Englebrecht argued that the non-association provision was unconstitutional because the size of the target area in *People v. Varrio Posole Locos* (1997) was significantly greater than the four-block target area of the *Acuna* decision. The appellate court found that the relative size of the target area was not a determining factor. The target area only needed to be narrowly construed to serve the significant government interest of abating the public nuisance caused by the gang. Because the target area was well defined by distinct boundaries and there was no showing that the target area was larger than needed to abate the public nuisance, the court concluded that the size of the target area alone would not make the non-association clause unconstitutional (*In re Englebrecht* 1998).

Target areas vary in both size and method of measurement. Because blocks differ in size between neighborhoods, the two measurements cannot be converted into a single measure. Therefore, the range of each measurement is considered separately.

Of thirty-four initiatives for which information is available, eighteen initiatives specify the target areas by blocks, ranging from one block to 112 blocks, with a median of 17.5 blocks. Six initiatives targeted less than ten blocks, five from ten to eighteen blocks, five from twenty to twenty-six blocks, and one each targeted fifty and one hundred and twelve blocks. Sixteen initiatives specify the target areas by square miles, ranging from .064 sq. mi. to 4.29 sq. mi., with a median of .82 sq. mi. Eight initiatives targeted areas less than one square mile, five from one to two square miles and three more than two square miles.[100]

The **number of target areas** indicates whether an injunction initiative targets one or more than one area. Although the majority of initiatives target only one area, there are certain conditions under which more than one area are targeted. An injunction might target two different gangs or gang cliques that claim separate turfs, several rival gangs involved in a gang war, or one gang which is active in two separate areas. The large majority of initiatives (37) are limited to one target area, while five initiatives target more than one area.

Of the five initiatives targeting more than one area, one enjoins two distinct cliques of one gang in two separate areas. The provisions of the injunction applied to both gangs in both areas because, as two cliques of the same gang, they might exchange territories to avoid the effects of the injunction on their activities. Another injunction targets two areas within the turf of a single gang. Originally there was a concern that the entire turf would be too large and the gang was relatively inactive in an area at the center of the gang's turf. When the injunction was implemented, the gang's activities were displaced into the area in between the target areas. Therefore, the prosecutor included the remaining area in the permanent injunction, effectively eliminating the displacement problem.

The remaining three initiatives are separate injunctions against single gangs in primary and secondary target areas. Two gangs that shared a territory were engaged in a gang war with a neighboring rival. All injunction provisions applied to each gang in their primary target area, and each gang was enjoined from entering the turf of the rival, designated as the secondary target area, with an associate from the same gang. The secondary target area was included to eliminate the problem of drive-by shootings, which generally require at least two gang members, a driver and a shooter.

Summary of Analysis Variables

The variables related to analysis displayed less variation than the problem identification variables. Most initiatives targeted a single gang simply because it was the only active gang in the target area. This is consistent with the strong emphasis by prosecutors on territoriality as the most important gang characteristic for the effectiveness of an injunction. Also consistent with the emphasis on territoriality is the targeting of traditionally turf-oriented Hispanic gangs and multigenerational gangs. However, the relative size of the gang and number of named defendants varied greatly, implying that neither are a significant consideration by prosecutors. Large gangs, with greater than 450 members, were no more likely to be targeted than smaller gangs, with less than 100 members. The number of named defendants ranged from nine to ninety-two. Initiatives did tend to target the lower part of that range because prosecutors generally named only the most active hardcore gang members as defendants. Prosecutors are also more likely to name the gang as an unincorporated association, giving them the flexibility to add named defendants to the injunction order as investigators identify them as gang members or they become more active in the target area.

The characteristics of the target area show slightly more variation than the gang characteristics. Consistent with the emphasis on territoriality, the majority of initiatives targeted a single geographic area. However, the characteristics of the target area deemed important to the effectiveness of the injunction are well distributed, with the isolation of the target area, the most frequent response, emphasized in less than half of the initiatives. The size of the target areas also displayed great variation, from one to 112 blocks or from .064 to 4.29 square miles, while tending toward the lower end of the range in order to construe relief as narrowly as possible.

Part of the analysis includes anticipation by prosecutors of legal opposition to the injunction initiative. Contrary to popular belief, gang members are slightly more likely to have, than not to have, some form of defense representation. Over half of the initiatives encountered legal opposition from defense counsel and/or *amicus curiae* interests. The preponderance of some form of defense representation suggests that prosecutors cannot systematically rely on default judgments, since arguments by an attorney on behalf of one defendant can place the injunction at risk of being denied for all defendants.

The tendency toward less variation in the analysis variables, particularly those associated with territoriality, can be partially explained by the status of the gang injunction as a response of last resort, which must be narrowly tailored to address the specific public nuisance activities of the targeted gang within a defined geographical area. Injunction initiatives generally target only "the worst of the worst" gangs and gang members. Many of these gangs, especially the turf-oriented Hispanic gangs, have controlled their territory for several decades, making the task of rooting them out even more difficult. To pass judicial scrutiny, the proposed injunction must be narrowly tailored, leading to a tendency to name only hardcore members as defendants and to limit the target area as much as possible, rather than naming all gang members and targeting the entire territory claimed by the gang.

Response

The goal of problem analysis is to develop the tailored response that holds the greatest potential for eliminating, or at least reducing the effects of, the underlying problem (Goldstein 1990). It is likely that an appropriately tailored response will consist of a blend of different alternatives, rather than a single alternative, suggesting that gang injunction prosecutors should search for alternate responses both within and beyond the confines of the criminal justice system. Depending on the underlying problem, the search for alternatives may involve agencies from various fields of law enforcement – the local police, county, state and federal law enforcement, probation and parole, the courts, and prison authorities – as well as non-law enforcement governmental and private agencies. When the underlying problem is based on the structural or economic deficiencies typically associated with gang problems, law enforcement efforts are generally only able to influence the proximate cause, or symptoms, of the problem. The participation of non-law enforcement entities is necessary to comprehensively attack the root cause of the problem.

One resource often untapped by law enforcement officials is the affected community, which holds "the potential for invoking informal legal controls that are more permanent and more effective than any measures the police themselves are in a position to implement" (Goldstein 1990: 45). However, mobilizing and engaging the community to help reduce gang activity may be both impractical and dangerous in neighborhoods taken over by gangs. Engaging the community after the proximate cause of the problem is ameliorated may be a more reasonable alternative for community involvement.

One alternative advanced by Goldstein is greater use of legal controls beyond the traditional approach of arrest and prosecution. Non-traditional legal controls fashioned specifically to the problem may allow law enforcement authorities to address the problem more directly, while avoiding the "potential for unfairness and abuse that always exists if the police response is unnecessarily broad" and overly powerful (Goldstein 1990: 45).

An example of the potential for unfairness and abuse in dealing with gang activity is the City of Chicago's *Gang Congregation Ordinance*, which resulted in over 42,000 arrests and 89,000 dispersal orders over a three-year period. In 1999, the ordinance was held unconstitutionally vague by the United States Supreme Court because it afforded "too much discretion to the police and too little notice to citizens" (*Chicago v. Morales* 1999: 1863). To avoid claims of bias against certain groups of citizens, traditional statutes and ordinances must apply to all person in a jurisdiction, often reaching innocent conduct by targeting those who look and dress like gang members.

In contrast, gang injunctions fall squarely into the alternative of a non-traditional legal response, dealing specifically with gang activities identified by prosecutors as problematic after the situation is analyzed. Gang injunctions also limit enforcement to named defendants and for specific violations occurring within a well-defined target area. When conducted as a collaborative effort among law enforcement agencies, non-law enforcement organizations, and entities from the community, the gang injunction is only one part of a holistic response that potentially can relieve the neighborhood of violence and disorder, while hopefully addressing some the root causes of the gang problem. In this sense, the injunction provides the community with 'breathing room' to allow the rebuilding of the community structures and informal social controls needed to maintain a sense of order, prevent future violence, and rebuild the economic base of the neighborhood. This examination of the gang injunction as a response provides a preliminary exploration into the issue of community involvement through the analysis of the decision-making process, the consideration of alternatives to an injunction, the role of the gang injunction in larger collaborative programs, and plans for implementing the injunction.

Participants

Participants are the entities involved in the decision to seek an injunction, as reported by prosecutors. Although the legal decision to seek an injunction is ultimately in the hands of prosecutors, they do not have the resources to obtain an injunction without the involvement of other entities. These entities collaborate in varying degrees in the decision-making role. Law enforcement officials, such as police and probation officers, provide prosecutors with evidence of gang activity, assist prosecutors in investigating the gang problem, and implement and enforce the injunction. Without the support of law enforcement officials, an injunction initiative by a prosecutor would be futile. Governing bodies, such as the city manager/mayor or the city council, are often involved in the decision to fund injunction initiatives.[101] Non-governmental community-based organizations may be involved in funding comprehensive gang intervention projects with an injunction component. Prosecutors may consult community-based organizations or the community, through community meetings, to give the community a sense of ownership in the project and to obtain the cooperation of residents in gathering necessary evidence.

The categories of **participants** are inclusive. The category *law enforcement officials only* indicates that prosecutors collaborated only with law enforcement officials on the injunction decision. All injunction initiatives in this study included law enforcement agencies, either solely or in conjunction with other entities. *Including governing bodies* indicates that governing bodies participated in the decision-making process with prosecutors and law enforcement officials. Although elected officials were identified as the initiators of some initiatives earlier in this study, there are no reports by prosecutors of their decision-making participation outside their role in a governing body. The category *including community entities* is particularly salient the question of community involvement. This category includes the involvement of community organizations or the community, as well as law enforcement and possibly governing bodies. The final category, *unknown*, includes cases in which prosecutors were not privy to who made the decision to seek an injunction. Prosecutors in these cases were generally mandated to seek an injunction after the decision had been made by supervisors (Table 5-30).

Prosecutors for only two initiatives did not know who participated in the decision. Over one-half of the initiatives (24) resulted from the decision of prosecutors in collaboration with *law enforcement officials only*. One-quarter of the initiatives (11) involved the municipality's *governing body* in the decision. Non- government *community entities* were included in the decision-making process in four initiatives. Two of these initiatives involved community organizations and two involved the community in the injunction decision. These four initiatives will be fully discussed in Chapter VI.

TABLE 5-30: Participants

Participants	Frequency	Percent
Unknown	2	4.9
Law enforcement officials only	24	58.5
Including governing bodies	11	26.8
Including community entities	4	9.8
Total	41	100.0
Missing cases: 1		

When examining **participants** by **category**, only *high crime* initiatives fail to include *community entities* as decision-makers (Table 5-31). Eleven *high crime* initiatives involved only law enforcement officials, while two *high crime* initiatives involved *governing bodies* in a decision-making role. *Community entities* participated in the decision in one *high disorder* initiative, compared with eight *high disorder* initiatives involving *law enforcement officials* and six involving *governing bodies*.

TABLE 5-31: Participant by Category

PARTICIPANTS	CATEGORY High Drug	High Crime	High Disorder	Row Frequency
Law enforcement officials only	5	11	8	24
Governing bodies	3	2	6	11
Community entities	3	-	1	4
Column Frequency	11	13	15	39

Missing: 3 cases

Somewhat surprising is the relatively high level of participation of community-based organizations in *high drug* initiatives. Of eleven *high drug* initiatives in which the prosecutor was knowledgeable of decision-making participants,[102] three included *community entities* as decision-makers. The greater participation of community entities in deciding to seek *high drug* injunctions than in the other categories tends to discredit the criticism that gang injunctions are merely a law enforcement tactic used to avoid the constitutional protections of the criminal law in addressing activities related to illegal drug trafficking.

TABLE 5-32: Participant by Office

PARTICIPANTS	OFFICE Other	LADA	LACA	Joint	SJCA	SDDA	SBCA	Row Freq.
Law enforcement officials only	4	2	7	2	3	4	2	24
Governing bodies	5	4	-	2	-	-	-	11
Community entities	-	3	1	-	-	-	-	4
Column Frequency	9	9	8	4	3	4	2	39

Missing: 3 cases

When type of agency is included in the analysis, all three *high drug* initiatives involving *community entities* as decision-makers were conducted by *district attorney* agencies, while the only *high disorder* initiative involving *community entities* was conducted by a *city attorney* agency. *City attorney* agencies relied solely on *law enforcement officials* as decision-makers in fifteen of twenty initiatives in which participants are identified, while *district attorney* agencies did so in six of thirteen initiatives. This suggests that *city attorney* agencies tend to rely solely on law enforcement officials as decision-makers more than do *district attorney* agencies.

When examined by individual prosecutor's **office** (Table 5-32), the three city attorney offices conducting at least two individual initiatives relied heavily on *law enforcement officials* as decision-makers, to the nearly total exclusion of *governing bodies* and *community entities*. All five initiatives by the San Jose (*SJCA*) and San Bernardino (*SBCA*) city attorney offices and seven of eight initiatives by the Los Angeles City Attorney's Office (*LACA*) used only law enforcement officials as decision-making partners. None of these offices included governing bodies in the decision-making process.[103] All four initiatives by the San Diego District Attorney's Office (*SDDA*) used only law enforcement officials as decision-making partners, possibly because the *SDDA* only begins injunction initiatives after being approached by police officials.

In contrast, prosecutor's offices with single initiatives (*other*) and the Los Angeles District Attorney's Office (*LADA*) include *governing bodies* as decision-making partners more frequently. Of nine initiatives by *other* offices, five included *governing bodies* as decision-makers, while only four relied solely on *law enforcement officers* as decision-making partners. The *LADA* relied most heavily on *governing bodies* (4 of 9 initiatives), primarily because of the contractual arrangement required between the *LADA* and municipalities involved in the SAGE program. That three *LADA* initiatives also included *community entities* as decision-making partners was possibly a result of the emphasis placed on community involvement by the SAGE program (Office of the District Attorney 1996).

A significant relationship between **participants** and **initiator** exists in the categories of *governing authority* and *law enforcement*. Of the seven initiatives that originated through *governing authorities*, five included *governing bodies* as decision-making partners. Of the seventeen initiatives requested by the *police*, fifteen included only *law enforcement officials* in the decision-making role. There is little correlation between the involvement of *community entities* as decision-makers and *citizens* or *representatives of community organizations* as initiators.

Differing views

The variable **differing views** examines the unanimity of the injunction decision among decision-makers. A number of prosecutors failed to answer this question, primarily because of attorney-client confidentiality or a lack of inside knowledge. Of the twenty-three responses to this question, there were differing views among decision-makers in only two initiatives. In one of the initiatives, the prosecutor questioned whether an injunction would work because of the extremely violent nature of the gang's activities. Law enforcement officials were the only decision-making collaborators in this initiative. The other initiative was the first gang injunction, which was conducted as an experiment. Decision-makers questioned whether a gang injunction would work, whether a judge would sign it, and what effect it would have. Decision-making participants in this initiative included community entities. The nearly unanimous decisions to seeking an injunction in the majority of initiatives suggest that law enforcement officials had exhausted all other measures to control the local gang problems, which begs the question of whether other alternatives were considered.

Alternatives

Fashioning the most appropriate response to a problem includes searching for alternatives (Goldstein 1990). Prosecutors were asked whether any alternatives to an injunction were considered and, if so, the type of alternatives. Of thirty-four initiatives for which data are available, over two-thirds (24) did not consider any alternatives. In nineteen of these initiatives, prosecutors determined that all alternatives were exhausted prior to the initiation of the injunction initiative. Under this reasoning, the injunction becomes a last resort response to the gang problem. Eight of the ten remaining initiatives limited alternatives to law enforcement suppression tactics. The other two initiatives considered alternatives beyond law enforcement suppression.

In one initiative, the grandfather of one of the defendants owned a house in which the gang problem was centered. The alternative was to have the house sold so the gang would have no place to congregate in the neighborhood, as most of the gang members were not from the neighborhood. The police contacted the son of the homeowner and the house was sold, eliminating the base for the gang's activities. Around the same time the house was sold, several of the hard-core members were incarcerated for gang-related crimes, diminishing the leadership of the gang. In this case, the alternative was a speedier solution and eliminated both the problem and the need for an injunction.

The other initiative considered a combination of law enforcement suppression and non-law enforcement alternatives. A gang coordinating council was formed to consider alternative interventions to coordinate with the injunction. Alternatives included vertical prosecution by the city attorney's office, coordination with a graffiti abatement program to allow graffiti to be documented before it was removed or painted over, improved intelligence gathering, school intervention through two full-time school resources officers, a tattoo removal program, and job placement and training. This initiative, entitled the *Lennox Gang Violence Suppression Program*, will be further discussed in Chapter VI.

<u>Part of a larger program</u>

The emphasis on collaborative partnerships, especially with non-law enforcement partners, suggests that injunction initiatives should be part of a larger program that includes a non-suppressive component, particularly when the causes of gang involvement – poverty, alienation from the larger society, and lack of education and employment opportunities – are considered for intervention. The variable **larger program** refers to whether the injunction initiatives are part of broader programs and, if so, the nature of those programs.

Prosecutors identified over one-half (24) as stand-alone law enforcement initiatives unconnected, either formally or informally, to a broader program. However, six of these initiatives were reported to have provided the impetus for broader post-intervention programs in the target areas. Seventeen initiatives were identified as a component of larger programs, eleven formally and six informally.

Of the seventeen initiatives linked formally or informally to larger programs, law enforcement suppression was the primary goal of eleven. Although these initiatives may include some social service aspect, their thrust was law enforcement suppression through either the criminal law or civil remedies, such as building code enforcement and narcotics nuisance abatement, in addition to injunctive relief.

Five initiatives were a component of CLEAR (Community Law Enforcement and Recovery) projects in Los Angeles, a federal and state funded multi-agency task force including the police, sheriff, district attorney, city attorney, mayor's office, and probation/parole. The goal of CLEAR is to bring together law enforcement and other government and community agencies to rid neighborhoods of street violence.

Although the CLEAR program claims to have a community involvement component, one prosecutor of a CLEAR injunction stated that he/she never saw any evidence of such collaboration.

Another initiative was spawned from the TARGET (Tri-agency Resource Gang Enforcement Team) program in Westminster, a multi-agency task force comprised of the Westminster Police Department, the Westminster City Attorney's Office, the Orange County District Attorney's Office, and the Orange County Probation Department. Although TARGET focused on removing gang leaders and chronic recidivists from the community, assistance to the Boys and Girls Club in Westminster, evictions by landlords, and a grant to retrofit street lighting were included in the program.

Four initiatives were components of police-led suppression programs, three of which are part of formal programs. The Westside Improvement Project was a problem-oriented policing project of the National City Police Department to improve the quality-of-life in a neighborhood. In addition to the injunction initiative, the Westside Improvement Project hosted a community clean up project and worked with property owners to improve their property. The Beat Health unit of the Oakland Police Department conducted a narcotic nuisance abatement program, using building code violations to close crack houses in the City of Oakland. The Peacemaker Program was a multi-agency program headed by the Stockton Police Department that targeted at-risk youths. Both programs employed gang injunctions as part of their strategy. The fourth police-led program was an informal collaboration between the prosecutor's office and a community policing project to target gang activity in Redondo Beach, which led to a gang injunction.

The final initiative was part of an informal suppression program in Long Beach. The prosecutor combined the injunction initiative with additional enforcement against probation and parole violators. The prosecutor constantly updated a list of gang members on probation or parole and the terms of their probation/parole. This list was circulated to patrol officers, with the goal of removing hard-core gang members from the community.

Six injunction initiatives were connected with programs that combined law enforcement efforts with social service programs. In Salinas, the injunction initiative was informally linked to a building code enforcement program, administered by the city attorney, and the Second Chance program, a social service program targeting at-risk youths. One of three initiatives in San Jose was informally tied to the city's Strong Neighborhood Initiative. The Strong Neighborhood Initiative provided resources from the City of San Jose, the San Jose Redevelopment Agency, private investment, and public-private partnerships to improve neighborhood conditions, enhance community safety, expand community services, and strengthen neighborhood associations.[104]

The Inglewood injunction initiative was a gang suppression component of the Youth Firearms Violence Initiative (YFVI), a federally funded program of the Inglewood Police Department's Community Oriented Policing and Problem Solving unit. The goal of the initiative was to reduce handgun violence through the disruption of gang activities, using a combination of the injunction, probation searches, and preventive measures. The prevention component, entitled Rights of Passage, was an after-school mentoring program using volunteer police officers, firefighters, and community leaders as role models. The curriculum focused on "civic values, self-esteem, conflict mediation, aesthetic and martial arts, academic support, and healthy male/female relationships." After federal funding for the YFVI had expired, the Rights of Passage component continued through donations from business and community interests (Office of Juvenile Justice and Delinquency Prevention 1999).

Two injunction initiatives in Pasadena were an outgrowth of the Community Partnership Against Gangs program, headed by the Pasadena City Prosecutor's Office. This program is a multi-agency approach to gang violence focusing on prevention, intervention, enforcement, and education through a partnership between community coalitions, law enforcement, schools, and human services. The program began after a 1993 Halloween night shooting, in which six non-gang youths were mistaken for gang members and ambushed. Three of the youths died. The common denominator of the program is for prosecutors to respond to the needs of the community through: preventive intervention, targeting youths who appear in court for delinquent and criminal offenses; education of the community about indicators of gang involvement among youths; and enforcement of the provisions of the injunction and violations of the penal code. Many of the city's non-profit organizations are involved in various aspects of the intervention and education components. The program includes a Graffiti Task Force, which enforces the city's Graffiti Ordinance and participates in anti-graffiti education in the schools. The injunctions addressed areas of the city where the gangs congregated to the point of taking over the areas and creating havoc for the neighborhoods. The injunctions were acquired by a SAGE deputy from the LADA under the oversight of the city prosecutor.

The Lennox injunction was a component of the Lennox Gang Violence Suppression Program, a collaborative project funded by the State of California's Office of Criminal Justice Planning. The program, which was in its sixth year at the time of this study, includes five collaborative partners – the LADA, the Los Angeles County Sheriff's Department, the Los Angeles County Probation Department, the Lennox School District, and the Richstone Family Center, which is the lead agency. The program is a holistic approach to gang violence, providing intervention through mental health counseling in the schools and at the Richstone Family Center, mentoring, community education and training, and enforcement. The injunction targeted an area near the Lennox Middle School, through which all the students had to walk to get to the school. There had been many incidents of gang-related violence in the target area, and the gang constantly recruited students traversing to and from the school.

Six initiatives did not originate as part of larger programs. Instead, the injunction provided the impetus for post-injunction intervention and/or community revitalization programs. Two San Jose injunctions targeted areas that have since been included in the city's Strong Neighborhoods Initiative, which was discussed earlier. As a result, all three of San Jose's injunctions have been tied to an initiative to revitalize the neighborhoods, suggesting that San Jose uses the injunctions to give the neighborhoods some breathing room from the disorder caused by gangs to allow for the building of community.

One of two injunctions in Oceanside was the impetus for improvements in Libby Lake Park, which a gang had taken over. According to the prosecutor, the police were responsible for instigating the revitalization of the park after the injunction was granted. The city funded a $317,000 resurrection of the park, including a central plaza for concerts and performances and adjacent picnic pavilions (Sherman 2001a). On May 12, 2001, two years after the preliminary injunction was obtained, a celebration of the resurrection of the park took place (San Diego Union-Tribune 2001b). Low-income housing has also been proposed as part of the concerted effort to revitalize the neighborhood (Sherman 2001b).

In San Diego, an injunction by the city attorney's office provided the impetus for an intervention program headed by the Southeastern Criminal Justice Coalition, a collaboration of community organizations chaired by the injunction prosecutor. The intervention occurred after community members recognized that something more than an injunction would be needed to deal with the gang problem. The coalition, which had been discussing doing something for high-risk kids, targeted injunction defendants who indicated a desire to make a lifestyle change. The original intervention occurred through an intermediary, a drug-counseling program where a coalition member, who was familiar with many of the defendants, worked. The program eventually expanded to include a job counselor with the California Corrections Department, who helped the defendants obtain employment. According to the prosecutor, intervention under the coalition continues in the targeted neighborhood.

In Burbank, an injunction initiative evolved into the rehabilitation of its target area and the surrounding neighborhood. After the gang was dislodged from the target area, the city's redevelopment agency bought several buildings and initiated a management program that included zero tolerance for drug dealing and gang members. A state law required the city to set aside 20% of tax revenues obtained from commercial redevelopment projects for construction and rehabilitation of public housing. The city was looking for a place to spend this money at the time the injunction was granted. As one of the few blighted areas in the city, the target area provided a perfect place for the city to use these funds.

In 1995, three years after the injunction was granted, the city council voted to spend $1.7 million to improve the quality-of-life of and to create affordable housing in the neighborhood. Improvements included a new playground and landscaping, repair and maintenance to nine apartment buildings owned by the redevelopment agency, the hiring of a property management firm to oversee the apartments, and the employment of an education director for after-school programs in the neighborhood. In 1999, the Elmwood Achievement Center and the Burbank Housing Corporation organized a celebration acclaiming four years of a beautiful and crime-free neighborhood. Streets had been repaved and lined with trees and flowerbeds, buildings had been sandblasted and painted, a gated playground was built, and bars were removed from the windows of residences. Although the gang still exists and their graffiti still mars some buildings in Burbank, a police lieutenant claimed that they are "out of their old turf for good" (Huffaker 1999).

The best-known initiative to provide impetus for post-injunction intervention is the injunction against the Blythe Street gang in the San Fernando Valley of the City of Los Angeles, where the largest neighborhood reclamation project connected to an injunction continues. The prosecutor emphasized that the injunction was a law enforcement effort, while the community effort to respond to the gang problem concentrated on bringing other resources into the area, not on helping the prosecutor sue the gang. The prosecutor stated:

> [It is] like two rivers running down the same geography at the same time that sometimes met, but most often were doing things on separate tracks. ... The long-term problem of a small percentage of the young male population that do not take advantage of schools, jobs, or training is a social service problem that law enforcement and correctional agencies can [only] nudge.

The history of the demise of Blythe Street and its eventual reclamation goes back to the mid-1970's, when a 100-acre General Motors complex located near the Blythe Street neighborhood was closed. As a result, jobs and support for local businesses disappeared and the surrounding neighborhood deteriorated. The deterioration continued through the 1980's, spurred on by an influx of Mexican-American immigrants lured by cheap rents and by a police division strained by shortages of manpower and resources.

Since the preliminary injunction was granted, Blythe Street and the surrounding area have seen an influx of funds and services. Numerous grants have been obtained by social service agencies. The vacant General Motors plant was bought by a property management group and refurbished into a $100 million center called 'The Plant', containing a mall of retail stores, a theater complex, a Home Depot, and an industrial complex. Today, the center provides nearly 2000 jobs, furnishing the surrounding area with badly needed economic infrastructure. As of 1999, more than $4 million in federal and local money had paid for everything from building renovations to increased police patrols in the Blythe Street neighborhood (*Los Angeles Times* 1999d).

News articles from 1985 to the present reveals a steady progression of reports of a preponderance of drug dealing in the late 1980's, through incidents of violence and the resulting injunction in the early 1990's, to revitalization and hope in the late 1990's and early 2000's. A 1999 declaration by Officer Willis of the Los Angeles Police Department, given in support of the request for a permanent injunction, lists over forty public and private organizations that have dedicated personnel and funds to projects in the Blythe Street neighborhood (Table 5-33).

TABLE 5-33: List of Agencies Contributing to Blythe Street Neighborhood Projects, 1985 – 2001

1	Los Angeles Housing Department
2	San Fernando Valley Partnership
3	North Hills Community Coordinating Council
4	Hermandad Mexicana Nacional
5	Casa Esperanza
6	Center for Substance Abuse Prevention
7	Boys and Girls Club of the San Fernando Valley
8	Pacoima Community Youth Culture Center
9	Blythe Street Prevention Project
10	Jobs for our Youths and Homeboy Industries
11	Blythe Street Youth Leadership Group
12	San Fernando Valley Opportunity through Education Scholarship Fund
13	The GM Project
14	The Peace Treaty Council
15	Head Start Program
16	Latin American Civic Association
17	Nelson Network Inc.
18	Los Angeles County Office of Education's Friday Night Live Program
19	California Wellness Foundation
20	Business Watch
21	Economic Development Incentive Task Force
22	Immaculate Heart Community
23	Familia Unidas
24	Blythe Street Sports Club
25	ITT Gilfillan of Van Nuys
26	City Attorney's Office
27	FBI, ATF, DEA, INS task forces
28	Parole
29	Probation
30	American Civil Liberties Union
31	LAPD (CRASH, FALCON, CNAP, Jeopardy)
32	L.A. Bridges
33	City Council (Councilman Bernardi) $82 thousand
34	Health Department (Public Health Nurse)
35	Los Angeles Unified School District (Shuttle Bus program)
36	Blythe Street Community Impact Team
37	Community Development Department (Youth Employment Training Program)
38	Los Angeles Community Center (Food Bank)
39	Business and Professional Center at L.A. Mission College (Street Vendor Training)
40	The Agricultural Foundation
41	The Don Aragon Scholarship Fund
42	Anheuser Busch Foundation
43	Blythe Street Improvement Association (street beautification)
44**	Home Depot
45**	Shalom Zone
46*	L.A. Parks and Recreation Department
47**	California Branch of Tzu Chi's Great Love Mobile Clinic (free medical care)

Sources: *People v. Blythe Street Gang*, Declaration of Officer Willis in Support of Request for Judgment for Permanent Injunction, March 16, 1999 (compiled from the Los Angeles Times).

*Los Angeles Times 2000d.

**Garcia 1999a, 1999b, 2001.

Although efforts to reclaim the Blythe Street neighborhood are continuing, there is evidence that Blythe Street remains a high-risk gang neighborhood seven years after the preliminary injunction was obtained. On Sunday, November 26, 2000 at 3:30 p.m., a woman believed to be an innocent bystander was killed in a drive-by shooting on Blythe Street. One resident was quoted as stating: "We have very heavy gang activity here. A few days ago, they burned mattresses and a grocery cart in the neighborhood. There's been a lot of shooting, graffiti everywhere. They [have] been pretty bad the last couple of weeks" (Kandal 2000).

Several prosecutors have pointed out that injunctions in challenged neighborhoods that, like Blythe Street, have transient populations living in non-owner occupied, multi- resident properties and have been given up on by authorities for a long period of time, require maintenance for longer than the normal honeymoon period experienced by most injunctions. Problems that have existed for twenty years are not going to be fixed in six months, or even in six years. It would be interesting to look at the Blythe Street neighborhood in five years to see if there is a lasting improvement, particularly with all the resources presently being devoted to the area.

Enforcement

Part of the response to a problem includes plans for implementation. The implementation of injunctions that have been granted by the court includes serving notice of the injunction order to defendants and enforcing the provisions of the injunction. When questioned about the plans for enforcement, prosecutors generally stated that the police are given special training on how to serve defendants with the injunction order and on the enforcement of a civil court order.[105] In some cases, a book was distributed to the officers responsible for enforcement. The book contained a list of defendants subject to the injunction order, along with addresses, physical descriptions, photographs, criminal records, proof of service, and other pertinent information about the defendants.[106]

Some prosecutors also offered information about the prosecution of violations. In Los Angeles County, the district attorney's office is generally responsible for felonies and the city prosecutor's office for misdemeanors. Therefore, unless a violation is linked to a felony, deputy city attorneys prosecute all contempt violations.[107] Prosecutions for contempt in other counties vary. In San Bernardino County, the District Attorney agreed to aggressively prosecute all violations of the injunction and to request a mandatory $20,000 bail for all violators, which the judge agreed to impose. In Salinas, the deputy city attorneys were deputized by the district attorney's office to allow them to prosecute injunction violators for associated felonies.

One prosecutor emphasized the importance of having the appropriate personnel to implement the injunction. Because all the injunction defendants were in the city attorney's computer files, the prosecutor was notified whenever a citation for a misdemeanor against an injunction defendant came through the office. The prosecutor would then determine whether a contempt charge should be added. In addition, there originally was coordination with the District Attorney's gang unit for felony cases involving injunction defendants. A key deputy in the District Attorney's gang unit would add the contempt charge to any felony cases involving injunction defendants if the circumstances also violated the injunction. However, when that key deputy district attorney left the gang unit, there was no follow-up on injunction violations associated with felony charges. Presently, unless a police officer knows the violator is an injunction defendant and passes the information on to the deputy district attorney, the contempt charge most likely will not be pursued.

This same prosecutor highlighted the importance of the right personnel for street enforcement. A detective in the gang unit was a key person in obtaining and enforcing the injunction. Three years after obtaining the injunction, the detective was reassigned. With nobody pushing enforcement on the street, the patrol officers no longer prioritized enforcement of the injunction. Presently, there is a new gang detective covering the enjoined gang, and, as he learns who the defendants are, he sends their criminal cases to the prosecutor, who adds the misdemeanor contempt charge.

Enforcement of the injunctions was conducted by four categories of police personnel: *regular police patrols*; *special units*, with only peripheral employment of patrol officers; a *combination* of patrol and special units; and a *coalition* of law enforcement agencies beyond the local police agency, such as a task force. Of the forty-one initiatives for which data were available, almost one-half (20) used a *combination* of special units and regular police patrols, while almost one-quarter (10) used only *special units*, seven used regular *police patrols* only, and four initiatives used a *coalition*, or task force, of law enforcement agencies. All four of the initiatives using a task force were CLEAR projects in Los Angeles, funded by state and federal funds earmarking a collaborative approach.

Summary of Response Variables

Response variables, describing the circumstances related to the decision to seek an injunction, give a mixed picture of variation. Slightly over half of the initiatives were unilateral decisions, with only law enforcement officials involved in the response decision. Injunctions were generally the only alternative considered. In most of these initiatives, all other interventions had previously been exhausted, leaving the injunction initiatives as last resorts to reclaim the neighborhoods. When alternatives were considered, they were generally limited to law enforcement suppression tactics. However, the inclusion of injunction initiatives in a broader program varies considerably. Less than half of the initiatives were formally or informally part of a broader program. While more than half were not part of a broader program, it was significant that one-quarter of these initiatives provided the impetus for post-injunction interventions. This finding is consistent with the explicit goal of gang injunctions – to give targeted neighborhoods 'breathing room' from the disorder caused by gangs, allowing residents the opportunity to physically improve neighborhood conditions and develop informal social control mechanisms. Plans for enforcement also vary considerably. While almost half of the initiatives used a combination of regular patrols and special units, enforcement for the other half was dispersed between special units, regular patrols, and a coalition of law enforcement agencies.

Assessment

Assessment refers to an evaluation of a response. Assessment is important to avoid merely replacing one ineffective response with another (Goldstein 1990: 49) and to prompt further efforts by the responding agency or other agencies to resolve similar problems. However, law enforcement agencies often lack the expertise in research methodology to make a valid assessment, and the cost of assessment is prohibitive for an agency with limited resources and other pressing problems to resolve. As a result, assessment is one area in which problem-oriented interventions are particularly weak, especially in smaller agencies that do not have crime analysis capabilities. Prosecutors often must rely on crime statistics from the police, when they are available, to assess the effectiveness of a prosecutorial intervention.

Problem-oriented interventions seek the most effective response within the confines of both the law and professional ethics. Evaluating the effect of a response is often difficult because of the large number of variables that can affect the outcome, some of which are not readily apparent. A controlled experiment, which compares outcomes in controlled and experimental areas, is often costly, difficult to set up, and raises the ethical dilemma of taking measures to improve one neighborhood while disregarding intervention in another equally needy neighborhood. Therefore, controlled experiments are not expected for the evaluation of gang injunctions, except where they might occur naturally.

Assessment is not limited to the evaluation of the impact of an injunction. Intervening events that significantly influence the initiatives or alter the activity level of the gang during the acquisition process are also relevant to assessment, as are displacement effects that result in the public nuisance merely being moved to another neighborhood. Therefore, five variables related to assessment are examined: *plans for assessment*, *intervening events*, *decrease in activity* during the acquisition process, prosecutors' *perceptions of effectiveness*, and *displacement*.

Plans for assessment

Prosecutors have grappled with the issue of assessment since the inception of the gang injunction strategy. Criticism of gang injunctions has often focused on the lack of empirical evidence of their effectiveness in decreasing gang activity. Beyond the common problems associated with police-generated crime statistics, the assessment of gang injunctions has been hampered by constantly changing populations of residents, gang members, and police officers in the target areas. Highly transitory populations plague the low-income neighborhoods commonly claimed by gangs. People are drawn to these neighborhoods by relatively low rents, often leaving as soon as they find more adequate affordable housing. Gang membership is also very fluid. New gang members are constantly recruited to replace members who are incarcerated, killed, mature out of the gang lifestyle, or leave the area for other reasons. In addition, police officers often transfer to better assignments or to increase the chances of promotion. According to one prosecutor in Los Angeles, there are institutional pressures on LAPD officers to move from one job to another every couple of years, resulting in a lack of neighborhood expertise, and similar pressures probably occur in other police departments.

Statistics are a questionable measure of effectiveness. As discussed earlier, gangs differ in the nature of their activity and their effect on different neighborhoods (Thornberry and Burch 1997; Huff 1998; Esbensen and Huizinga 1996; Battin-Pearson et al. 1998; Thrasher 1927/1963; Klein 1996). Indicia of law enforcement activity, such as arrest and field interrogations, are a poor measure of effectiveness because law enforcement agencies control their occurrence. The frequency of arrests and field interrogations may vary greatly between neighborhoods, regardless of the level of crime and gang activity. Even when scrupulously maintained, police statistics do not always correlate with unreported crimes and the fear factor resulting from the intimidation that cripples gang-plagued neighborhoods.

There is a general lack of an emphasis by prosecutors on **plans for assessment**. Responses for nine initiatives indicated no plans for assessment. Another nine responses reported that their assessment consisted of anecdotal evidence, obtained by talking to residents and police officers, as well as feedback from community meetings and personal observations. Prosecutors for these initiatives state that increased community activity in a neighborhood, such as children playing in streets and parks where they were seldom seen prior to the injunction, is sufficient evidence that an injunction is effective. However, anecdotal evidence tends to be very subjective, not the kind of information that can easily be documented to provide data for a rigorous evaluation.[108]

Eight initiatives relied on crime statistics, generally through pre- and post-injunction comparisons of crime in the target areas. Two of these initiatives stand out. One prosecutor used pre- and post-injunction calls-for-service, a statistic not controlled by police activity. This method assumes that an increase in calls-for-service results from opening the lines of communication between law enforcement and the community due to a reduction in community intimidation by gang members. This assumption contrasts with that used in the ACLU's evaluation of the Blythe Street injunction, which assumed that increased calls-for-service indicate increased crime and the failure of an injunction to curb gang activity (ACLU Foundation of Southern California 1997).

Another prosecutor had the benefit of a natural experiment. The target area was a discrete territory of a single gang that was heavily involved in the illegal sales of drugs. Over forty different gangs sold drugs in an area directly across a major thoroughfare from the injunction target area. The large number of gangs using the same turf made an injunction impractical in the area, making it an ideal control area for the comparison of changes in narcotics arrest statistics in both locals, without the ethical dilemma of ignoring intervention in the control area for experimental purposes. There was a 56% decrease in arrests for sales and purchases of narcotics and a significant decrease in graffiti in the target area in the three month following implementation of the injunction, compared with little change in the control area.

Twelve initiatives used a combination of anecdotal evidence and crime statistics, uniting subjective and objective indicators of effectiveness. Using both subjective and objective measures may give a more comprehensive picture of the impact of the injunction by using statistics – arrest data, reported criminal incidents, documented police contacts with gang members, and calls-for-service – supported by observations and the perceptions of residents and police officers.

The first initiative to obtain a gang injunction, which originated as an experiment, was the only initiative to attempt a relatively objective assessment of the impact of the injunction on the lives of residents through a community survey. There originally were no plans for assessment. After the injunction was in place, the LACA and the LAPD mailed 200 surveys to neighborhood residents, asking them to judge the effect of the injunction. Of the 50 surveys that were returned, 40 responses indicated that the injunction helped deter criminal activities in the neighborhood (Harris 1988).

Intervening events

The acquisition process generally takes six months to a year from the inception of the injunction initiative to filing for a preliminary injunction. During that time, various factors may alter the extent and seriousness of the gang's activities. The gang may become embroiled in a conflict with a rival gang, resulting in a marked increase in violence in the target area; it may increase other activities for various reasons; or it may go underground because of stepped-up enforcement action. Because of the relatively long time from decision to filing, it is anticipated that intervening event or incidents would significantly affect many of the injunction initiative.

Fifteen initiatives experienced some type of **intervening event**, thirteen of which reported an increase in violence in the target area. In nine cases, the violence made the case for an injunction more compelling without altering the course of the process. For example, in one case, seventeen shootings occurred in or near the target area just two weeks prior to filing for the preliminary injunction. At least half of the shootings were tied to the targeted gang, convincing the police department to maintain its resources in the target area.

Intervening violence altered the course of the process in four cases. Two initiatives were accelerated due to an increase in gang-related shootings. Intervening violence led to additions to the requested relief in two cases. In one, the gang members were targets of drive-by shootings while sitting on a wall in front of a strip mall, causing the prosecutor to add a provision prohibiting defendants from the area of the shopping center unless actively engaged in legitimate business. In the other initiative, the gang's activities primarily consisted of low level nuisance behavior until the gang began firebombing the residences of Afro-Americans to drive them from the neighborhood. This resulted in the addition of a prohibition on the possession of Molotov cocktails.

Non-violent intervening incidents occurred in two initiatives. One initiative experienced an increase in a gang's non-violent activities, making the case for an injunction more compelling. Another initiative was terminated when the gang's activity ceased. The house at the center of the activity was sold and several gang leaders were incarcerated, leading to a marked decrease in gang activity in the area.

Decrease in activity

The process of gathering evidence and filing for an injunction may lead to a **decrease in activity** by the gang prior to the implementation of an injunction. Gang members may go underground after learning that some extraordinary action is afoot. The process of serving notice[109] that legal action has been filed against the defendants may also result in reduced activity in the target area.

Prosecutors for over one-half (24) of the initiatives reported no decrease in gang activity prior to a ruling by the court. Slightly more than one-half of these initiatives (13) did not obtain a temporary restraining order (TRO), suggesting that the mere service of notice had little effect on the gangs. In the eleven initiatives that obtained a TRO, the lack of any decrease in activity prior to the TRO was most likely due to attempts by prosecutors to keep the operation secret so that the TRO could be served on the defendants.

Prosecutors for fourteen initiatives reported some decrease in the gang's activities prior to a ruling on the preliminary injunction. In nine cases, service of notice of the pending lawsuit was most likely the reason for the decrease. The remaining five initiatives had been granted temporary restraining orders, meaning that there was no service of notice prior to the first ruling by the court. In these cases, either the operational security of the initiative was breached or officials purposely made the initiative known to the public.

In one initiative, the prosecutor announced the injunction effort at a public meeting and continued other suppression interventions against the targeted gang. This prosecutor raised an ethical dilemma. Where a suppression effort might be so successful that abatement by injunction might not be necessary, there has been a subtle undercurrent among injunction prosecutors to leave the neighborhood alone so that a high level of gang activity could be documented. Because the injunction team for this initiative did not feel comfortable ignoring neighborhood problems to allow documentation of crime and blight, the injunction was conducted openly in conjunction with other suppression efforts.

The existence of this undercurrent was supported by an anecdote from another prosecutor. While at a meeting just prior to filing for and injunction, a member of the injunction team announced something to the effect of "Good news, there was another murder last night". Realizing what he/she said, the announcer immediately clarified that the murder made the case for an injunction more compelling, not that he/she was thrilled about another murder in the neighborhood.

One prosecutor frankly stated that injunction initiatives are often kept at a low profile to maintain the operational security of the initiatives. This prosecutor avoided involving the community in any manner and refused to use civilian declarations as evidence of the public nuisance caused by targeted gangs.

Perceptions of effectiveness

Effectiveness is the most frequently raised issue regarding any controversial intervention, including gang injunctions. As previously noted, prosecutors have been criticized for their inability to provide statistical evaluations of effectiveness. On the other hand, statistical evaluations are not always reliable or relevant.

Prosecutors for thirty-seven initiatives shared their perceptions of the effectiveness of their injunction initiatives. All believed the injunctions were effective (see Table 5-34 for examples of effectiveness and the methods used for assessment).[110] Several prosecutors stated that they did not know of any neighborhood that did not want an injunction. According to one prosecutor, by the time an injunction is proposed, the neighborhoods are usually in such bad shape that the residents are very glad to have the initiative.

Five cases provided a natural pre/post intervention experiment on the short-term impact of gang injunctions. In a case previously described, the prosecutor had a natural control area across a main thoroughfare from the target area with which to compare the effect of the injunction. Because the control area was controlled by a number of gangs, the prosecutor was able to assess the effect of the injunction through a comparison of narcotics arrests and instances of graffiti, finding significant decreases in each.

Unfortunately, the difference in gang activity is often noted only after enforcement ceases and the gang returns to the streets. Two cases had a preliminary injunction denied after a temporary restraining order was in effect for several weeks. The prosecutors for both cases observed a dramatic difference in gang activity while the temporary restraining order was in force. In one of these initiatives, the police saw the level of gang-related incidents decline significantly while the restraining order was in force, but return to the level experienced before the injunction within a month of the dissolution of the restraining order (Eljera 1993).

The enforcement of two injunctions was suspended as a direct result if the Rampart corruption scandal in Los Angeles. According to a news report, gang-related violence in the Rampart area, which contained the target areas for both injunctions, increased nearly 40% after suspension of the injunctions. In a two-month period in which the injunctions were in force, police reported 108 violent gang-related crimes, ranging from extortion to rape and murder. During the same months of the following year, after the injunctions were suspended, police recorded 151 violent gang-related crimes in the same area, a nearly 50% increase. A police captain of the Rampart Division offered three possible reasons for the large spike in crime: gang members became more brazen since the injunctions were lifted, a gang conflict was smoldering beneath the surface while the injunction was in force, or there was merely a blip in crime in the area. The president of the Police Protective League argued that lifting the injunctions made gang members "feel they've been given the green light to go back and terrorize people" (Associated Press 2000b).

Several prosecutors discussed the reasons they thought gang injunctions were effective, while the criminal law was not effective. They speculated that the injunction has a psychological effect on the gang members, who are dealing with an 'unknown' and do not understand what is at risk. According to one prosecutor:

> [There was a] psychological effect on the gang, in that they thought somebody was watching them, and they took their

activities and moved them to less conspicuous forms of activity, so that they weren't on the street corners, harassing cars – less violence, less vandalism.

TABLE 5-34: Effectiveness and Methods of Assessment

- An increase in calls-for-service from 1740 in the prior year to almost 1900 in the year following the injunction, attributed to opening communications between the community and the police.
- In a very small target area, an average of 12 calls-for-service per day in the 3 to 4 months prior to the injunction decreased to 12 call-for-service per week, with no reports of gang activity, in three to four months following the injunction, attributed to a decrease in crime.
- In a very small target area, 28 assaults in the 12 months preceding the injunction decreased to 7 assaults in the 24 months following the injunction.
- Comparing the three months following the issuance of the injunction with the same three month period of the preceding year, a 26% decrease in calls-for-service in the target area compared with a 2% decrease citywide, and a 38% decrease in police incidents, both attributed to a decrease in gang activity.
- "There was a park in the target area that nobody ever used, and a year after the injunction was in place people walked down there and had a neighborhood barbeque for the first time – like a huge coming out".
- In three months after the injunction was granted, no narcotics complaints from the target area.
- From 1992 to 1998, Part 1 crimes decreased from 450 to 350, Part 2 crimes decreased from 215 to 150, and patrol calls decreased from 1850 to 1475 (*People v. Blythe Street* 1993, Declaration of Officer Leon in Support of Request for Judgment for Permanent Injunction (1999)).
- For an injunction granted in December 1998, gang-related calls-for-service in the same three month period decreased from 30 in 1997 and 18 in 1998 to 3 in 1999 (*People v. Alcala* 1998, Declaration of Sergeant Lanny Roark in Support of Application for Permanent Injunction (1999)).
- Arrests for sales and purchases of narcotics down 56% in the quarter following the injunction from the same quarter of the previous year, compared with the same level of activity right across the street from the target area.
- No homicides in the year following the injunction compared with 19 over several previous years.
- Newspaper articles about the revitalization of Libby Lake Park, videotapes of people in the parks, and no murders in the target areas.
- Over the ensuing year, no gang presence or activity reported.
- "A decrease of 74% in total 'Rocksprings' arrests, a decrease of 81% in both the total 'drug arrests' and the total 'reported incidents' involving drugs, and a decrease of 63% in the total 'reported incidents,' when comparing pre-gang –abatement statistics with post-gang-abatement statistics" for similar one-month periods (*People v. Avalos* 1994, Declaration of Linda Hernandez).
- "The proof is in the pudding. Within three or four months, you could drive down the street, there was no graffiti…and there weren't all these homies hanging out".
- Not a lot of contacts with defendants and a low number of prosecutions for violations.
- "Crime went down, residential burglaries practically stopped, and the neighborhood complaints went down".
- Analyzing six months before and after the injunction, violent crime decreased 89.89%, gang contacts decreased 70.73%, and graffiti decreased 75.5%.

Source: Response to the Prosecutor Survey (unless otherwise noted).

This view was supported by an anecdotal report about one targeted gang going underground. The gang had been heavily involved in the street sales of narcotics. After the injunction was granted, the street presence disappeared, as the gang started using the telephone to make drug deals. This allowed the federal Drug Enforcement Agency (DEA) to accumulate wiretap evidence against the gang. As a result, the DEA obtained an indictment against the gang and some gang members under the federal Racketeer Influenced and Corrupt Organizations (RICO) Act (Rosenzweig 2000).

Another prosecutor opined that the effectiveness of gang injunctions stem from the defendants' ignorance of the civil law. According to this view, gang members are not afraid of the law in the criminal context because they are used to the criminal system. However, the civil context scares them because they do not know the civil law.

A third prosecutor agrees with both the psychological factor and the ignorance factor:

> I have a couple of theories. I think one of the factors is the fear of the unknown, the ignorance factor. It's a civil case, and most of their knowledge about civil cases comes from: "they're going to take my Mom's house away, they're going to take custody away, my parents are going to get sued for money." So they don't completely understand what's at risk, where they understand the criminal system better. I think that's part of it.
>
> Probably the biggest factor is that the gang mentality allows these guys to hang out on the street, drink beer, smoke dope, and do whatever they want with very little heat brought on them, unless they get involved in a full-scale gang war, where the cops will put a strike team together and do some probation searches in their houses. But generally there's not a lot the cops can do, because by the time the cop pulls up and gets out of the car, they've dumped the beer and stashed the joint…So the reason they abide by the injunction for the most part is because you're suddenly preventing them, not from committing crimes like the penal code does, but from hanging out together…So the association clause is very, very powerful because you're bringing heat onto them even when they're not committing some kind of serious crimes, and they don't like it. Nobody likes being in the spotlight, even when you're doing

> something wrong, and I think that's what the injunction does. It really focuses the spotlight on them and makes it harder to be a street thug hanging out on a street corner doing what street thugs do…That's the whole purpose of putting the names on the injunction, not just the names of the gang…it has a significant psychological impact.

Another prosecutor put a different spin on the reasons for effectiveness, placing the focus on attention to the gang problem and the involvement of the community in addressing it:

> [Injunctions] bring outside attention to a problem area and make everyone call the problem by its real name…The injunction process focuses the intelligence gathering part of the law enforcement job for a discrete period and brings resources to that task that may by otherwise unavailable to a resource-strapped institution…It brings knowledge to the community that *the gang* is part of their problem, not *the police*…Injunctions provide an opportunity for the community to figure out what their problem is and try to take care of it themselves, [providing] a period of peace and the focus of other city agencies because of the attention they get…[Injunctions] put these places on the map so that innocent people stay away from them.

Displacement

The final variable related to assessment is evidence of displacement, an issue that has often been raised regarding gang injunctions. In its study of the Blythe Street injunction, the American Civil Liberties Union (1997) argued that displacement is a serious concern which may negate any positive impact of gang injunctions by shifting crime elsewhere. Gang researcher Professor Malcolm W. Klein (1998) has also raised the issue of displacement, arguing that gang injunctions merely cause gang members to take their activities to adjacent neighborhoods, while doing little to change the structural causes of gang life. In contrast, Professor Jeffrey Grogger (2000) of UCLA found no significant evidence of displacement around fourteen injunction target areas in Los Angeles County.

Prosecutors generally agree that displacement is, at most, a minor issue because many gangs are hemmed into their territory, especially in urban areas that are claimed by contiguous rival gangs. Areas not infiltrated by gangs are not susceptible to incursions by outside gangs because they contain the essential infrastructure and informal social control mechanisms to defend against serious gang involvement by area youths. Residents of upper and middle class areas do not tolerate the disorder that goes along with rampant gang activity. The frequency of territoriality as a significant gang characteristic suggests that prosecutors often consider the issue of displacement when analyzing gang problems.

Prosecutors for thirty-seven cases reported data on displacement, based on the perceptions of prosecutors and often supported by anecdotal evidence. Over three-quarters of the initiatives (30) showed no evidence of displacement. There was some indication of displacement in six initiatives, while the issue was premature for one initiative at the time of the study. If the perceptions of prosecuted are valid, the fear of displacement is vastly overstated (Table 5-35).

TABLE 5-35: Displacement

Displacement	Frequency	Percent
No evidence of displacement	30	81.1
Some evidence of displacement	6	16.2
Premature	1	2.7
Total	37	100.0
Missing cases: 5		

Prosecutors for three of the six initiatives in which there was some evidence of displacement indicated that some of the gangs' activities began occurring in adjoining areas. One of these cases enjoined activities in two target areas separated by an area not included in the injunction. The adjacent area was subsequently added to the permanent injunction because the gang had moved its activities into that area. Two cases resulted in the gang moving its activities to another jurisdiction, a neighboring city in one case and the city in which the gang had originated in the other. The prosecutor for one initiative indicated that the displacement effect was minimal, with no further information. Although prosecutors for several cases stated that some gang members relocated their residence, they did not indicate that the gang activity was relocated.

Summary of Assessment Variables

Assessment is an important, but often ignored, component of the problem-solving process. The issue of effectiveness is often controversial for any innovative initiative, let alone for initiatives resulting in serious implications for the civil rights of a select group of individuals. As with many problem-oriented interventions, the assessment of gang injunctions is predictably weak, primarily based on anecdotal evidence and comparative official statistics.

Although the assessment stage occurs after the acquisition of the gang injunction, plans for assessment should be made prior to obtaining the injunction. Plans for assessment were fairly evenly distributed between no plans for assessment, the use of anecdotal evidence, the use of crime statistics, and the use of a combination of anecdotal evidence and crime statistics. Only one initiative attempted to determine the community's perception of effectiveness through a community survey, which was planned and conducted in retrospect. In fairness, it should be noted that this was the first initiative as defined by this research and was conducted as an experiment.

There tended to be no significant intervening events that had an influence on the response. Decreases in gang activities prior to a ruling by the court were also scarce, most likely due to the importance of operational security to allow for the gathering of sufficient evidence to support the request for the injunction and for the service of notice to gang members.

Perceptions of effectiveness by prosecutors did not vary at all. All responding prosecutors reported that their initiatives were effective, including those who obtained a temporary restraining order but were denied a preliminary injunction. Prosecutors for less than one-quarter of the initiatives reported some evidence of displacement of a targeted gang's activities to a location outside the target area, mainly because of the territorial nature of the targeted gangs. This finding was in keeping with the findings of Grogger (2000) and contrary to the position of critics, whose position that gang injunctions merely displace gang activity into adjoining areas, which was supported by the findings of the Blythe Street study (ACLU 1997)

UNPURSUED INJUNCTION INITIATIVES

The examination of injunction initiatives that did not come to fruition may further define the circumstances necessary for a viable injunction effort. To explore this issue, prosecutors were asked whether they had been involved in any cases where a gang injunction had been seriously considered but rejected by their agency, and, if so, to describe the circumstances and reason the initiative did not take place.

The most frequent response was that the gang problem was successfully addressed by other means, making an injunction unnecessary. Injunction relief is an extraordinary remedy that should be limited to situations where the criminal law or other less drastic remedies have proven inadequate. If traditional law enforcement or less drastic civil remedies can solve the gang problem, there is no need for an injunction. Several prosecutors cited a well-known example of addressing the gang problem by other means. In an area where a gang war over drug turf was taking place, an injunction initiative was terminated after six months of investigation when a truce between the warring gangs was negotiated, eliminating the need for an injunction. Unfortunately, the truce did not hold, and injunctions against three gangs in the area were obtained within six years of the truce. Another case was solved by the sale of the house in which the gang's activities were centered and the incarceration of several gang leaders, eliminating the public nuisance and the need for an injunction. The legal action was withdrawn at the request of the prosecutor.

Respondents often mentioned the lack of necessary resources as one circumstance inhibiting injunction initiatives. One prosecutor stated that the process of deciding to seek an injunction is more a matter of prioritizing resources than of rejecting an injunction as a response. According to this prosecutor, the process includes determining the problem to be addressed, analyzing the available resources, and determining the chances of solving the problem with the available resources.

The LACA and the LAPD have developed a protocol under which area commanders submit injunction requests to the four geographic bureaus. The operations committee, consisting of all the deputy chiefs of the department, prioritizes the requests and sends the list to the supervisor of the City Attorney's Hardcore Gang Unit. To determine whether an injunction would work, a deputy city attorney is sent to the priority areas to evaluate the crime picture and gang statistics. If an injunction is feasible, a request is made for the necessary resources, which generally consists of two prosecutors and two police officers dedicated to the initiative for one year. If the necessary resources are not available, an injunction is not pursued. One prosecutor has investigated three priority areas in the past year. Although determining that an injunction was feasible in all three areas, injunction initiatives were not commenced because dedicated police investigators were not available.

Several prosecutors mentioned the inability to meet legal requirements as a primary reason for not pursuing an injunction. To prove a public nuisance, continuous nuisance-related activity must be present on a daily basis within a well-defined area. Without continuous nuisance activity, there is no public nuisance to abate. Personal information about the potential defendants is also necessary to make a successful case for an injunction. In one case, the police requested an injunction in a park that was constantly being tagged with graffiti and used to 'jump in'[111] new gang members, but there were no documented prior police contacts with members of the gang within the park. Because the police were not writing up field interrogation reports, the prosecutor could not prove that the gang members caused the problems in the park. Another prosecutor felt that the legal requisites were not present in one case because there was no personal information on the gang members and the nuisance-related activities of the gang were not continuous.

Because the injunction must be as narrowly defined as necessary to meet the government's interests, discreteness of territory is an important consideration. Territory must be both well defined and amenable to an injunction. In one case, an Afro-American gang was being targeted for an injunction, but the gang's territory was poorly defined. The gang was friendly with the surrounding gangs, increasing the potential for displacement. The territory was centered on a housing project surrounded by an iron fence that limited police access, and most of the gang members lived in the project. The prosecutor ultimately decided that the injunction would be difficult to enforce and most likely ineffective.

The type of activity must be amenable to an injunction. In one case, the United States Border Patrol requested an injunction against a gang of Mexican youths engaged in smuggling illegal aliens across a freeway located on the border with Mexico. In the previous year, cars had killed five gang members while they were crossing the freeway. Prosecutors determined that this activity was not amenable to injunctive relief and that serving notice on Mexican juveniles who lived across the border would pose serious implementation problems. Another case involved a gang that was robbing and assaulting passengers on a city trolley system. The gang members would get off the trolley with the chosen victim, assault and rob the victim, and get back on the trolley to get away. Prosecutors determined that this activity did not lend itself to an injunction.

Finally, one prosecutor, who had successfully obtained injunctions in another city, mentioned the political climate of the jurisdiction. Because of the conservative climate in the city presently employing the prosecutor, a gang injunction would most likely be too controversial for the governing body.

CHAPTER VI

The Dimension of Community Involvement

The engagement of the community in the decision-making process is the second major dimension of problem-oriented interventions. According to Goldstein, widening the procedures for addressing neighborhood problems to include the community in the decision-making process allows greater visibility for the procedures used to tackle problems. Greater visibility encourages and facilitates accountability by informing the community about the limited alternatives available to law enforcement officials and the constraints under which they work. Visibility also results in wider recognition of the risks associated with developing and implementing responses to community problems (Goldstein 1990: 47-8).

As applied to civil gang abatement, risks are inherent in a preference for the safety and quality-of-life of an entire neighborhood over the individual liberties of the "one-half of one percent" of the community members who facilitate the disorder that destroys neighborhoods. There is no doubt that the individual liberties of named defendants are at risk. These liberties include behaviors and activities normally considered non-criminal, which are often proscribed by injunction orders because they facilitate the gang's control over the neighborhood. Accountability for both the positive impact of the injunction on the neighborhood and the negative risk of decreased liberties for a small minority of community members is partially assumed by the community when community entities are decision-making partners in the initiatives. Community ownership of the initiative may make the negative risks more palatable to non-participating members of the community. The problem-oriented perspective advocates criminal justice initiatives involving collaborative partnerships between law enforcement agencies and various community entities, with community entities ideally playing a decision-making role in the partnership. Whether civil gang abatement initiatives live up to this ideal is examined in this chapter.

The concept of community involvement has various connotations, primarily because of the ambiguity in the meanings of both *community* and *involvement*. *Community* is a "contested concept" (DeLeon-Granados 1999: 134) with both spatial and social connotations. A spatial community describes a specific geographic area where people are clustered. In the social sense, community implies the sharing of some characteristics, interests, and/or associations (Warren 1971). These two connotations are often combined to yield a pragmatic definition of community: "shared interests and behavior patterns which people have by virtue of their common locality" (Warren 1971: 6). This definition of community includes four elements: people, interaction, shared ties, and a specific locality (Lyons 1987: 5; Duffee 1997: 85).

This pragmatic definition of community is often used by law enforcement agencies in addressing programmatic objectives (DeLeon-Granados 1999: 135). To prosecutors and police officers, community refers to the people who are affected by the explicit problem being addressed or the specific program being launched (Goldstein 1990: 25), giving them a shared interest in that problem or program. Because law enforcement problems and programs are often limited to particular locations, this shared interest is frequently united with location specificity. As a result, law enforcement programs identify communities using three common factors: (1) a geographically defined location, bounded by natural or man-made barriers or distinguished by some other criteria, such as police beats or precincts; (2) a shared character or identity that cause people to identify with one another, such as ethnicity or socio-economic status; and (3) common concerns or problems (Flynn 1998).

This study employs the pragmatic definition of community used by law enforcement agencies. Community refers to a community-of-interest within the spatial neighborhood targeted for intervention by injunction. The community-of-interest shares the common goal of, and stands to derive a common benefit from, ameliorating the gang activity causing the public nuisance in the spatial neighborhood. This sense of community includes property owners, tenants, business owners and employees, and public and private organizations/agencies operating within the targeted neighborhood. This sense of community is consistent with the problem-oriented objective of expanding the role of community entities in addressing local crime and disorder problems (Goldstein 1990: 48).

This sense of community excludes gang members. Although arguably gang members constitute the segment of the community most affected by injunctions, their interests lie in perpetuating disorderly conditions and enhancing the gang lifestyle, in contrast to the goal of the community-of-interest in ameliorating disorder. Gang members are also distinguished from community entities that oppose the use of gang injunctions on constitutional and/or strategic grounds, while supporting the general goal of eliminating the local public nuisance. Because the objective of this study is to determine the nature of an official response to a local gang problem, directly including gang members in the community involvement phase of the research would be inappropriate, even though their activities may have great influence on the acquisition and implementation of the injunction orders. The influence of gang members on the acquisition process is accounted for through the presence and scope of any legal defense raised against injunctive relief.

The *involvement* of the community in law enforcement interventions generally takes place at four levels. The lowest level is an absence of community involvement, which generally occurs for several related reasons: (1) the failure of law enforcement officials to reach out to the community to gain its participation in an intervention; (2) the failure of the community to participate, because of fear of retribution from the targets of intervention, a historically poor relationship between the community and law enforcement officials, or apathy on the part of the community; and/or (3) the lack of active community groups around which to organize community participation (Grinc 1994). The second level of community involvement is as informants, conveying information to law enforcement officials. At this level, the community is limited to being "the eyes and ears" of law enforcement officials, with no participation at a decision-making level. The third level is as supporters, legitimizing a law enforcement strategy through the allocation of resources and public displays of support (Buerger 1994b),[112] while leaving the decision to employ a strategy to law enforcement officials. At the highest level of involvement, the community assumes a collaborative role, participating with law enforcement officials in the process of identifying the problem and its causes and of choosing the most appropriate response(s) from the available alternatives. The collaborative role is most consistent with the problem-oriented goal of law enforcement responding to a problem *for the community*, as opposed to responding *to the community* through unilateral decisions by law enforcement officials.

Recently, the research team of Maxson, Hennigan, and Sloan conducted a survey of gang officers from twenty-five Southern California cities to determine how law enforcement officials viewed the role of gang injunctions as an intervention tool. Included were thirteen jurisdictions that had been involved in thirty injunctions. Part of the survey addressed the question of community involvement. According to the results, community members played an important supporting role in the decision to pursue a gang injunction in roughly one-half of the jurisdictions. Although community leaders met with police and residents submitted declarations documenting gang activities, the decision to seek a gang injunction was generally made unilaterally by law enforcement officials. There was no indication that community members participated in the decision-making process. The researchers concluded that the pivotal role for the community in gang injunction initiatives is not yet fully appreciated (Maxson, Hennigan, and Sloane 2003).

The second goal of the present study is to examine whether the promise of community involvement in the decision-making arena is fulfilled in gang injunction initiatives. The community prosecution and gang injunction literature (American Prosecutors Research Institute 1995, Coles 1997, Boland 1998, Office of the District Attorney 1996, Los Angeles City Attorney Gang Prosecution Section 1995) advocates the formation of collaborative partnerships between the community and law enforcement officials. However, despite good intentions, community participants in law enforcement ventures are often relegated to the roles of informants and/or supporters, with officials making response decisions unilaterally. Therefore, the second question examined by this research is: *Are injunction initiatives collaborative partnerships between law enforcement agencies and the community, with a decision-making role for community participants, or are the initiatives unilateral responses by law enforcement, with a limited role for the community*?

The original research design relied on participation by community organizations as a proxy for the involvement of the entire community. Because of the large number of injunction initiatives, the length of time covered in the study, and the transitory nature of the population of many target areas, a survey of community members was impractical. Therefore, a limited survey of community organizations involved in nine to twelve initiatives was originally proposed, using a snowball sampling design relying on information provided by prosecutors and by the community organizations identified by prosecutors. Contact information originating from prosecutors was deemed vital to this design, as many grassroots organizations do not have established headquarters, office locations, or telephone listings, making it impossible to identify and contact representatives of these organizations without knowledge of their existence or contact information. It was anticipated that prosecutors would provide the contact information to initiate the sample of community organizations, with the remaining information to come from representatives of those organizations.

As the research progressed, it quickly became apparent that information about the direct involvement of community organizations in injunction initiatives would be insufficient to conduct a meaningful survey. Although all prosecutors were very forthcoming with information requested by the survey, some may have been reluctant to provide contact information on community organizations. For example, the prosecutor for two initiatives explicitly refused to provide information on community organizations out of concern for the safety of organization members. At the time of this study, enforcement of the injunctions had been suspended as a result of the Rampart corruption scandal in the LAPD. Such reluctance is understandable in light of the conditions in most injunction target areas. Despite the perceived success of injunction initiatives in reducing gang activity, injunction target areas remain dangerous neighborhoods in which targeted gangs continue to maintain a presence and gang members continue to reside. Assurances of confidentiality may have been insufficient to allay prosecutors' fears of placing organization members at risk. Therefore, the analysis of the dimension of community involvement is conducted from information obtained from the case files and the Prosecutor Survey. Because the prosecutors provided most of the data used in this analysis, the results are *from the perspective of prosecutors*, not from the perspective of representatives of community organizations or of the community.

As used in this study, community involvement refers to the role of community organizations or groups of community members, through the medium of community meetings, in the process of acquiring a gang injunction. Although individuals often became involved in the acquisition process by submitting civilian declarations, the involvement of individual community members is a relatively weak measure of community involvement. The submission of a citizen declaration is an act by an individual acting on his/her own and does not necessarily represent the support of the community for the injunction initiative. The involvement of community organizations and groups of community members is a far stronger indicator of community involvement. Due to the strength of numbers, community organizations and meetings of groups of community members have a greater potential influence on policy decisions in general, and on a prosecutor's decisions to seek an injunction in particular, than individual citizens acting independently.

The Prosecutor Survey requested prosecutors to rate the level of the involvement of community organizations in injunction initiatives. When it became apparent that community organizations would be involved in few injunction initiatives, the question was amended to include the involvement of the community. This ad lib amendment was necessary to obtain some indication of community involvement. A definition of community was not provided to the respondents. Therefore, the study relies on the pragmatic definition of community usually employed by law enforcement officials when initiating location specific programs.

ANALYSIS OF COMMUNITY INVOLVEMENT

Participating Organizations

Participating organizations are organizations that collaborate in some manner in the injunction initiatives. Problem-oriented interventions are envisioned as collaborative efforts involving agencies and organizations from both within and outside the field of law enforcement. Collaboration recognizes multiple interests in the problem, allows the identification of underlying causes that may not be readily apparent to law enforcement officials, and increases the alternatives and resources to address the problem.

Two categories of **participating organizations** are identified. In the first category, participation is limited to *government entities*, including law enforcement agencies, governing bodies, non-law enforcement government agencies, and elected officials. The second category includes participation by non-governmental *community-based organizations*. Participation was limited to *government entities* in almost three-quarters (30) of the initiatives, with twenty-one of these initiatives involving only law enforcement agencies.

The participation of the community was indicated in eleven initiatives. Community organizations were peripherally involved in the injunction process in four initiatives. In one case, a business association and some homeowners gave support to the initiative. A second case involved a community court-watch group that supported the initiative by attending the injunction hearings. In the third initiative, organizations from outside the target area assisted the prosecutor in approaching target area residents for support. In all these initiatives, community organizations played a supporting role.

In the fourth initiative, local organizations were instrumental in the genesis of the 'carve-out'. Carve-outs are locations within the target area that house social service programs aimed at at-risk youths. The concern is that the non-association provision would be enforced against defendants while attending or working at gang prevention programs. The non-association provision would effectively exclude the defendants from participation in these programs, severely limiting the alternatives to the gang lifestyle that were available to them. These locations are 'carved out' of the target area, allowing defendants to associate at these locations under certain conditions.

In this initiative, the executive director of the school board met with prosecutors to discuss how defendants could participate in these programs without violating the injunction. Specific locations were 'carved out' of the target area, in which defendants could associate if they were legitimately enrolled in or employed by a program held at the locations. However, the defendants were not allowed to walk or drive to and from the program in a group.[113] The prosecutors saw the 'carve-outs' as an opportunity to allay criticism that the injunctions failed to provide for prevention programs for at-risk youths and gang members. Since this initiative, 'carve-outs' have been used to help provide defendants with an alternative to gang life in four other injunction initiatives. The carve-out is a prime example of how injunction orders can be tailored to meet the needs of both the community and the defendants.

Five cases include direct involvement by community organizations or the community in the effort to obtain an injunction. In one case, an association of landlords and residents requested in writing that the city attorney seek an injunction after violence became intolerable within the target area. The violence culminated in the daytime murder of a popular landlord by members of the targeted gang. Residents were so intimidated by the gang that the dead victim was left in the street for forty-five minutes before the police were called. Aware of past injunction initiatives, members of the association thought an injunction would work in their neighborhood. Although the association requested the injunction initiative, it was not involved in the actual decision to pursue an injunction, which was made by law enforcement officials based on legal requisites and available evidence.

Community organizations or the community were directly involved in the decision-making process in the other four initiatives. In one case, the injunction initiative received the blessing of a neighborhood association prior to the inception of an injunction initiative. The prosecutor had experienced serious opposition to an earlier initiative in which community organizations had not been consulted. To avoid similar opposition, the prosecutor approached the association prior to the inception of the initiative, explaining the injunction process to association members. If the association had been opposed to the injunction, the initiative would not have gone forward.

The prosecutor of a third case was invited to speak about gang injunctions at a community meeting. The prosecutor had previously been involved in three successful injunction initiatives under the SAGE program. After the meeting, the residents collectively demanded that the city and the sheriff's department pursue an injunction in the neighborhood, resulting in the city contracting with the district attorney's office for an injunction initiative under the SAGE program. This was the only injunction initiative that targeted a middle class neighborhood. Of four initiatives conducted by the prosecutor, this was the one most fueled by residents. Residents came together without any formal organization to demand action, supporting the perception of some prosecutors that middle and upper class communities do not tolerate the type of behavior that facilitates gang control over a neighborhood.

A fourth injunction initiative was the result of a state grant to a coalition of organizations led by a private social service agency. The coalition also included the local school department, the sheriff's department, the district attorney's office, and the county probation office. The decision to seek an injunction was made by a steering committee, after several community meetings conducted to determine whether the community supported an injunction initiative. This program, entitled the *Lennox Gang Violence Suppression Program*, is further discussed at the end of this chapter as a model for gang injunctions as community prosecution interventions.

The fifth case is the first injunction initiative identified in this study. It was primarily conducted as an experiment in response to open-air drug trafficking by a local gang. The police and prosecutors held a community meeting at which they proposed an injunction to help alleviate gang activity in the neighborhood. After explaining what would be needed from residents to support the initiative, the community cooperated directly with the prosecutor. Approximately twenty civilian declarations were obtained from residents in support of the injunction. According to the prosecutor, the input of the community was vital to the decision to seek the injunction. If the community did not support the initiative, the prosecutor would not have sought an injunction.

One prosecutor claimed that two initiatives included participation by community-based organizations, but refused to identify the organizations or the nature of their involvement. This reluctance to identify participating community organizations is understandable. The target areas for injunction initiatives are dangerous, and injunctions are not expected to cure all the ills in these neighborhoods. Despite the existence in an injunction, the gang usually continues to exist to some degree and gang members continue to reside in the target areas. If the identities of collaborating community organizations were revealed, it would not be difficult for defendants or their associates to learn the identities and addresses of members of those organizations. Compounding the danger of the disclosure of organization members, the enforcement of these two initiatives was suspended as part of the fallout from the Rampart corruption scandal, resulting in an increase in violent gang crime in the target areas during the period of this study.

When **participating organizations** are examined by **office** (Table 6-1), initiatives involving the LADA are most likely to involve community-based organizations or the community. Five of the nine initiatives by the LADA and two of the five joint initiatives involving the LADA included some form of community participation. In contrast, only three of nine LACA initiatives and only two of nine initiatives by agencies conducting a single initiative involve participation by a community entity. Other agencies that conducted multiple initiatives (the SDDA, SJCA, and SBCA) also failed to include community entities as participants.

Collaboration by various interests in an intervention infers that all stakeholders, including community entities, are willing participants in the intervention. However, some important stakeholders may choose not to participate or limit their participation to a superficial level, which may limit the impact of the intervention on the problem. This issue is especially important to injunction initiatives because of the general lack of community participants. To explore whether any interests vital to the injunction initiatives failed to participate as expected, prosecutors were asked if there were any organizations that were expected to participate, but did not. Of the thirty-two initiatives for which information was available, twenty-seven indicated that all organizations participated as expected. In twenty-one of those initiatives, participation was limited to government entities, while six included participation by community entities.

TABLE 6-1: Participating Organizations by Office

	OFFICE							
PARTICIPATING ORGANIZATION	Other	LADA	LACA	Joint	SJCA	SDDA	SBCA	Row Frequency
Government entities	7	5	6	3	3	4	2	30
Community-based organizations	2	4	3	2	-	-	-	11
Column frequency	9	9	9	5	3	4	2	41
Missing: 1 case								

Office:
Other = prosecutor's offices conducting a single injunction initiative.
LADA = Los Angeles District Attorney's Office
LACA = Los Angeles City Attorney's Office
LADA/LACA = Joint initiative between the LADA and the LACA
SDDA = San Diego District Attorney's Office
SJCA = San Jose City Attorney's Office
SBCA = San Bernardino City Attorney's Office

Prosecutors for five initiatives indicated that one or more organizations failed to participate as expected. The prosecutor for two initiatives indicated that the local councilman's office was expected to participate more than it did. The prosecutor did not elaborate on the reasons for the lower-than-expected level of participation.

In one initiative, the prosecutor expected the area schools to be helpful in the initiative. School staff often retains excellent information on gang membership among students, and schools can be a convenient meeting place for the community. However, in this case the schools were extremely uncooperative, refusing to allow the prosecutor to use schools to meet with residents or to participate in any manner in the injunction initiative. The lack of cooperation was, at least in part, due to an understanding between the school administration and the gang that administrators did not want to disrupt (Maxson and Allen 1997). The lack of participation by the schools reinforced the prosecutor's perception of the extent and the strength of the gang's stranglehold over the community.

The prosecutor of another initiative experienced tension with a neighborhood association run by a "hard-core left-wing prevention person" who did not agree with the injunction initiative. Through city funding, the neighborhood association provided services to the neighborhood, including jobs for gang members. According to the prosecutor, the association was counterproductive to efforts to ameliorate the gang problem. In seeking an injunction, the city was saying it would not tolerate gang activity, while it was funding an association having a completely different attitude about gangs. From this experience, the prosecutor concluded that, although in the abstract it may seem productive to bring different elements together to target a problem neighborhood, involving different elements can sometimes be counterproductive, depending on the personalities and philosophies that are brought to the table.

A third initiative experienced inadequate participation by the gang unit of a county probation department. The probation officer initially involved in the initiative had to withdraw for personal reasons, and the gang unit's subsequent participation in the initiative was only peripheral. The prosecutor highlights an important, yet often ignored, aspect of the injunction process:

> It's interesting how much sometimes this depends on people, because without [the probation officer] we were never able to get the kind of involvement or support necessary. Involvement by the probation department throughout this process would have made it better. A lot of this is so dependent on having the right people available at the right time.

Opposition

Opposition to a neighborhood initiative is a valid role for community stakeholders. Opposition may indicate that government officials are imposing the initiative without the support of the community or merely that there are differing views on the propriety of the initiative. An attempt by community entities to influence a law enforcement response through opposition may also be read as an indication that the neighborhood is ready for a participatory role in law enforcement decision-making (Duffee, Fluellen, and Roscoe 1999).

Opposition can come from both outside and within the community. Opposition to injunction initiatives from organizations outside the immediate community is evidenced in the provision of legal representation to defendants, either through private attorneys or via *amicus curiae* briefs by civil libertarian organizations. Opposition from both outside and within the community is evident when there are community protests against an injunction. Particularly in neighborhoods that have poor relations with law enforcement officials, opposition from neighborhood entities offended by the draconian restrictions placed on disadvantaged neighborhood youths may lead other residents to perceive that something is being done *to* the community, as a suppressive force, rather than *for* the community, as a facilitator of community building (Goldstein 1990: 22). Therefore, prosecutors should attempt to address the concerns injunction opponents, especially those from within the community, so that all legitimate interests can be represented in the initiatives. While organizations opposed to injunctions are not expected to be involved in the decision-making process, they do counteract unequivocal support for injunction initiatives.

Twenty initiatives experienced no legal or community **opposition**. In nineteen initiatives, **opposition** was limited to legal defense, either through the representation by defense attorneys or by legal organizations focused on preserving civil liberties. Only three initiatives experienced a significant degree of organized opposition from entities within the community. Two of those initiatives targeted Afro-American gangs and one targeted a Hispanic gang.

In one of the initiatives targeting a predominately Afro-American gang, the local branch of the National Association for the Advancement of Colored People (NAACP) unsuccessfully filed for an injunction to block the issuance of the gang injunction. The NAACP claimed that the injunction was racist (Kariak 1995, *Pasadena Weekly* 1995), despite the fact that Afro-Americans were among the victims of gang violence in the racially mixed target area. According to the prosecutors, NAACP members living in the target area urged the organization to cease its opposition, claiming that the injunction would help all residents, including Afro-Americans. Although the NAACP eventually withdrew its opposition to the injunction, it submitted an *amicus curiae* brief requesting the appointment of counsel for the defendants.

The opposition resulted in an expansion of the community aspect of the injunction, including enhanced social services to help gang members obtain job training. A program entitled "Injunction Conjunction" was initiated to provide gang members with an alternative to gang life. Some of the gang members took advantage of the program. In addition, the city prosecutor's office initiated a gun recovery program based on consent searches, and proposed several additions to the municipal code, including gambling, trespassing, and loitering/curfew ordinances. Partially as a result of the opposition to this injunction, the prosecutor consulted a community group for its blessing prior to the commencement of a second initiative in this city, this one against a Hispanic gang.

In a second initiative targeting an Afro-American gang, significant opposition by a large portion of the community arose because many of the residents viewed the injunction as a racially motivated tactic aimed at eliminating Afro-Americans from the neighborhood. The community, which was about fifty percent Afro-American and twenty-five percent white, was experiencing the forces of gentrification at the time of the initiative. With many white residents from the entertainment industry relocating into the area, gentrification was a hot issue in the neighborhood prior to the initiative, and many Afro-Americans saw the injunction as furthering the forces of gentrification. The opposition made it difficult for prosecutors to obtain declarations from citizens. Many of the Afro-American residents favored the injunction initiative, but feared retaliation from residents opposed to the injunction more than retaliation from gang members. As a result, some residents were publicly opposed to the injunction, while telling the prosecutor in confidence that they favored it. The Nation of Islam led the opposition and provided lawyers for about one-half of the defendants, as well as forming a community program emphasizing job training, self-improvement, and community building (Piccalo 1999a). The prosecutor was puzzled that the initiative took on a racial aspect because most of the murder victims were Afro-American, the result of black-on-black disputes over drug-selling territory.

The third initiative that experienced significant community opposition targeted a Hispanic gang. The opposition culminated in a protest by a number of residents, including parents of some defendants, outside the courthouse while the hearing for the preliminary injunction was taking place (Larrubia 1999). According to the prosecutor, opposition came from both inside and outside the community. While the trying to address the concerns of all, the prosecutor differentiated between the outsiders and the insiders, being more attentive to the concerns of the people residing within the target area. One local organization was entangled in a power struggle between parents of the defendants, who were opposed to the injunction, and the majority of members, who supported the injunction. The prosecutor successfully overcame the opposition by addressing the concerns of the residents, but paid little attention to opposition originating outside the target area.

When **opposition** is examined by prosecutor's **office** (Table 6-2), initiatives by the Los Angeles City Attorney (LACA), the San Jose City Attorney (SJCA), and the San Diego District Attorney (SDDA) experienced the most opposition. Two-thirds of the initiatives by the LACA and the SJCA experienced either legal or community opposition, and all the SDDA initiatives experienced legal opposition. In contrast, only one-third of the LADA initiatives experienced opposition.

TABLE 6-2: Opposition by Office

	OFFICE							
OPPOSITION	Other	LADA	LACA	Joint	SJCA	SDDA	SBCA	Row Frequency
None	6	6	3	3	1	-	1	20
Legal defense only	4	2	5	1	2	4	1	19
Community opposition	-	1	1	1	-	-	-	3
Column Frequency	10	9	9	5	3	4	2	42

When **opposition** is examined by **participating organization** (Table 6-3), slightly over one-half of the initiatives with participation by a community entity experienced legal opposition. While one half of the initiatives having no community participation had no opposition, it is significant that all the initiatives experiencing community opposition (3) limited participation to law enforcement or government agencies. Community opposition was not present in any initiatives that had some form of community participation.

TABLE 6-3: Opposition by Participating Organization

PARTICIPATING ORGANIZATION

OPPOSITION	Government entities	Community-based organization	Row Frequency
None	15	5	20
Legal defense only	12	6	19
Community opposition	3	-	3
Column Frequency	30	11	41

Missing cases: 1

TABLE 6-4: Opposition by Initiator

INITIATOR

OPPOSITION	No request – self initiated	Local governing authority	Elected official	Community Organization	Individual citizen(s)	Police	Combination	Row Frequency
None	-	4	4	1	3	7	1	20
Legal defense only	3	2	2	1	-	10	-	18
Community opposition	-	1	1	-	-	-	1	3
Column frequency	3	7	7	2	3	17	2	41

Missing: 1 case

When **opposition** is examined by **initiator** (Table 6-4), only one of the five initiatives requested by community entities experienced any opposition, and none experienced community opposition. Although no clear pattern of legal opposition emerges, these results suggest that community opposition is more likely to occur against initiatives in which the community entities are not included as participants in the injunction process. These results tend to support the problem-oriented thesis that community ownership of law enforcement initiatives, including gang injunctions, tends to allay opposition within the community.

Civilian Declarations

One relatively objective, although admittedly weak, indicator of community involvement in gang injunction initiatives is the number of civilian declarations gathered in support of the injunction. By submitting a declaration, civilian declarants implicitly support the decision to seek injunctive relief. To guard against witness intimidation and retaliation by gang members, the declarations are generally submitted to the court under seal and, therefore, are seldom accessible to the public. The *orders to seal civilian declarations*, which often indicates the number of declarations entered into evidence under seal, are available in the publicly accessible court records, and, in some case files, the declarations are referred to by number in the *memorandum of points and authorities*. In addition, many respondents to the Prosecutor Survey specified or approximated the number of declarations gathered as evidence. Therefore, the exact or approximate number of civilian declarations was available for most injunction initiatives, including those cases in which the declarations were not submitted to the court.[114]

However, as noted earlier, the number of citizen declarations is a relatively weak measure of community involvement because it does not necessarily indicate community support for the initiative. The decision to submit a declaration is made by an individual acting on his/her own accord, not as a representative of the community. The declarants' role in the acquisition process is limited to that of an informant, providing evidence establishing the existence of the public nuisance in the target area and its nexus to the targeted gang. Although the existence and number of civilian declarations provides little evidence of community involvement beyond the individual decision to act as an informant, they are an important part of the acquisition process. Many prosecutors believe that they would not have obtained injunctions without civilian declarations because of the importance to judges of the descriptions of the neighborhood conditions by those who live and work there.

Prosecutors use different methods to obtain civilian declarations. To protect the declarant from retaliation, declarations are often given covertly, usually outside the neighborhood. One agency used a team consisting of a prosecutor and an investigator, both Hispanic, who 'dress down' as gang members to solicit the neighborhood. According to one prosecutor, investigators generally approached twenty-five to thirty people to obtain ten civilian declarations.

In some cases, prosecutors do not seek citizen declarations because they cannot guarantee confidentiality to declarants. According to one prosecutor, civilian declarations sealed by the court may be accessed by who choose a *pro se* defense, in which a defendant represents himself in court. In one initiative in which a defendant chose a *pro se* defense, the prosecutor withdrew the civilian declarations as evidence even though they were under seal, because the defendant could have asserted his right to examine all the evidence offered against him. Because of the risk of retaliation to civilian declarants, the LACA had ceased obtaining declarations from civilians at the time of this study.

Data on civilian declarations are available for thirty-five initiatives. The number of civilian declarations range from zero to thirty-two. Information on three initiatives indicates only that some declarations were gathered, but did not specify the number of declarations gathered. In two of these initiatives, the declarations were withdrawn because the judge either refused to seal them or refused to accept them, due to the risk to declarants and/or the overwhelming evidence otherwise presented by the prosecutors. Seven initiatives did not gather any civilian declarations, thirteen initiatives submitted between three and ten declarations, and twelve initiatives gathered more than ten declarations, with the prosecutor for one of the latter withdrawing the declarations when a defendant chose a *pro se* defense.

When **civilian declarations** are examined by **category** of injunction initiatives (Table 6-5), seven of the twelve initiatives that gathered over ten declarations fell into the *high disorder* category, while only one of the seven initiatives that gathered no declarations fell into that category. This suggests that prosecutors are more likely to obtain declarations for injunctions focusing on disorder, possibly due to the emphasis by many residents on the disorderly activities of the gangs. There may also be a lower threat of retaliation by gangs that concentrate on low-level nuisance activity. At the other end of the spectrum, four of the seven initiatives that gathered no declarations fall into the *high crime* category, implying that prosecutors do not seek declarations in target areas in which criminal activity is emphasized, possibly because of the greater threat of retaliation by gangs more heavily involved in criminal activities.

When the number of **civilian declarations** is examined by **agency**, initiatives involving city attorney offices are more likely to not rely on citizen declarations than initiatives by district attorney offices and private firms. All district attorney and private firm initiatives used civilian declarations, while five city attorney initiatives did not seek any civilian declarations.

TABLE 6-5: Civilian Declarations by Category

	CATEGORY			
CIVILIAN DECLARATIONS	High Drug	High Crime	High Disorder	Row Freq.
No declarations	2	4	1	7
Yes – number unknown	2	-	1	3
One to ten	5	5	3	13
More than ten	1	4	7	12
Column Frequency	10	13	12	35

Missing: 7 cases

Table 6-6 illustrates that three of those initiatives were by the LACA, which has enacted a policy to not seek civilian declarations because of the danger of retaliation. Joint initiatives by city and district attorney offices also did not seek declarations in two of five cases, only one of which involved the LACA. The San Diego District Attorney' Office (SDDA) submitted the most declarations. In all three of the SDDA initiatives, more than ten declarations were submitted. A prosecutor for these initiatives stated that the judge would not grant an injunction without the civilian declarations.

TABLE 6-6: Civilian Declarations by Office

	OFFICE							
CIVILIAN DECLARATION	Other	LADA	LACA	Joint	SJCA	SDDA	SBCA	Row Frequency
No declarations	3	-	3	1	-	-	-	7
Yes – number unknown	-	3	-	-	-	-	-	3
One to ten	3	3	1	3	2	-	1	13
More than ten	4	1	3	-	-	3	1	12
Column Frequency	10	7	7	4	2	3	2	35

Missing: 7 cases

Prosecutors' Perceptions of Community Involvement

The original survey instrument requested prosecutors to rate both the degree of involvement in the injunction initiative by non-law enforcement community organizations and the impact of those organizations on the decision to seek an injunction. However, while the survey was being conducted, it quickly became apparent that there was a lack of involvement by community organizations. Although most prosecutors stated that the community was involved in varying degrees, many initiatives did not have any involvement by community organizations. Therefore, the assumption that community organizations can be used as a proxy for the community is incorrect, at least in the neighborhoods that are taken over by gangs to the extent that an injunction effort is initiated.

To account for the role and effect of the community in the initiatives, the survey instrument was amended to include the degree and impact of the involvement of the community, including community organizations. Therefore, the **degree of community involvement** refers to the role of community organizations or the community in the injunction process, on an ordinal scale ranging from no community involvement (*none*), through limited to providing information and/or declarations (*informant*) and providing political/community support for or opposition to the injunction (*supporter/opponent*), with participated in making the decision to seek the injunction (*decision-maker*) as the highest level of involvement. The community **impact** on the decision to seek an injunction was left open for prosecutors to interpret, ranging from *none*, through *small* and *moderate*, to *large*. For each question, prosecutors were asked to explain the reasons for their response. Data are available for forty-one initiatives for the **degree of community involvement** and for thirty-nine initiatives for community **impact**.

An examination of the **degree of community involvement** reveals that prosecutors for five initiatives reported no involvement by either community organizations or the community. Community involvement for almost one-half of the initiatives (19) was limited to providing information and/or declarations. In these initiatives, community participants are the eyes and ears of law enforcement agencies, or informants (Buerger 1994), not participants in the decision-making process. In slightly more than one quarter of the initiatives (11), community organizations and the community served either a supporting or opposing role for the initiatives. Although considered a step above providing information and/or declarations on the participatory scale, these initiatives also did not involve the community in the decision-making process. Included in this category are initiatives that experienced some degree of organized community opposition.

There is evidence that six initiatives involved either community organizations or the community as participants in the decision-making process. Four of these initiatives have previously been described in the section on *participating organizations*, so only a summary will be given here. In one, residents of a largely middle class neighborhood invited a SAGE deputy to give a presentation on injunction and subsequently demanded that officials address the gang problem in their neighborhood with an injunction initiative. In the second, an organization of landlords and residents was asked for its blessing for the injunction initiative before the decision was made. In this case, an earlier initiative in the same city had met with significant opposition, prompting the prosecutor to ask the organization for its opinion on the subsequent initiative. In the third, a private social service agency served as the lead agency for a state grant to suppress gang violence in the neighborhood. The fourth initiative resulted from the support of the community after a community meeting at which prosecutors announced their intent to seek an injunction. Community input was important in the decision to seek the injunction, as the injunction would not have been sought if the community did not support and cooperate with the initiative.

In one of the two remaining initiatives, residents requested an injunction through the police department. The residents wanted members of a gang banned from the neighborhood. The gang was heavily involved in drug trafficking, and few, if any, gang members lived in the neighborhood, which was populated primarily by elderly people and young families. The prosecutor had been working with the police department on narcotics nuisance abatements targeting crack houses in the neighborhood. The prosecutor and the police discussed the desired outcome with the residents, who indicated that they wanted the gang members banned from the neighborhood. Abiding by the consensus of the community, the prosecutor included a provision banning gang members from coming within one thousand yards of the target area. Although a temporary restraining order was issued, the judge denied the preliminary injunction, reasoning that the criminal law provided sufficient remedies for the public nuisance caused by the gang's activities. According to the prosecutor, the provision banning the defendants was an underlying reason for the denial. In fairness to the prosecutor, it should be noted that the initiative was one of the earlier efforts, occurring during the *pre-Acuna period* when prosecutors had little judicial guidance on gang injunctions.

The final initiative in which the community played a decision-making role was the direct result of a community meeting organized by a community policing officer and attended by the prosecutor. The residents of the target area complained of gang activity in and around a local park. A gang war had resulted in three recent homicides near the park, raising great concern in the neighborhood about public safety. The park was covered with gang graffiti, and residents did not feel safe using the park. After observing the graffiti and gang members congregating in the park, potential buyers of property around the park would rescind or refuse to make offers, causing property values in the area to plummet. The prosecutor, who had previously worked in another jurisdiction where an injunction had been sought, suggested that an injunction might help. The gang had already been documented by the district attorney's office as a criminal street gang under the Street Terrorism Enforcement and Prevention Act (STEP Act).[115] Other gang interventions employed in the area had not worked. The decision to seek an injunction was the direct result of the community meeting, as the residents were very receptive to the prosecutor's suggestion.

When **degree of community involvement** is examined by **category** (Table 6-7), three of the six initiatives in which the community played a decision-making role fall into the *high drug* category. In fact, of the thirteen *high drug* initiatives, nine rate within the two highest degrees of community involvement. In comparison, only two of thirteen *high crime* initiatives and six of fifteen *high disorder* initiatives are rated in the two highest degrees of community involvement. This rating is contrary to what would be expected if gang injunctions were being used to avoid constitutional protections in the effort to suppress illegal drug sales. One would presume that the degree of community involvement would be highest in *high disorder* initiatives because of the importance that many residents place on the disorderly conditions accompanying gang activity. Even when the three cases in which prosecutors experienced community opposition are eliminated, sixty percent of the *high drug* initiatives experienced a significant degree of community involvement, compared to only forty percent of *high disorder* initiatives. If the perceptions of prosecutors are correct, the community is more involved in initiatives targeting drug offenses than in initiatives targeting crime and disorder.

TABLE 6-7: Degree of Community Involvement by Category

	CATEGORY			
DEGREE OF COMMUNITY INVOLVEMENT	High Drug	High Crime	High Disorder	Row Freq.
None	1	4	-	5
Informant	3	7	9	19
Supporter/opponent	6	1	4	11
Decision-maker	3	1	2	6
Column Frequency Missing: 1 case	13	13	15	41

TABLE 6-8: Degree of Community Involvement by Initiator

	INITIATOR							
DEGREE OF COMMUNITY INVOLVEMENT	No request – self initiated	Local governing authority	Elected official	Community Organization	Individual Citizen(s)	Police	Combination	Row Frequency
No community involvement	1	-	1	-	-	3	-	5
Limited to providing information/declarations	-	4	1	-	1	13	-	19
Provided community support or opposition	1	2	5	1	-	-	2	11
Participated in the decision to seek an injunction	1	1	-	1	2	1	-	6
Column Frequency Missing: 1 case	3	7	7	2	3	17	2	41

The **degree of community involvement** is also examined by **initiator** to determine whether prosecutors' perceptions of community involvement are consistent with the initiators of injunction efforts. As Table 6-8 illustrates, the initiatives that were requested by community entities rate high on degree of community involvement. In four of the five initiatives requested by community entities, the community played at least a supporting role, and in three of these initiatives community entities had a decision-making role. In the two initiatives that originated from a general outcry by both officials and the community, the community played a supporting/opposing role. In contrast, police-requested initiatives generally rank low on community involvement. With one exception in which the community played a decision-making role, the initiatives requested by the police either used the community as an informant or there was no community involvement at all.

TABLE 6-9: Degree of Community Involvement by Office

DEGREE OF COMMUNITY INVOLVEMENT	OFFICE: Other	LADA	LACA	Joint	SJCA	SDDA	SBCA	Row Frequency
No community involvement	2	-	3	-	-	-	-	5
Limited to providing information/declarations	4	4	2	-	3	4	2	19
Provided community support or opposition	1	2	3	5	-	-	-	11
Participated in the decision to seek and injunction	2	3	1	-	-	-	-	6
Column Frequency	9	9	9	5	2	4	2	41

Missing: 1 case

When the prosecutor's **office** is considered (Table 6-9), all offices that rely on the police as initiators rated the role of the community as that of an informant. The initiator was the police in all the injunctions by the San Jose City Attorney (SJCA), the San Diego District Attorney (SDDA), and the San Bernardino City Attorney (SBCA). All three agencies rated the degree of community involvement as limited to providing information and/or declarations, in other words as an informant. This is consistent with community policing research that indicates that the police often see the community role as being "the eyes and ears" of the police (Buerger 1994).

Prosecutors were also requested to rate the **impact** of the community on the decision to seek an injunction. The **impact** is rated on a scale of *none*, *small*, *moderate*, and *large*, with meanings of the rates purposely left open to interpretation to see what prosecutors would emphasize. Thirty-nine prosecutors responded to the question.

There is no perceived impact by either community organizations or the community in nine initiatives. Prosecutors perceive a small impact in ten initiatives and a moderate impact in five initiatives. Prosecutors perceive a large impact in fifteen initiatives (Table 6-15).

Prosecutors indicating the impact of community involvement as moderate to large generally perceived that they were responding to the needs of the community. The community was considered the driving force behind these injunction initiatives, providing the impetus for government to become creative in dedicating resources to the problem. In many of these cases, prosecutors stated that they would not have commenced the injunction initiatives without the support of the community.

On the other hand, the initiatives that indicated an impact of none to small generally emphasized the unwillingness of the community to get involved or to call the police. These prosecutors tended to be approached by the police. Aware of the intimidating effect of the gangs on these neighborhoods, the prosecutors waited for the police to request an injunction or limited any involvement to law enforcement agencies in order to reduce the risk to civilians, as well as to maintain operational security.

TABLE 6-10: Impact by Degree of Community Involvement

	DEGREE OF COMMUNITY INVOLVEMENT				
IMPACT	None	Informant	Supporter/ opponent	Decision-maker	Row Frequency
None	3	5	1	-	9
Small	1	7	2	-	10
Moderate	-	2	2	1	5
Large	-	5	5	5	15
Column Freq.	4	19	10	6	39

Missing: 3 cases

There is a strong relationship between the **degree of community involvement** and the **impact** of the community on the injunction decision. As Table 6-10 illustrates, initiatives that are rated low in degree of community involvement tend to be rated low in impact. In all four initiatives that prosecutors rate as having no community involvement, the community is rated as having either no impact or only a small impact on the injunction decision. Prosecutors of twelve of nineteen initiatives in which community involvement is rated at the level of an informant also rate the impact of the community on the injunction decision as none to small. Conversely, initiatives rated high in degree of community involvement generally score high on the impact of the community on the injunction decision. For five of the six initiatives for which the degree of community involvement is rated as a decision-maker, the community had a high impact on the injunction decision, with the one remaining initiative having a moderate impact. For seven of the ten initiatives in which community involvement plays a supporting/opposing role, the community has a high or moderate impact in the injunction decision.

TABLE 6-11: Impact by Initiator

IMPACT	INITIATOR: No request-self initiated	Local governing authority	Elected official	Community Organization	Individual citizen(s)	Police	Combination	Row Frequency
None	-	1	2	-	-	6	-	9
Small	1	2	3	-	-	4	-	10
Moderate	1	2	-	-	-	2	-	5
Large	1	2	2	2	3	4	1	15
Col. Freq.	3	7	7	2	3	16	1	39

Missing: 3 cases

The **impact** of the community on the injunction decision is also consistent with the **initiators** of the initiatives (Table 6-11). Of the nine initiatives in which prosecutors perceived no impact by the community, the police requested six, a governing authority requested one, and elected officials requested two. No initiative in this category was requested by a community entity nor initiated by a general outcry by various entities, including the community. At the other end of the spectrum, all initiatives requested by community entities score large on community impact. In addition, the large impact category contains at least one injunction from every category of initiator, supporting the perception of prosecutors that the government is responding to the needs of citizens even when they are not directly involved with the prosecutor in the injunction process.

TABLE 6-12: Impact by Office

OFFICE

IMPACT	Other	LADA	LACA	Joint	SJCA	SDDA	SBCA	Row Frequency
None	2	-	3	-	-	4	-	9
Small	2	3	2	2	-	-	1	10
Moderate	3	2	-	-	-	-	-	5
Large	2	4	3	2	3	-	1	15
Col. Freq.	9	9	8	4	3	4	2	39

Missing: 3 cases

When **impact** is examined by **office**, a discrepancy between some prosecutors' perceptions of the degree of community involvement and the impact on the injunction decision is evident. In particular, the initiatives by the San Jose City Attorney's Office (SJCA) and the San Diego District Attorney's Office (SDDA) show inconsistency between degree and impact. Recall that all the initiatives for these offices were rated as limited to the role of informant on degree of community involvement. However, Table 6-12 illustrates that in all the SJCA initiatives the community impact of the injunction decision is large, despite the somewhat limited role of the community in the acquisition process. In contrast, the impact of the community on the injunction decision was rated as none in every SDDA initiative, all of which rate the degree of community involvement as informant. Despite this discrepancy, prosecutors for both agencies stressed the consideration of the needs of the community as paramount in the decision to seek an injunction.

When examining impact by category (Table 6-13), the *high drug* category again stood out. Prosecutors of over 50% of *high drug* initiatives rate the community impact on the injunction decision as large. This is significantly higher than the large impact ratings of *high crime* and *high disorder* initiatives, which are 30% and 33% respectively. If prosecutors use gang injunctions as drug enforcement tools to avoid the constitutional protections of the criminal law, one would expect the impact of the community on the injunction decision to be small to none.

TABLE 6-13: Impact by Category

CATEGORY

Count
Column Pct.

IMPACT	High Drug	High Crime	High Disorder	Row Frequency
None	1 9.1%	4 30.8%	4 26.7%	9 23.1%
Small	4 36.4%	2 15.4%	4 26.7%	10 25.6%
Moderate	-	3 23.1%	2 13.3%	5 12.8%
Large	6 54.5%	4 30.8%	5 33.3%	15 38.5%
Column Frequency	11	13	15	39
Missing: 3 cases				100%

TABLE 6-14: Impact by Date Filed

DATE FILED

Count
Column Pct.

IMPACT	Pre-*Acuna*	Appellate	Post-*Acuna*	Row Frequency
None	1 12.5%	1 14.3%	7 29.2%	9 23.1%
Small	1 12.5%	2 28.6%	7 29.2%	10 25.6%
Moderate	2 25%	-	3 12.5%	5 12.8%
Large	4 50%	4 57.1%	7 29.2%	15 38.5%
Column Frequency	8	4	24	39
Missing: 3 cases				100%

Finally, an examination of **impact** and **date filed** reveals a change in prosecutors' perceptions of the community impact on injunction decisions over time. Table 6-14 illustrates that the initiatives with a large community impact diminished in the *post-Acuna period*, while those rated as none significantly increased. Almost 30% of the initiatives were rated large in the *post-Acuna period*, significantly lower than the 50% and 57% in the pre-*Acuna* and *appellate* periods respectively. Conversely, the initiatives rated as none rose to almost

30% in the *post-Acuna period*, compared with approximately 12% and 14% in the preceding periods. This may be due to the lower reliance by prosecutors on the community in the *post-Acuna* injunctions. Indeed, the LACA has recently formulated a policy to no longer to seek civilian declarations from the community because of the serious threat of retaliation by gang members. If this trend continues, the gang injunction phenomenon may be leaning away from a problem-oriented/community justice approach toward a war-on-crime/suppression approach.

THE LACK OF COMMUNITY INVOLVEMENT

It is clear that the majority of injunction initiatives lacked participation by community organizations or the community, especially at the decision-making level. Prosecutors for thirty initiatives reported participation by law enforcement efforts only, while eleven initiatives were reported as having some degree of participation by a community entity. Of those eleven initiatives, only four initiatives involved community entities in a decision-making role, of which community organizations had a decision-making role in two. Finally, of the fifteen initiatives in which the prosecutor perceived community entities as having a large impact on the decision to seek an injunction, only two identified a community organization as an initiator. In short, community organizations are involved in very few injunction initiatives as decision-makers or initiators, begging the question of whether community organizations should be used as a proxy for the community in research on gang injunctions.

When prosecutors were asked to explain the lack of community organizational involvement in injunction initiatives, three explanations surfaced: (1) there was a strong concern for the safety of target area residents, including members of community organizations; (2) the necessity for the operational security of the injunction initiative precluded involving community organizations in the initiatives; and (3) there was an absence of community organizations in many of the target areas. Although the lack of community organizational involvement was often attributed to a combination of all three explanations, each explanation will be discussed separately.

The first explanation offered by prosecutors is a strong concern for the safety of residents, including organization members. Neighborhood intimidation by gang members has been documented as a serious problem in areas controlled by gangs. Finn and Healey (1996) reported that gang-inspired fear of retaliation is a particularly pervasive problem causing community-wide witness intimidation:

> Both case-specific and community-wide fear of retaliation are often fed by the fear that incarcerated gang members will return quickly to the community after serving brief sentences, or will be able, from behind bars, to arrange for friends or family members to threaten potential witnesses...Prosecutors note that the mere fact that a crime is gang-related can be sufficient to prevent an entire neighborhood from cooperating (Finn and Healey 1996: 2).

The chilling effect of retaliation on community involvement has also been noted in the literature on community policing. In a study of community policing programs in eight cities, Grinc (1994) found that residents frequently offered fear of retaliation from drug dealers as an explanation for the lack of community involvement in community policing initiatives. Kennedy (1993) reported that one of the goals of a problem-oriented/community policing approach to controlling the illicit drug trade in Tampa, Florida was preventing retaliation against cooperating citizens. Pogrebin and Poole (1989) cited fear of retaliation among the factors hampering reporting of crime by Korean immigrants.

Gang injunction prosecutors explained that the gangs targeted by injunctions are usually considered "the worst of the worst" and, according to one prosecutor, "gang members mean business". For this reason, the police and prosecutors are vigilant to avoid putting residents and other community stakeholders, such as business owners and landlords, at risk. Citizen declarations are generally obtained covertly under the promise of confidentiality, with the caveat that they be submitted as evidence only under seal. Some prosecutors do not solicit any declarations from citizens, preferring to rely on community policing officers as a conduit for information from civilians. Members of community organizations are equally, and perhaps more, at risk if a targeted gang learns that a community organization is participating in the injunction initiative. Gang members can target members of the organization for retaliation, even those members having little involvement in the injunction initiative, and it would not be difficult for gang members to learn who the members are and where they live.

An extreme example of the danger of retaliation for assisting authorities against gangs is the murder of community activist James Richards. Richards was a zealous anti-crime activist living in the Oakwood section of Venice, which was included in the target areas for two gang injunctions. Richards was well known in the neighborhood for responding to crime and accident scenes, often arriving before the police. He watched suspected drug corners and photographed illegal drug transactions. He was a Neighborhood Watch block captain, participated in the Model Neighborhood Program, and a member of the Community Police Advisory Board. He also published an online newsletter, *Neighborhood News*, which focused on crime and community issues, sometimes naming offenders and displaying their photographs on the internet website. Richards was assassinated at 4:15 a.m. on October 18, 2000, shot several times in his driveway when he returned home from a twenty-four hour gym (Morrison 2000, Piccalo 2000, Piccalo and Streeter 2000, Streeter 2000).

It is unknown whether Richards was a declarant in either of the two injunctions in the Oakwood area or whether the murder was connected to one of the injunctions. However, two issues of the *Neighborhood News* were quoted in the memorandum of *Points and Authorities* submitted in support of the injunction against the Venice 13 gang (*People v. Venice 13 Gang* (2000), Points and Authorities, p. 8). The injunction was granted approximately six months before his death. Los Angeles police have alleged that two gang members, one from the Venice Shoreline Crips and the other from Venice 13, collaborated in a unique partnership to commit the murder because Richards was considered a snitch and a threat to their illegal narcotics trade (Leovy and Kay 2002).[116]

The second explanation for the lack of community organizational involvement is the concern of prosecutors for the operational security of the injunction initiative. To show the necessity for injunctive relief, there must be continuous nuisance activity by the targeted gang in the target area. If nuisance activity has ceased prior to filing for an injunction, the judge may see the injunction as unnecessary and deny relief. Therefore, it is advantageous to keep the initiative low-keyed so that the activity continues until the first court hearing.

In an initiative not included in this study,[117] flyers about the proposed injunction were distributed and other interventions were employed during the acquisition phase. As a result, the gang left the target area prior to filing for an injunction. Because the public nuisance caused by the gang in the target area was eliminated, there was no need for injunctive relief and the complaint was never filed.

Operational security is also relevant to the legal requirement of notice, under which named defendants are required to be served with official notice that they are subject to a lawsuit. Service of notice consists of giving the defendants a packet of legal documents containing the complaint, the pleadings and prayer for relief, and any order granted by the court, such as a temporary restraining order. If a defendant does not respond to the complaint at the Order to Show Cause (OSC) hearing for a preliminary injunction, the court may grant a default judgment against the defendant. If a defendant is not served prior to the OSC hearing, he/she will not be subject to the injunction order. Because defendants have been known to go to great lengths to avoid service, injunction initiatives are often kept at a very low profile to allow the service of notice on each defendant.

The most frequent explanation given by prosecutors for the lack of community organizational participation is lack of community organizations in the areas targeted by injunctions. Neighborhoods vulnerable to gang control are generally 'high-risk' neighborhoods, characterized by poverty and unemployment, high numbers of school-dropout youths, many single parent and unmarried person households, predominantly multiple-unit dwellings, and a transient population (Esbensen and Huizinga 1996: 70). The high levels of crime and social disruption in these neighborhoods "attest to the relative weakness of their social organizations" (McGabey 1986: 253). Frederick Thrasher, a pioneer in gang research, referred to these neighborhoods as "interstitial regions" in which "fissures and breaks in the structure of social organization" allow gangs to develop (Thrasher 1927/1963: 20).

According to the prosecutors, most of the neighborhoods targeted by injunctions are in urban environments in which people often do not know their neighbors and community organizations are relatively weak. They rank low on the socio-economic ladder, are densely populated, and contain highly transitory populations. In addition, many injunction target areas have high concentrations of new immigrants, some in the country illegally, who are reluctant to become involved with law enforcement because of the fear of deportation and/or bad experiences with the police in their native country. In such highly disorganized neighborhoods, community organizations focusing on addressing quality-of-life issues are scarce (Grinc 1994).

One prosecutor, who was involved in four injunction initiatives, stated that the target areas simply have no community organizations.

Another prosecutor was quoted in another study as stating "there is no there, there" (Maxson and Allen 1997), meaning that no community structure exists in the target area to support community organizations. The community was basically a population of homeowners and residents who were incredibly intimidated by the gang. The only structure that existed was the local school, which was totally uncooperative with the prosecutor because school administrators feared the gang.

Several prosecutors opined that the lack of any community structure on which to build grassroots community organizations is the main reason gangs are able to take control of these neighborhoods. According to one prosecutor, there is a basic irony to the idea of using community organizations in gang injunctions. The neighborhoods that have community organizations aimed at improving the quality-of-life are already doing pretty well without an injunction. The neighborhoods that need the most help are so oppressed that residents do not get together to do anything about community problems. The irony is that prosecutors want the help of community organizations, but if the neighborhood already has one, it generally does not need an injunction. Another prosecutor stated:

> I think the reason the gangs take hold in these neighborhoods is because there aren't any neighborhood organizations. I've seen neighborhood organizations that were viable and real cohesive, and they don't tolerate much. They don't tolerate their neighbors littering their front yards, and they certainly are not going to tolerate a bunch of gangsters taking control of their neighborhood. So, [the gangs] have a way of finding these [disorganized] neighborhoods and taking them over because people don't know enough to keep them out. Of course, by that time it's too late, because they don't know their neighbors and don't work together. Everybody just stays inside and allows this stuff to happen.

The social science literature on communities supports this view. Lyons (1987) asserts that the loss of social infrastructure in communities is the result of the decline of both social interaction within the community and the territorial conception of community. The decline of social interaction is characterized by the estrangement of personal relations between community members. The decline of the territorial conception of community results in the spatial community ceasing to be a place that matters. Because social interaction within the community and the territorial conception of community tend to reinforce each other, apathy toward the spatial community is augmented by the alienation of personal relations.

Warren (1972) also recognized the problems of apathy and alienation, claiming that they contribute to "the general problem of the inability of the community to organize its forces effectively to cope with its specific problems" (Warren 1972. 15). According to Warren, the inability of some communities to sustain the interest and activity of a sufficient number of people over a sufficient period of time for the purpose of remedying community problems is a paramount stumbling block to community organization, particularly where there is a large number of significant debilitating concerns.

The finding of the lack of community infrastructure in neighborhoods targeted for gang injunctions is consistent with research on community involvement in community policing initiatives. In a review of the literature on community policing projects in urban settings, Duffee, Fluellin, and Roscoe (1999) found that community policing is least effective in neighborhoods most in need of effective police service. The task of building a constituency of citizens actively engaged in the processes of their own governance was found to be particularly difficult in urban areas experiencing the most poverty and crime. According to the authors, constituency building requires social capital to facilitate coordination and cooperation for the mutual benefit of all members of the community. Social capital is derived from associational life, which is most scarce in poor, diverse, urban neighborhoods. Without social capital, neighborhoods lack the processes and structures that support the active involvement in governance. Concerted action by neighborhood groups and organizations is critical to strengthening neighborhoods. Crime prevention is most successful when integrated with existing community associations and least successful in neighborhoods with little associational life. Although the police are able to improve conditions in some neighborhoods without significant participation by residents or changes in the structure of neighborhood life, sustaining those gains in neighborhoods with little social capital resources requires long-term changes to the social infrastructure of the community. Thus, the areas most in need are the least able to participate in the co-production of public safety (Duffee, Fluellin, and Roscoe 1999).

In his study of eight community policing projects, Grinc (1994) commented on the reasons for the inability of police departments to organize and maintain active community involvement in community policing initiatives. Among the reasons is the highly disorganized nature of the areas targeted by community policing initiatives, making it difficult to find well-organized community groups focused on quality-of-life issues. Most residents interviewed in the research stated that the level of community organization in their neighborhood was either low or average, attributing the absence of active community groups to fear of crime and to the burden of day-to-day survival in highly disorganized neighborhoods.

There may be other reasons for the lack of involvement by community organizations that were not mentioned by prosecutors, but were implied by the circumstances surrounding some injunction initiatives. According to Grinc (1994), the assumption that community residents and organizations will actively participate in community policing initiatives "largely ignores or grossly underestimates the level of hostility that has existed between the police and members of poor and minority communities who have often borne the brunt of police abuses" (Grinc 1994: 446). The community opposition reported in three initiatives and the reluctance by key community organizations, such as a school and a community outreach service, to participate in injunction initiatives support the possibility of hostility and suspicion about the intentions behind injunction initiatives.

Another potential explanation involves neighborhood and cultural loyalty. Regarding neighborhood loyalty, Finn and Healey state:

> Many communities in which gangs operate are worlds unto themselves – places where people live, attend school, and work all within a radius of only a few blocks beyond which they rarely venture. As a result, victims and witnesses are often the children of a defendant's friends or relatives, member of the same church as the defendant, or classmates or neighbors (Finn and Healey 1996: 4).

Neighborhood loyalty may be especially strong in multigenerational gang neighborhoods, which are targeted by two-thirds of the initiatives.[118] In addition, the sense of cultural loyalty among some minority and ethnic groups often leads to reluctance to testify against other members of the group. Although this study attempted to account for these kinds of loyalties by inquiring about organizations that were expected to participate but did not, prosecutors did not identify any minority or ethnic organizations that failed to participate as expected.

It is also possible that community organizations were present in the target areas, but failed to step forward to participate in injunction initiatives. In a review of the research on the involvement of community organizations in crime prevention efforts, Skogan (1988) noted that community organizations usually have a broader agenda than crime prevention. More importantly, he distinguished between two types of community organization by differences in demographics, agendas, and attitudes toward law enforcement initiatives. *Preservationist* organizations are typically found in stable, homogeneous middle-class areas with high levels of home ownership by residents. They generally focused on preserving the status quo and maintaining property values. Because of the homogeneous character of their constituents, the agenda of preservationist organizations consists of maintaining the established neighborhood interests, customs, and values and preserving property values and the racial mix of the neighborhood population. Although they seldom form in response to crime, preservationist organizations generally support law enforcement initiatives (Skogan 1988).

In contrast, *insurgent* organizations focus on upsetting the current distribution of status and property. They most commonly arise in low-income, high-crime areas that contain high-density, deteriorated neighborhoods with heterogeneous, highly transitory, tenant populations. Insurgent organizations are least likely to feature crime prevention programs for two reasons. First, residents of low-income areas are more concerned about paying their rent and putting food on the table than about participating in anti-crime efforts. Because constituents tend to rank crime prevention as low on their list of priorities, insurgent organizations are under pressure to produce agendas having a higher priority and supplying material benefits, such as jobs and clinics. Insurgent organizations typically pursue a broad agenda that focuses on the root causes of crime, such as poverty, poor education, employment opportunities, and racial discrimination, as opposed to the proximate causes of crime, such as 'hanging out' by youths and young adults. Second, the relationship between the constituents of insurgent organizations and law enforcement agencies, particularly the police, is often antagonistic. Because their constituents often fear and resent the manner by which law enforcement officials exercise their authority, insurgent organizations are often more interested in monitoring police misconduct and pressing for police accountability than in obtaining greater resources to fight crime and disorder. Therefore, insurgent organizations may be hesitant to participate in an initiative that would legitimize the role of law enforcement, especially if the initiative lacks a component to address the root causes of the crime problem. As a result, insurgent organizations may refuse to become involved in a strategy viewed as suppressive and discriminating, which has been a frequent criticism of gang abatements by injunction (Skogan 1988).[119]

This study attempted to address reluctance by community organizations to participate in injunction initiatives by asking prosecutors if there were any organizations that failed to participate as expected. Prosecutors for only two initiatives stated that community organizations failed to participate as expected. However, because of their law enforcement role, prosecutors may not be in the best position to identify existing community organization in high-risk neighborhoods or to request their involvement in an innovative and controversial initiative targeting neighborhood youths with proscriptions against normally legal activities.

It is also probable that the combination of low-profile operations and the disorganized character of injunction target areas is responsible for the general lack of participation by community organizations. In his analysis of public involvement of the Chicago Alternative Policing Strategy (CAPS), a community policing initiative, Skogan reported that attendance rates at community meetings was highest in poor high-crime communities, which contrasts with the historical poor police-community relations in low-income and disenfranchised areas. The community meetings, which were run by police officers, were the principal forum for airing and tackling neighborhood issues and formulating joint police-citizen action plans (Skogan 2000).

Although Chicago's experience indicates that it is possible to generate interest in anti-crime programs in disorganized neighborhoods, the CAPS program differs significantly from gang injunction initiatives in both focus and publicity. CAPS is a long-term, citywide program that does not focus on a single problem. It is also the subject of an aggressive, multi-component, citywide marketing campaign to significantly raise the public's awareness of the program. In contrast, gang injunction prosecutors focus on a single problem in a limited geographic area and generally avoid publicity prior to filing the case in court. In most cases, prosecutors run a low-profile operation because of strong concerns about the operational security of the injunction initiatives and the safety of cooperating citizens.

The combination of low-profile initiatives and predominately disorganized neighborhoods most likely significantly reduced the level of participation in injunction initiatives by existing community organizations. Community organizations that existed in the target areas most likely were insurgent groups that would be hesitant to legitimize law enforcement efforts by participating in the initiatives. In addition, prosecutors might not be in the best position to identify insurgent organizations or to bring them 'on board'. Therefore, it is questionable whether community organizations should be used as a proxy for the community in research on gang injunction initiatives, or on any problem-oriented intervention in highly disorganized neighborhoods.

MODEL FOR COMMUNITY INVOLVEMENT

One injunction initiative, the *Lennox Gang Violence Suppression Program*,[120] is prominent in the involvement of community organizations. The injunction *People v. Lennox 13* (1996) is the gang suppression component of the Lennox Gang Violence Suppression Program, which is presently in its sixth year of funding by the Governor's Office of Criminal Justice Planning. The intent of the initiative is to provide gang intervention and suppression in the unincorporated area of Lennox. The program has five collaborative partners: the LADA, the Los Angeles County Sheriff's Department, the Los Angeles County Probation Department, the Lennox Unified School District, and the Richstone Family Center, which is the lead agency.

The state program, entitled the *Gang Violence Suppression Program*, is a multi-component program to reduce the level of gang violence in communities and to divert potentially dangerous gang activity into a more positive and constructive behavior. The Law Enforcement and Prosecution Components attempt to swiftly identify, prosecute, and remove violent perpetrators from the community, while the Probation Component exercises intensive supervision in the community to prevent incidents of violence (Office of Criminal Justice Programs 2001). Funding is available to law enforcement agencies, schools, district attorney's offices, and community-based organizations.

This program is unique for an injunction initiative, in that a community-based organization took the lead in forming the coalition of agencies and applying for the grant. The Richstone Family Center, the lead agency for the program, is a private, non-profit, community-based social service agency located in Hawthorne, which neighbors Lennox. Its mission is the treatment and prevention of child abuse and the reduction of violence in families and communities. In existence for approximately twenty-eight years, the Center was originally formed to prevent and provide treatment for child abuse. However, the staff came to realize that, to make the world safer for children and to be advocates for children and families, it needed to deal with violence in the community and the schools, as well as in families. Therefore, the Center broadened its mission statement to include community and school violence.

The Office of Criminal Justice Planning (OCJP) sought a program in Lennox because of the community's long-standing reputation for gang problems. It is a unique area under the flight path of the Los Angeles International Airport, very poor and depressed because of the noise of planes constantly flying overhead. A small, very tight community of approximately 1.3 square miles and 30,000 residents, the community is ninety percent Hispanic, with many illegal immigrants, few businesses, and few community organizations. It is an unincorporated part of Los Angeles County, with no municipal organization and few services. At the time of the injunction, there was little infrastructure to support an effective community organization, and any organizations that were present had been ineffective at improving the quality-of-life in the community. As a result, gangs and drugs thrive in Lennox, with eight to ten percent of the population actively involved in multigenerational gangs.

To qualify for funding from the OCJP, a district attorney's office, a probation department, a local law enforcement agency, a local school district, and a local community-based organization had to jointly apply for the grant. Although the collaborative partnership was mandated by the grant, it was up to the partners to determine the needs of the community and the roles of the various agencies. An advisory body for the grant, the Lennox Gang Violence Suppression Council, which is chaired by the representative from the Richstone Center, was formed.

Once funded, the council examined the gang activity in the community and discussed what interventions would be effective. Although they could do things in the schools and the home aimed at prevention, the council realized that suppression of the gang activity in the community was vital to give the community a sense that something positive could be done and to elicit its support for the prevention programs. Without suppression, the residents would still have to live in a community heavily impacted by a gang that was terrorizing the neighborhood, and any positive experience from counseling in school or in the Richstone Center would be negated as soon as the client returned to the community. Therefore, suppression was recognized as an equally important component as prevention and other interventions.

The role of the LADA was to reduce gang violence and suppress gang activity in the Lennox community. When the partners met to talk about options and successful potential interventions, the prosecutor assigned to the program suggested a gang injunction. The LADA had recently completed a successful injunction in Norwalk. To introduce the injunction initiative to the community, a series of community meetings was held, during which the issue of the injunction – what it would mean and what would be needed from the community – was explained.

A very specific area on the pathway that feeds the middle school from Lennox, which the Lennox 13 gang controlled and through which all students from Lennox had to walk to get to school, was initially targeted for the injunction. There had been numerous incidents of gang-related violence on one particular street corner and the adjacent area, through which the school pathway traversed. Students were constantly hassled, robbed, and recruited by the gang while walking to and from the middle school.

The prosecutor explained in detail what area was being targeted, what the injunction entailed, what would be needed from the community – that people would have to come forward anonymously to provide information and declarations and that the safety of informants and declarants would be accommodated as much as possible. The prosecutor also dispelled myths about gang injunctions, such as allowing the police to stop anyone who looked like a gang member instead of only defendants named in the injunction order. When the council stated that the injunction component would not go forward without the support of the community, there was an overwhelmingly positive response by residents in favor of the injunction.

The response was surprising because the community was very small and tight, with a high amount of multigenerational gang membership, the kind of place where everyone knows what is going on, but nobody talks about it. There was community-wide intimidation against speaking out against the gang or calling the police. If a police car showed up at a complainant's house, somebody across the street would know, and the caller was likely to experience some kind of retaliatory action from the gang. So the overwhelmingly positive response in a very intimidated community suggested that the injunction would be valued, supported, and desired by the community, and the council decided to go ahead with the injunction. Had the community been hesitant or negative, the council would not have gone forward with the injunction.

The primary gang problems identified by the prosecutor were violence, especially gang-related shootings, and huge groups of gang members hanging out on every corner on the pathway to the middle school. The activity was centered on a hamburger stand. Often, thirty or more 'dressed-down' gang members would hang around the hamburger stand and in the adjoining areas. Besides hassling, robbing, and recruiting middle school students, the area drew violence from rival gangs, who knew where to find Lennox 13 members.

The injunction was only one component of the program, which has expanded in the six years since its initiation. Each of the partner agencies has its own objectives and goals within the broader program. The Richstone Center provides mental health counseling on school campuses and at the center. It also coordinates with the Lennox Unified School District to provide mentoring and with the other agencies to provide community education and training, as well as sponsoring community events. The school district identifies at-risk youths who are beginning gang involvement and provides counseling and other intervention services to the youths and their parents. The school district also provides many after-school programs, often in conjunction with the Boy's and Girl's Club, as positive alternatives to gangs. A computer lab was set up in the school under the program.

Initially a deputy probation officer was assigned to provide counseling in the school. That position has been translated into a hardcore probation officer to deal exclusively with Lennox 13 gang members, providing immediate intervention for probation violators. The Sheriff's Department currently provides enforcement of the injunction and other gang-related crimes. During the injunction acquisition process, deputy sheriffs assisted with the investigation and acted as translators to help the prosecutor obtain civilian declarations. Although there were few community organizations in the target area, other community entities that were involved to some extent in the program include a church, a community coordinating council, and a Catholic charity organization involved in counseling.

Besides obtaining the injunction and prosecuting injunction violators, the LADA vertically prosecutes gang violence in the area. One prosecutor handles the case from beginning to end, facilitating both convictions and community support for the prosecutions by making victims feel comfortable when coming forward to report gang-related crimes. According to the prosecutor, there is a strict 'no tolerance' policy on witness intimidation. Witness intimidation is prosecuted as a 'life' crime under Proposition 21, which imposes a life sentence for witness intimidation by gang members, even for lesser crimes such as auto theft.[121]

While each partner has its own objectives and goals, the collaboration acts together to provide a comprehensive anti-gang program. For example, if a youth is cited for a curfew violation, counseling is provided to both the youth and his/her parents by the Richstone Center so that the parents are aware of the youth's gang involvement.

The target area for the injunction consisted of two areas, separated by an adjoining area in which the preliminary injunction was initially not in force. The adjoining area was not included in the initial target area because, at the time, the court was reluctant to enjoin large areas, causing the prosecutor to be conservative in delineating the target area. After the preliminary injunction was granted, the gang's activities displaced into the adjoining area. Because larger target areas had been enjoined in other cases, the prosecutor expanded the target area to include all of the territory claimed by the Lennox 13 gang in the request for a permanent injunction.

According to the chairperson of the Council, there has been an immediate change in the target area since the injunction was granted. Although gang violence is still a major problem in Lennox, there have been fewer shootings, mainly because the large groups of gang members are no longer hanging out on the street corners and providing easy targets for rivals. Before the injunction, Lennox 13 had a large street presence – hanging out, writing graffiti, blocking the sidewalk, and harassing residents. Today, in places where thirty or more gang members used to be hanging out, gang members are rarely seen at all or, when visible, are only seen in small groups of five or six. While still present in the neighborhood, graffiti is considerably less frequent, and the number of minor infractions is lower. The injunction immediately made the pathways around the school safe and cleaned up the area, which was one of the primary goals of the entire program. While some gang members did move their activities into neighboring Hawthorne, expanding the target area with the permanent injunction solved any displacement problems within Lennox. The Sheriff's Department is credited with contributing to the success of the injunction because of its commitment to file charges against injunction violators.

CHAPTER VII

Policy Implications

Civil gang abatement is one of the most creative legal interventions that has been developed by California prosecutors to address the persistent gang problems facing many California communities. However, chronic and emerging gang problems are not limited to California. Gangs and the accompanying violence and disorder have proliferated in urban, suburban, and rural settings in every state (Maxson 1998), causing affected communities to search for innovative responses. In the wake of the U.S. Supreme Court's decision in *City of Chicago v. Morales* (1999), there may be increasing interest in gang injunctions as a policy response by communities experiencing chronic or accelerating gang activity. This increased interest is evident in former Vice President Al Gore's proposal to "provide federal assistance for the establishment of gang-free zones . . . created under federal court injunctions banning the wearing of gang-related clothing in specific areas and imposing curfews on gang members there" (Gerstenzang, 2000).

Civil gang abatement fulfills Packer's (1968) vision of law enforcement agencies employing civil remedies to alleviate their reliance on the criminal law in the fight against crime and disorder. Although it does not, nor was it ever intended to, replace criminal prosecutions of gang members, civil gang abatement does give the police and prosecutors a powerful tool in their attempts to ameliorate the destructive influences of gangs on vulnerable neighborhoods. Gang injunctions attack the group dynamics that are so vital to the gang's power over a neighborhood, as well as the numerous low-level nuisance activities that add to the disorder and reduce the quality-of-life in a neighborhood. As Packer envisioned, the gang injunction puts named defendants on notice that they are being watched as individuals, while allowing them to remain free members of society within the predetermined restraints of the injunction order (Packer 1968: 253-55). However heavy-handed gang injunctions may appear, they are not nearly as suppressive as criminal remedies aimed at curbing gang activity, such as Chicago's now-defunct *Gang Congregation*

Ordinance, which resulted in approximately 40,000 arrests over three years. In contrast to such ordinances, gang injunctions are not applied against all gangs, but only against gangs shown to cause a serious public nuisance in a limited geographic area. In addition, the provisions of gang injunctions do not apply to all citizens, or even to all members of the targeted gangs. The restraints of the injunctions are generally limited to hard-core members of the targeted gangs – the "worst of the worst."

Gang injunctions are far less draconian than other civil remedies used to curb gang activity. Cicero's ordinance effectively banishing identified gang members from the city and the eviction ordinances targeting gang members affect not only the gangster, but also the members of his/her family. In contrast, the restrictions under gang injunction only apply to named defendants, based on their predetermined threat to the community.

Are gang injunctions effective? Although not the focus of this study, this is a controversial issue that is addressed through the perceptions of the prosecutors, who assessed effectiveness primarily through anecdotal evidence and/or crime statistics. All responding prosecutors reported that their initiatives were effective, including those in which a temporary restraining order was obtained but a preliminary injunction was denied. Prosecutors for less than one-quarter of the initiatives reported some evidence of displacement of a targeted gang's activities to a location outside the target area. The lack of displacement was mainly attributed to the territorial nature of the targeted gangs, which generally were hemmed into the target area by physical barriers and/or rival gangs. This finding is in keeping with Grogger (2000), who found a 5 to 10% reduction in serious crime with no evidence of displacement, and contrary to the position of critics that injunctions merely displace gang activity into adjoining areas, which was supported by the Blythe Street study (ACLU 1997).

The real controversy over gang injunctions turns on a central concept of the American legal tradition – equal treatment under the law. The nature of any government response that, under the guise of the common good and community safety, imposes greater restrictions on the liberty of a distinct group of individuals is an important policy issue for both criminal justice administrators and affected communities. If the response is intended to generically suppress offensive conduct, it is appropriate that it be applied equally to all citizens through statutory enactments and traditional law enforcement techniques. However, if the response is intended to address a particular and persistent problem by an identifiable group of individuals in a localized context where the criminal law has proven ineffective, disparate application of the response may be justified.

Since Goldstein (1990) first advanced the concept of problem-oriented policing, the acceptance of the problem-oriented perspective as an operating philosophy for law enforcement agencies has accelerated. When addressing unremitting anti-social behavior, this philosophy will increasingly subject defined groups of individuals to tailored government interventions, some of which will fall outside the bounds of the criminal law. This study has focused on whether one type of tailored response, the gang injunction, fulfills the dimensions of flexibility and community involvement, which are central to the problem-oriented philosophy.

There is sufficient evidence of variation to conclude that gang injunctions fulfill the dimension of flexibility by addressing local gang problems with customized provisions based on specific local circumstances. There is a strong tendency toward variation in the problem identification and, to a lesser extent, the response variables. The lack of variation in the analysis variables can be explained by the fairly narrow targeting by gang injunctions. As a response of last resort, gang injunction initiatives tend to target gangs and neighborhoods with similar characteristics, due at least in part to legal status of the injunction as an extraordinary legal remedy to be used only when other legal remedies, such as the criminal law, have been exhausted. The strongest and most straightforward evidence of flexibility is observed in the categorization of injunction initiatives by the requested relief. The high level of variation in the injunction categories – high-drug, high-crime, and high-disorder – clearly indicates that the injunction provisions are tailored responses to a variety of localized gang activities.

The analysis of the dimension of community involvement paints a different picture. On the whole, there is little evidence of the involvement of the community in the decision to seek a gang injunction. The ideal of legitimizing gang injunctions through the involvement of local community entities in the decision-making process should be tempered by the structural realities of the neighborhoods most in need of injunctive relief, as well as the valid concerns about the operational security of the injunction initiative and the physical safety of participating community members. The assumption that community organizations can serve as a proxy for the community is incorrect, at least in the highly disorganized neighborhoods commonly targeted by gang injunctions. Although there was little involvement by community organizations, the needs of the community are an important consideration to prosecutors. Many prosecutors stressed that gang injunctions are intended to meet the needs of the communities, regardless of who requests the initiatives or the degree of community involvement in the initiatives.

Community involvement in law enforcement decision-making has generally been a weak area of problem- and community-oriented initiatives in similar neighborhoods. Perhaps the ideal of community involvement in the emerging field of community justice should be moderated so that initiatives in highly disorganized neighborhoods are not set up for failure. Law enforcement administrators should be aware that the constant pressure to "do something now" must be reconciled with the fact that what realistically can and should be done varies according to the neighborhood (Duffee, Fluellen, and Roscoe 1999). Gang injunctions may represent an acceptable policy response for communities facing serious gang activity as long as the limits of community involvement are kept in perspective according to the targeted neighborhood.

In addition, prosecutors should be more creative in trying to involve the community in the decision-making process. Where they exist, community organizations can be approach covertly by meeting representatives in locations that are removed from the target area. Attempts should be made to bring insurgent organizations (Skogan 1988) 'on board' through reasonable concessions, such as 'carve outs', that would reduce community opposition to injunction initiatives. Such concessions might also serve to reduce the historic hostility that exists between law enforcement agencies and members of poor and minority communities. The community legitimatization of injunction initiatives is important if the initiatives are to be perceived as supporting community change, rather than as merely more of the same suppression tactics imposed on vulnerable neighborhoods in the past.

The ultimate decision by a community to employ gang injunctions to abate local gang activity is ideological and beyond the scope of this study. Although the California Supreme Court has addressed the issue of constitutionality in *People v. Acuna* (1997), the decision to use the strategy depends on the community's perception of the proper balance between individual and community rights.[122] While the balancing of costs and benefits is an important concern for public agencies with limited resources, the issue of individual liberties versus community safety is most controversial when the propriety of any extraordinary criminal justice response to a problem is being considered. In a democratic society, the means used to achieve a goal are as, if not more, important than the end result.

Despite the limits of community involvement in highly disorganized neighborhoods, this study suggests that civil gang abatement is a problem-oriented intervention addressing neighborhood gang problems. The flexibility implicit in injunctive relief gives prosecutors the ability to customize injunction provisions to meet the needs of both the community and the police, regardless of how those needs are identified. Prosecutors are not merely making a rhetorical claim to using a problem-oriented response in order to mask purely suppressive intentions and to allay criticism. Injunctions have been successfully used to address many other forms of anti-social conduct, so why not combat destructive gang activity in vulnerable neighborhoods with injunctive relief? Such an approach to persistent neighborhood problems is a necessary departure from our traditional "one size fits all" approach to crime prevention, which casts a much larger net. The strategy of "policing by injunction" is an appropriate response to gang problems in communities that wish to tailor legal proscriptions against anti-social conduct by "the worst of the worst".

FUTURE RESEARCH

There is much research to be conducted if the civil gang abatement phenomenon is to be fully understood. It is difficult to obtain more than a general sense of the strategy through a retrospective study of the universe of gang injunctions based on court documents and the perceptions of prosecutors. Prospective studies of the acquisition process in several future injunction initiatives conducted by different agencies are needed. These studies should focus on the role of the community, to determine whether civil gang abatement meets the ideal of community involvement under the problem-oriented and community justice philosophies *from the perception of the community*. Short- and long-term impact studies are also needed to determine whether the injunctions give neighborhoods immediate relief from the destructive influence of gang activity and whether neighborhoods take advantage of the opportunity to re-establish informal social control in their public space. On a broader note, further research needs to be conducted on the capacity of high-risk neighborhoods to meaningfully participate in innovative criminal justice initiatives.

This study into civil gang abatement as a tool to "police by injunction" merely scratches the surface of research opportunities into gang injunctions in particular and community justice/problem-oriented initiatives in general. Research is lacking into the use of injunctions by community prosecutors for other persistent public order problems, such as prostitution. In addition, research is needed into other innovative measures employed by prosecutors under the rubric of both community prosecution and traditional case oriented prosecution. The time is ripe for practitioners and researchers to fully explore alternatives to the traditional "one size fits all" approach to crime prevention, such as civil gang abatement.

Appendices

APPENDIX A: Injunction List

Case Title	Case #	File Date	Location
1. People v. Eastside/Westside Wilmas	NC 030080	5/23/2001	LA - Wilmington
2. People v. Pacoima Project Boys	PC 027254 Y	3/20/2001	LA - Pacoima
3. People v. Linda Vista 13	GIC 745162	3/16/2000	San Diego
4. People v. Venice 13	SC 060375	2/10/2000	LA - Venice/Oakwood
5. People v. Harbor City Gang / Crips	NC 026769	11/12/1999	LA - Harbor City
6. City of Oceanside v. Varrio Mesa Locos	N 82223	8/18/1999	Oceanside
7. People v. Sur Crazy Ones	SCV 42552	6/24/1999	San Bernardino
8. People v. Venice Shoreline Crips	SC 057282	5/21/1999	LA - Venice
9. People v. Culver City Boys	SC 056980	4/23/1999	LA - Mar Vista
10. People v. Langdon Street Gang	LC 048292	3/26/1999	LA - North Hills
11. People v. Alcala	SB 7194	12/15/1998	National City
12. People v. Lincoln Park	725795	11/13/1998	San Diego
13. City Compton v. CompVarrio Tortilla Flats	TC 011598	8/25/1998	Compton
14. People v. Alcarez	115095	8/12/1998	Salinas
15. City of San Marcos v. Varrio San Marcos	N 78777	7/30/1998	San Marcos
16. People v. Original Bloods	CV 05505	7/28/1998	Stockton
17. People v. Harpys Gang	BC 192678	7/16/1998	LA - USC area
18. People v. Arroyo	CV 775225	7/10/1998	San Jose
19. People v. 18th St . Gang	BC 190334	5/1/1998	LA - Westside
20. People v. Mara Salvathrucha	BC 187039	3/1/1998	LA - E Hollywood
21. City of Oceanside v. Varrio Pesole Locos	N0 76652	11/24/1997	Oceanside
22. People v. 7th St. Gang	SCV42552	11/12/1997	San Bernardino
23. People v. 18th St. Gang	BC 175684	8/1/1997	LA - Pico-Union
24. City of Long Beach v. West Coast Crips	NC 021240	5/5/1997	Long Bch
25. People v. Brown Nation	VC 24170	3/27/1997	Bellflower/Long Bch
26. People v. 18th St. Gang	BC 167915	3/19/1997	LA - Alsace/Jefferson Park
27. City of Inglewood v. Crenshaw Mafia Gang	YC 028318	12/17/1996	Inglewood
28. City of Commerce v. Chopper-12	BC 155927	8/20/1996	Commerce
29. People v. Lennox-13	YC 027006	8/15/1996	Lennox
30. People v. Headhunters	SCV 30441	6/20/1996	Fontana
31. City of Pasadena v. Villa Boys, Krazy Boys	GC017109	6/13/1996	Pasadena
32. City Redondo Beach v. N. Side Redondo 13	YC 026580	4/30/1996	Redondo Beach
33. City of Pasadena v. Pasadena Denver Lanes	GC 015651	10/25/1995	Pasadena
34. City of Long Beach v. West Side Longos	NC 17601	10/6/1995	Long Beach
35. City of Norwalk v.Orange St. Locos	VC016746	7/21/1994	Norwalk
36. People v. 'B' St. Boys	735405-4	5/18/1994	Oakland
37. People v. Avalos	CV 739089	3/16/1994	San Jose
38. People v. Amaya	713223	6/30/1993	Westminister
39. People v. Acuna	729322	2/26/1993	San Jose
40. People v. Blythe St. Gang	LC 20525	2/22/1993	LA - Van Nuys
41. People v. Acosta	EC 010205	10/7/1992	Burbank
42. People v. Playboy Gangster Crips	WEC 118860	10/26/1987	LA

APPENDIX B: Behavioral Index -Variables, Coding, Frequencies

***Drug Index** (10 proscriptions) - Behavior associated with the illegal sale/possession/use of controlled substances (drugs):*

bicycle = use of a bicycle (mainly associated with the illegal sale of drugs).
Frequency present = 9

climbing = climbing trees, walls, fences, or roofs (mainly associated with theillegal sale of drugs).
Frequency present = 15

drugpres = knowingly being in the presence of another who is in possession of illegal drugs.
Frequency present = 19

drugproh = proscription on the illegal possession, sale, or use of drugs.
Frequency present = 30

infldrug = being under the influence of drugs.
Frequency present = 7

paraph = possession of drug paraphernalia.
Frequency present = 28

posscomm = possession in public of electronic communications equipment, including pager, beeper, cell phone, flashlight, and police scaner (mainly associated with the illegal sale of drugs).
Frequency present = 15

recwarn = recruiting othersas lookouts
Frequency present = 24

signalle = signaling to others about the presence of law enforcement officers.
Frequency present = 31

signveh = signaling, approaching, or stopping vehicles or communicating with the occupants of vehicles (mainly associated with the illegal sale of drugs).
Frequency present = 23

***Crime Index** (21 Proscriptions) - Behavior comprising crimes and ordinance violations:*

alcund21 = possession of alcohol by a defendant under 21 old.
Frequency present = 3

brandwpn = brandishing/displaying a firearm or any weapon.
Frequency present = 2

burgtool = possession of burglary and being in the presence of a person in possession of burglary tools, including those used to break into vehicles.
Frequency present = 12

exhbspd = exhibitions of speed with a motor vehicle.
Frequency present = 7

fighting = fighting or challenging to fight in any place open to public view or hearing.
Frequency present = 24

gambling = gambling in public, including being in the presence of gambling.
Frequency present = 7

graffiti = applying graffiti and defacing public/private property.
Frequency present = 34

graftool = being in possession of devices with which to apply graffiti, including aerosol paint containers, felt tip markers, or other marking substances.
Frequency present = 32

harbor = harboring, hiding, sheltering, or assisting another to evade law enforcement officers.
Frequency present = 8

homeintr = demanding or forcing entry into the home of another, including by the use of threats to gain access.
Frequency present = 9

intcompl = intimidating or contacting complainants/witnesses of any of the gang's activities, including complainants and declarants to the injunction.
Frequency present = 33

litter = littering.
Frequency present = 28

miscrime = miscellaneous crimes that do not fit into other categories, including "obey all laws".
Frequency present = 8

obstrpub = obstructing a public thoroughfare (street, sidewalk, etc.).
Frequency present = 39

possdw = possession of a dangerous weapon, including firearms, ammunition, or any illegal weapon.
Frequency present = 39
pubdrink = drinking or possession of an open container of an alcoholic beverage in any place open to public view.
Frequency present = 34
puburin = urinating or defecating in any place open to public view.
Frequency present = 23
shooting = discharge of any firearms.
Frequency present = 17
throwing = throwing objects at cars, persons, or animals.
Frequency present = 5
trespass = trespassing or being on the property of another without permission.
Frequency present = 39
vandal = vandalism to property, excluding graffiti.
Frequency present = 27

***Disorder Index** (23 proscriptions) - Non-criminal behavior associated with disorder:*

abandpro = being in or on abandoned property.
Frequency present = 14
assyesno = Presence of any proscriptions against associating or congregating.
Frequency present = 40
attschev = attending any event, on or off campus, sponsored by a designated school without prior consent from the school administration.
Frequency present = 5
bannedta = banned from entering the target area.
Frequency present = 2
carrepr = possession of auto parts without valid proof of purchase or performing maintenance or repairs to any vehicle unless the defendant is the registered owner or in possession of written permission by the registered owner.
Frequency present = 3
clothing = wearing clothing or accessories with lettering identifying one as a member of the gang.
Frequency present = 10
coopwpol = refusing to cooperate with the police, including giving false information to the police concerning one's name, date of birth, or probation status.
Frequency present = 2
curfadlt = curfew provisions for adult (18 years of age or older) defendants or all defendants regardless of age.
Frequency present = 29
curfmin = separate curfew provisions for minor (under 18 years of age) defendants.
Frequency present = 26
dogs = possession of a dog with the intent to harm another.
Frequency present = 2
handsign = flashing hand signs or other forms of communication indicating gang membership.
Frequency present = 9
harasint = harassing, annoying, intimidating, or threatening anyone within the target area.
Frequency present = 35
inflalc = being under the influence of alcohol.
Frequency present = 5
locrstr = special restrictions regarding presence in specific locations, including parks and specific addresses, excluding school property.
Frequency present = 3
loiter = loitering for any purpose, including the illegal sale of drugs and applying graffiti.
Frequency present = 7
noise = making excessive noise.
Frequency present = 25
noncrim = miscellaneous non-criminal proscriptions that do not fit into other categories, such as looking into an unoccupied parked vehicle, failure to attend school, or failure to carry valid identification.
Frequency present = 2
opencont = being within a certain proximity (10 feet, 100 feet) of an open container of alcohol.
Frequency present = 13

prespdw = knowingly being in the presence of another in possession of a dangerous weapon.
Frequency present = 25

separate = separate provisions for one or more named defendants.
Frequency present = 2

tarival = being in any vehicle, other than a public bus, with any other member of the gang while in a rival gang's defined turf.
Frequency present = 3.

toygun = possession of or knowingly being in the presence of another in possession of a toy gun, replica gun, or water gun.
Frequency present = 5

useveh = using a vehicle to store drugs, dangerous weapons, or other illegal material/contraband
Frequency present = 13

APPENDIX C: Assignment of Categories

Injunction	crime	disorder	drug	category
Eastside/Westside Wilmas	low	low	high	high drug
Pacoima Project Boys	high	low	high	high crime
Linda Vista 13	low	high	low	high disorder
Venice 13	low	high	high	high disorder
Harbor City/Harbor City Crips	low	low	high	high drug
Varrio Mesa Locos	high	high	low	high disorder
Sur Crazy Ones	high	low	low	high crime
Venice Shoreline Crips	low	high	high	high drug
Culver City Boys	low	low	high	high drug
Langdon St. Gang	low	low	high	high drug
Acala (Old Town National City)	high	high	low	high disorder
Lincoln Park	low	high	low	high disorder
Varrio Tortilla Flats	low	high	high	high drug
Alcarez (Vagos)	high	low	high	high crime
Varrio San Marcos	high	high	low	high disorder
Original Bloods	high	low	low	high crime
Harpys	high	low	low	high crime
Arroyo (Norteno/Sureno)	high	low	low	high crime
18th St / Westside	low	high	high	high disorder
Mara Salvathrucha	low	high	high	high drug
Varrio Pesole Locos	high	low	low	high crime
7th St	high	low	low	high crime
18th St / Pico-Union	low	high	high	high drug
West Coast Crips	low	high	high	high disorder
Brown Nation	low	low	high	high drug
18th St. / Alsace (Jefferson Park)	low	high	high	high disorder
Crenshaw Mafia	low	low	high	high drug
Chopper 12	low	high	high	high disorder
Lennox-13	low	low	high	high drug
Headhunters	high	low	low	high crime
Villa Boys/Krazy Boys	low	low	high	high drug
North Side Redondo 13	low	high	low	high disorder
Pasadena Denver Lanes	low	low	high	high drug
West Side Longos	low	high	high	high disorder
Orange St. Locos	low	high	low	high disorder
'B' St. Boys	high	low	high	high crime
Avalos (Varrio Mexicanos Locos)	high	low	high	high crime
Amaya (West Trece)	high	low	low	high crime
Acuna (Varrio Sureno Treces/Locos)	high	low	high	high crime
Blythe St.	low	high	low	high disorder
Acosta (Barrio Elmwood Rifa)	high	low	low	high crime
Playboy Gangster Crips	high	high	low	high disorder

Endnotes

[1]There have also been several injunctions targeting gang activities at county fairs, street festivals, and specific residences or other private property, such as a shopping plaza and pool hall (Schweizer 1999, Skipitares 2000, Wolcott 1999). Because these actions are limited to specific events or do not restrict activities on public thoroughfares or property, such as parks and recreation centers, they are not as controversial as gang injunctions that prohibit association and other non-criminal activities at all times on both public and private property.

[2] The only successful initiatives to obtain a gang injunction outside California were in Austin and San Antonio, Texas. Initiatives in New York City and Phoenix, Arizona were denied. The cities of Cincinnati, Ohio, Albuquerque, New Mexico, and Houston, Texas have contemplated, but have not commenced, injunction initiatives.

[3] Civilian declarants are persons providing sworn declarations who are not associated with law enforcement agencies.

[4] In two cases, a temporary restraining order was granted, but the preliminary injunction was denied. In one case, the action was dismissed at the request of the prosecutor because the nuisance activity had been abated by other interventions. One case was still in litigation at the time of this study.

[5] An *ex parte* proceeding is a judicial hearing brought for the benefit of one party, without notice to or the opportunity to challenge by the adverse party.

[6] An interlocutory order is an order made during the course of litigation. It does not dispose of the case, but addresses the exigency of the case and is, therefore, subject to change by a final decree.

[7] According to one prosecutor, *amicus curiae* status is generally "an appellate animal", which is requested at the appellate, rather than the trial, level. However, superior court judges have granted *amicus curiae* status at the trial level in several gang injunction cases because of the broad public interest in these cases.

[8] In one case, there was a seven-year gap between the preliminary and permanent injunctions, during which the prosecutor returned to court several times to add defendants to the action.

[9] In a recent initiative, the City Prosecutor of Long Beach obtained a permanent injunction within three weeks of filing the case (Los Angeles Deputy City Attorney James McDougal, personal communication, November 27, 2001; City News Service 2001). There is no indication that it was preceded by a preliminary injunction.

[10] *People v. Amaya* (1993) in Orange County and *People v. B Street Boys* (1994) in Alameida County.

[11] In *People v. Brown Nation* (1997), the prosecutor requested that the case be dismissed without prejudice after the public nuisance was eliminated prior to the issuance of the injunction. The gang activity ceased after four defendants were incarcerated, two moved out of state, and the house around which the nuisance was centered was sold (Castorena 1998a).

[12] At the time of this study, *People v. Eastside Wilmas and Westside Wilmas* (2001) was still in litigation.

[13] The groupings are assigned category labels representing the attributes, allowing the frequency of the presence of each attribute to be examined. The distribution of the frequencies of each attribute indicates the amount of variation in the variable. The process of 'pigeonholing' data into categories is very subjective, particularly for qualitative data for which the distinction between categories is often unclear. The choice of attributes on which to categorize variables is dependent on the goals of the research and the available information. The categorization of the variables in this study is based on the information provided by the data sources as interpreted by the researcher. In some cases, all categories of a variable apply to some degree, and the determination of the appropriate category is based on the general emphasis in the sources of data.

[14] Because this is a study of the identified universe of gang injunction initiatives, and not a random sample of a larger population, measures of statistical significance, such as the chi-square statistic often associated with contingency tables, are not meaningful and, therefore, not used in this study.

[15]The principal investigator visually inspected the case files in the records office of every Superior court house in which an injunction case was filed. For cases in which prosecutors supplied a copy of the case file, a visual inspection was still performed, unless the case file was incomplete or not available, primarily because the judge sealed the case or the file/document was missing from the court archives. In these cases, prosecutors either supplied pertinent documents at the request of the researcher or responded to questions regarding the contents of the case file. In most cases, prosecutors were very cooperative in supplying pertinent documents for the study.

[16] Prosecutors for only one injunction initiative failed to respond to the survey.

[17] The case file of *People v. Brown Nation* contains only three documents: the complaint, a notice of status conference, and a report on the status conference, which documents the dismissal of the case at the request of the prosecutor. Because the case did not reach litigation, there are no declarations or other evidence in the case file.

[18] An unincorporated association is defined as a voluntary group of persons, without a charter, formed by mutual consent for the purpose of promoting a common enterprise or prosecuting a common objective (*Black's Law Dictionary,* 6th ed., s.v. 'Unincorporated association').

[19] The STEP Act was enacted in 1988 to enhance the penal consequences against defendants "convicted of a felony committed for the benefit of, at the direction of, or in association with any criminal street gang with the intent to

promote, further, or assist in any criminal conduct by gang members." (Cal. Pen. Code, Sect. 186.22 (b)(1)). A criminal street gang is defined as "any organization, association, or group of three or more persons, whether formal or informal, having as one of its primary activities the commission of one or more [of 23 enumerated] criminal acts... having a common name or common identifying sign or symbol, and whose members individually or collectively engage in or have engaged in a pattern of criminal gang activity" (Cal. Pen. Code, Sect. 186.22(f)). The California Department of the Attorney General uses these criteria to document criminal street gangs, a procedure commonly called STEPing the gang.

[20] The senior lead officer is the LAPD's version of a community policing officer.

[21] Three entire cases were sealed, all police declarations were sealed in one case, and two cases were missing from the court archives. Occasionally, an expert declaration is sealed when it contains confidential information on juvenile defendants, such as juvenile criminal records. At least one of the cases was sealed because of the large number of juvenile defendants.

[22] A copy of the original article published in the *Atlantic Monthly* magazine (Wilson and Kelling 1982) is the first appendix in the Los Angeles District Attorney's training manual on civil gang abatement, entitled *S.A.G.E. – Strategies Against Gang Environments: A Handbook for Community Prosecution* (Office of the District Attorney 1996).

[23] In responses to the Prosecutor Survey, several prosecutors explicitly referred to *broken windows* theory, and many others alluded to it in their responses.

[24] On January 9, 2002, City Attorney Rocky Delgadillo proposed a neighborhood prosecutor program to target quality-of-life crimes. The program would employ eighteen prosecutors, assigned to each of the city's police divisions, to coordinate police and neighborhood groups to address minor offenses, such as graffiti and prostitution, which often fall between the cracks. Injunctions against gangs and other targets are among the remedies to be used by the program (Uranga 2002).

[25] See *Lanzetta v. New Jersey* 1939 – statute prohibiting being a 'gangster'; *City of Chicago v. Morales* 1999 city ordinance prohibiting loitering by gang members; *Nunez v. City of San Diego* 1997 – city curfew ordinance enforced for the express purpose of reducing gang activity; *Harvard, Ill. v. Gaut* 1996 – city ordinance prohibiting the wearing of gang clothing and insignias and the use of hand signals for gang-related communications.

[26] Only one initiative did not include an associational prohibition.

[27] *People v. Acuna* (Cal. 1997) is discussed in full in Chapter IV.

[28] The United States Supreme Court recently upheld a similar policy in public housing projects (*Department of Housing and Urban Development v. Rucker* (2002).

[29] Parents of juveniles who fall under the ordinance have the option of relocating the child, relocating with the child, or renouncing the child's gang

affiliation and agreeing that no further gang involvement will take place for at least one year, after which the sanctions may be waived.

[30] In its ongoing battle against gangs, Cicero has filed an $11 million lawsuit against two street gangs, the Latin Kings and the Noble Knights, alleging that both are involved in the sale of illegal drugs. The lawsuit is designed to take the profit out of crime and to compensate the townsfolk for the resulting fear and for damages from graffiti (Robinson 1999). The town had also passed an ordinance allowing the police to seize cars of suspected gang members (Sadovi 1999). After impounding over sixty cars in six weeks, the ordinance was withdrawn in response to a lawsuit filed by the American Civil Liberties Union and replaced with a curfew ordinance, which allows the police to impound cars driven by anyone under the age of seventeen caught out after curfew (Associated Press State and Local Wire 1999).

[31] An indictment is an accusation presented by a grand jury. An information is an accusation presented by competent public officer on his oath of office. In most states, an information may be used in place of a grand jury indictment to bring the accused to trial.

[32] *People v. Dogtown* is not included in this study because the injunction is limited to the graffiti activities of the gangs and is not confined to activity within a defined target area.

[33] Since the conclusion of this research on June 30 2001, there have been at least a dozen gang injunction initiatives in California: in Long Beach against the East Side Longos, the Insane Crips, and the West Side Longos; in Los Angeles against the 18th Street Gang, Canoga Park Alabama, KAM, the Avenues, the Rolling Sixty Crips, and the Bounty Hunters; in Escondido against the Westside gang and the Diablos; in San Bernadino, against the Five Time Hometown Crips, and in Sanger, against the Chankla Bulldogs.

[34] Litigation was pending in one case at the conclusion of this research. The LACA injunction against the Eastside and Westside Wilmas gangs (*People v. Eastside/Westside Wilmas* 2001) has since been denied because of insufficient evidence to support the injunction (Zahniser 2003).

[35] The gang sign provision prohibits "using words, phrases, physical gestures, or symbols commonly known as hand signs or engaging in other forms of communication which describe or refer to the gang known as 'VST' or 'VSL'" (*People v. Acuna* 1995: 596).

[36] The gang clothing provision prohibits "wearing clothing which bears the name or letters of the gang known as 'VST' or 'VSL'" (*People v. Acuna* 1995: 596).

[37] The non-association clause prohibits "standing, sitting, walking, driving, gathering, or appearing anywhere in public view with any other defendant, or any other known VSL or VST member" (*People v. Acuna* 1995: 597).

[38] The non-intimidation clause prohibits "confronting, intimidating, annoying, harassing, threatening, challenging, provoking, assaulting, battering residents, patrons, or visitors to Rocksprings, or persons known to have complained about

gang activity or provided information in support of the complaint" (*People v. Acuna* 1995: 599).

[39] See Note 34.

[40] The California State Senate has since rejected a bill that would have provided public defenders for indigents named as defendants in gang injunction cases, citing the potentially heavy costs to taxpayers, which could run into millions of dollars. Senator Tom Hayden introduced the bill, contending that gang injunction actions are civil in name only, as "the vast power of police and prosecutors is brought to bear on indigents who cannot properly defend themselves because they cannot afford lawyers" (New York Times 2000).

[41] According to the prosecutor, who had earlier objected to Englebrecht's release from the injunction, the judge determined that he had not been involved with the gang for a period of at least one year.

[42] Unless otherwise cited, the information in this section is from the SAGE manual (Office of the District Attorney 1996).

[43] The statutory law supporting the injunction may include the local municipal code if the code declares a violation to be a nuisance *per se*. Such a declaration establishes the activity as a public nuisance without the need of showing that it falls within the definition of a public nuisance.

[44] The fallout from the Rampart Scandal has been extensive. Perez accused approximately 70 officers of the Rampart Division CRASH unit of being involved in or knowing about crimes and/or misconduct (Berry, Glover and Lait 2001). More than a dozen officers resigned or were fired amid corruption-related charges (Berry et al. 2001). Nine officers, including Perez and Durden, were charged with crimes. More than 100 criminal convictions, many involving 18th Street gang members, were dismissed as a result of the scandal (Berry et al. 2001). The price tag to the city and the county for investigation of the scandal and the resulting liability is expected to be in the hundreds-of-million dollars (Riccardi 2000). The LAPD will operate under a court-approved federal consent decree with the Department of Justice for the next five years. Among the terms of the decree is the development of a computer system to keep track of complaints, use-of-force incidents, and other information for the purpose of identifying rogue cops (Duant 2001).

[45] The former city attorney, James K. Hahn, who is credited with pioneering gang injunctions, was elected mayor of Los Angeles in 2001.

[46] Although the study states that fourteen injunctions are represented, two targeted gangs, Shatto Park Locos and Columbia Little Cycos, are actually enjoined in two different target areas under one injunction, *People v. 18th Street Gang*, No. BC190334 (Cal. Super. Ct. Los Angeles County (1998)).

[47] Three Los Angeles County injunctions granted during the time period were not included because suitable data was not available (Grogger 2000: 2).

[48] The study used the reporting districts (RD's), or, in the case of Pasadena, census tracts that are similar to RD's. All are called RD's for the purpose of the study (Grogger 2000: 6).

[49] Adjoining areas are defined as all RD's that touch the boundaries of the RD's comprising the target areas. The design is described as a doughnut, with the target area RD's as the hole. The adjoining RD's are included to detect displacement (Grogger 2000: 10).
[50] Neighboring areas are RD's with boundaries touching the outer boundaries of the adjoining areas, or the outer edge of the doughnut. Neighboring areas are used to control for changes in reported crime due to factors other than the injunctions (Grogger 2000: 10).
[51] Matched comparison areas are "a separate comparison sample for each target area RD that consists of all RD's whose crime levels were similar to those of the RD's in the target areas" during the five quarters preceding the injunction (Grogger 2000: 19). The matched comparison sample was used to control for 'mean reversion', strong crime trends, and seasonal patterns that could erroneously attribute to the injunctions a decline in crime that would have occurred in the absence of the injunctions. As Grogger explains, 'mean reversion' refers to the possibility that injunctions may be imposed while the target areas are experiencing unusually high levels of crime, which would most likely fall to more typical levels (reversion to the mean) regardless of whether the injunction was imposed.
[52] Crime counts were employed because the population data needed to construct crime rates were not available for RD's and census population data were available only for 1990, which would necessitate the extrapolation of population data for the pre-and post-injunction periods and increase the likelihood of error. Using crime counts instead of crime rates also eliminated the measure of 'risk sets' for small areas such as RD's. 'Risk sets' refer to the number of people at risk of victimization in an area. Because many residents spend much time outside of their residential RD, reducing the risk of victimization within the RD, and the daytime populations of some RD's swell where there are many employers in the area, increasing the risk of victimization, crime rates based on the residential population of an RD may not be an accurate indicator of crime (Grogger 2000:12-13).
[53] The simple before-and-after method used a pre-injunction period of five quarters preceding the imposition of the injunction and a post-injunction period of four quarters following the imposition of the injunction, including the quarter in which the injunction was imposed. This relatively short pre-injunction period was used to allow the inclusion of the Blythe Street injunction, which was the subject of the only previous attempt to evaluate the effects of an injunction on reported crime. The sample period begins in 1992, and the Blythe Street injunction was imposed in April 1993. A longer post-injunction period would have resulted in dropping a substantial number of injunctions from the sample, as the sample period ended in 1999. Although longer periods would have provided a more reliable baseline and allowed the assessment of both short and long-term effects of injunctions, it would have resulted in a smaller sample of injunctions, reducing overall reliability. The research design is referred to as a case control design because the neighboring

areas and matched comparison areas were used as a control by pairing them with the target areas and the adjoining areas.

[54] Difference-in-difference estimation refers to subtracting the difference in pre- and post-injunction crime counts in the target area and adjoining areas from the difference in pre- and post-injunction crime counts in the neighboring (control) areas. The difference-in-difference indicates the reduction in crime counts controlling for factors extraneous to the effects of the injunctions.

[55] Fixed-effects regression was used to assess the match between the target/adjoining areas and the neighboring and matched comparison areas. The difference-in-difference format is too cumbersome for presenting the large number of results when the matched comparison areas are included in the analysis. Fixed-effects regression is essentially another way to compute difference-in-difference estimates and yields the same estimates of the effects of the injunctions. It controls for trends and seasonal patterns in crime counts and for time-invariant factors (fixed effects) that differ among RD's and contribute to differences in crime, including natural geographic features, man-made features (such as an RD's mix of residential and commercial properties), and, over relatively short time periods, daytime and resident populations and demographic make-up of RD's. Thus, it "provides more precise estimates of the effects of injunctions than the difference-in-difference approach" (Grogger 2000: 22-23).

[56] The expert declarations from the case files emphasize the group nature of drug dealing. According to many of the police experts who gave declarations, drug transactions by gangs involve at least three gang members – one to make the sale, a second to get the drugs, and a third to lookout for the police and signal their presence. Some expert declarations suggest that there are often at least six gang members involved in every drug transaction.

[57] DiMaggio and Powell (1983) discuss three isomorphic (having the same form or appearance) processes – coercive, mimetic, and normative – that, in the process of organizational innovation driven by a desire to improve performance, paradoxically result in organizations becoming increasingly similar without necessarily becoming more efficient. Mimetic processes result from uncertainty, which encourages imitation.

[58] To be consistent, the *Complaint* is the source of the requested relief whenever possible. Where the *Complaint* is not available or does not contain the necessary information, the *Proposed Preliminary Injunction* or the *Memorandum of Points and Authorities* are substituted. Any amendments to the above documents are also utilized as a source. In some cases, only the *Preliminary Injunction* is available. This occurred in cases for which the court files were not available to the researcher for various reasons: the case file was sealed by the court, to be viewed only by the attorneys of record; the case file was missing from the courthouse records room and its whereabouts was unknown; and the case file obtained by the researcher did not include the complaint or the complaint was otherwise unavailable. In all these cases, prosecutors verified that there were no substantive changes made by the court

to the requested relief. In one case, the requested provisions were specified only in the *Order to Show Cause.*

[59] "The illegal sale, possession, or use of a controlled substance" may also be divided into three distinct activities – sale, possession, and use. However, because most injunctions that prohibit such drug-related activities place these three activities together, they have been considered one activity for the purpose of this study. This is evidence of the inherently subjective task of teasing out distinct activities in order to make an objective assessment of the variation in the pleadings.

[60] A commonly used measure of variation based on all observations is the variance, computed by summing the squared differences from the mean from all observations divided by one less than the number of observations. If all observations are identical, the variance equals 0 because there is no variance from the mean. The variance is greater as the observations spread out from the mean. However, this statistic is not very clear for the purpose of this study because one must think in terms of squared units, or the number of provisions squared. The variance of the behavioral index is 48.63, which is somewhat meaningless to the reader not versed in statistics. In contrast, the standard deviation, which is the squared root of the variance, is much more appealing because is expressed in the same units of measurement as the observations (Norusis 1993: 173). For the behavioral index, the standard deviation is 6.97, meaning the average variation in number of provisions from the mean is approximately 7 provisions.

[61] Proscriptions that are present in only one injunction are grouped into a miscellaneous variable in each sub-index. Therefore, the smallest number of frequencies for each provision is two.

[62] The different degrees of associational proscriptions are not differentiated in the behavioral index and will be discussed in more detail later in this study.

[63] This provision is often coupled with the intimidation of complainants and witnesses. For the purpose of this study, these provisions are considered separately, as the intimidation of complainants/witnesses is clearly a violation of the criminal law, while harassment/intimidation of persons not involved in official police action is generally not a crime.

[64] Although it may be argued that there is no drug activity in the target areas for these injunctions, it is highly unlikely in the disenfranchised areas that gangs control. Interviews with some of the prosecutors of initiatives that did not include drug proscriptions revealed that drug violations in their jurisdictions were sufficiently pursued under the criminal law, leaving no necessity for injunctive relief for illegal drug activity.

[65] This is considered as a different provision from intimidation/harassment of residents. See Note 63.

[66] There are two general cluster analysis techniques – hierarchical and partitioning. Hierarchical cluster analysis refers to the creation of a series of clusters, proceeding from one cluster for each case to a single cluster containing all cases (agglomerative) or in the opposite direction (divisive).

Partitioning cluster analysis refers to a defined number of clusters, selected in advance of the analysis and based on the goals of the research. If the research calls for a specific number of partitions, the procedure groups the cases through an iterative process that seeks the best fit of the data to the desired number of partitions. Hierarchical cluster analysis provides a more objective technique than partitioning cluster analysis by removing the subjective decision on the optimum number of categories.

To achieve a meaningful cluster analysis, the sub-indexes were weighted to represent the proportion of each index in the behavioral index. Weighting the sub-indexes was necessary to equalize the requested relief of all injunctions. Because the number of proscriptions in the injunctions ranges from four to thirty-seven, the use of the raw number of proscriptions for each index would have resulted in categories that closely correlate to the total number of proscriptions in the behavioral index. Injunction initiatives with a lower number of proscriptions would have tended to score low in each category, while those with a high number would have tended to score high in each category. Weighting was achieved by dividing the number of proscriptions in each sub-index by the total number of proscriptions in the behavioral index. The weighted sub-indexes are expressed in decimal form, indicating the proportion of requested relief that is associated with each of the three categories of behavior. After being weighted, the sub-indexes for each case are classified as high or low, depending on whether the ratio falls above or below the mean value of the sub-index, using the standardized score (z-score) for each index. Z-scores measure the sub-index in terms of the standard deviation from the mean. Z-scores above the mean (0.00) represent a high proportion of the index in the requested relief, and z-scores at the mean and below represent a low proportion of the index in the requested relief.

Several analyses were performed, using various methods of agglomerative hierarchical cluster analysis. Agglomerative hierarchical cluster analysis using the *Pearson correlation coefficient* and the *median clustering method* produced the best fit. The *median clustering method* is a centroid method, which combines two clusters of cases by equally weighting the computation of the centroid, or average score for each cluster, regardless of the number of cases in each cluster. It allows clusters of a smaller number of cases to have an equal effect on the characterization of clusters into which they are merged. Identical clusters were also produced using the cosine measure, another similarity measure, supporting the validity of the resulting categories.

The differences in the fusion levels, or the levels at which two different clusters are combined, indicate that the optimal partitioning location is at stage 39. There was a greater difference between the fusion levels of the correlation coefficients at stages 38 and 39 than in other stages, except stage 40, which would result in two clusters. Because the fusion levels of stages 39 and 40 were so close, with stage 40 being only .01 larger, and because three categories were more appropriate to the goals of the research than two categories, stage 39 was chosen as the optimal stage for partitioning, resulting in three categories of injunction initiatives.

[67] This analysis does not include the denial of the injunction against the Eastside and Westside Wilmas. The case was still in litigation at the time of this research. See Note 34.

[68] The Los Angeles District Attorney's Office (LADA) was the only district attorney agency that has conducted gang injunctions under contract. Incorporated municipalities paid the county $95,000 per year for a deputy district attorney dedicated to the injunction initiative. According to one respondent to the Prosecutor Survey, this arrangement was initiated in 1993 between the LADA and the City of Norwalk. The city administration requested a specialized prosecutor to prosecute gang cases because it felt that intimidation by gang members was resulting in increasing victimization of residents. The city wanted a deputy district attorney with specialized training and a lower caseload to concentrate on these crimes. However, under the general services agreement, a contract under which the LADA was already responsible for the prosecution of felonies in the city, but not necessarily with a specialized prosecutor, the LADA could not accept additional funds for job responsibilities it was currently performing. The head deputy in charge of the Hardcore Gang Division suggested seeking a gang injunction, which had already been successfully used by other prosecuting agencies to reduce street-level gang activity. The city paid additional funding for a dedicated deputy district attorney to obtain an injunction. This was the genesis of the LADA's SAGE (Strategy Against Gang Environments) Program and resulted in the first LADA gang injunction, *City of Norwalk v. Orange Street Locos* (1994).

[69] The preliminary injunction was denied in this initiative, which may account for the lack of any further initiatives by the Orange County District Attorney's Office.

[70] One deputy city attorney stated that the gang injunction initiative originated in part due to the increasing frequency of gang-related misdemeanors or ordinance violations that were being prosecuted by the agency.

[71] Two of the early injunction, *People v. Playboy Gangster Crips* and *People v. Blythe Street Gang*, did not have named defendants. The gang itself was the defendant, named as an unincorporated association. *Playboy Gangster Crips* was the first gang injunction as defined in this research and, according to the prosecutor, was an experiment. *Blythe Street Gang*, the third gang injunction, did not name defendants because of the large number of juveniles in the gang. According to the prosecutor, there was a concern about labeling specific juveniles as gang members in court documents that would be open to public viewing.

[72] The Los Angeles Times is riddled with stories of gang members and innocent victims being shot and killed. For example, in an October 9, 2000 article, a 10-year-old girl was fatally wounded as a bystander in the killing of an 18 year old gang member. In a separate incident, a 9-year-old girl was wounded after a bullet intended for a gang members pierced the wall of her house (Los Angeles

Times 2000c). In a March 6, 1999 article, a 19-year-old man was shot to death in his driveway while bringing in trashcans, after gang members mistook him for a rival (Los Angeles Times 1999c).

[73] Two cases contained more than one non-association provision. For each case, the most severe provision is used in this analysis.

[74] The frequency of the presence of some form of associational restriction in the disorder index, which was used to conduct the cluster analysis, does not coincide with the frequency used in the present analysis. The total ban from the target area was considered as a location restriction, not an associational restriction, in the disorder index. The frequency of the associational restriction in the disorder index is forty cases, while forty-one cases are considered to have some form of associational restriction, including the total ban, in the present analysis.

[75] The prosecutor stated that, when it was learned that almost all the named defendants were on probation, it was believed that nobody was going to challenge a provision requiring all defendants to obey the conditions of their probation, and all probation conditions have a 'do not associate' clause.

[76] The genesis of the 'carve-out' is *People v. Harpys Gang* (BC192678, Los Angeles Superior Court 1998). Representatives of local organizations that had prevention programs requested exceptions to the associational ban for defendants employed by the programs. Prior to *Harpys*, the final 18th Street gang injunction (*People v. 18th Street Gang*, BC190334, Los Angeles Superior Court 1998) had permitted defendants validly enrolled in the local high school to associate on the campus during the individual's regular school schedule.

[77] Although the judge is not specifically mention this provision in his written decision, the prosecutor believes that the total ban may have strongly influenced the judge to deny the preliminary injunction.

[78] SDDA, SBCA, and joint LADA/LACA initiatives did not begin until the *post-Acuna period.*

[79] A prosecutor from a county agency noted that gang injunctions are the only proactive interventions by the agency.

[80] California ranks first in the United States in the number of gangs (4,927) and gang members (254,618) (Office of Juvenile Justice and Delinquency Prevention 1997). With forty-two identified injunction initiatives against fifty gangs statewide, only approximately one in one hundred gangs (1%) have been targets of gang injunction initiatives during the period of this study.

[81] The Los Angeles City Attorney's Office has designed a protocol with the Los Angeles Police Department (LAPD) to extract the LAPD from the political process of initiating gang injunctions. Once a year the four geographic bureaus are asked to prioritize their injunction requests, which filter up to the bureau level from the eighteen different area commands. LAPD's Operations Committee, which is composed of all the deputy chiefs, determine which of those areas gets priority and send the prioritized list to the Assistant City Attorney in charge of the Hardcore Gang Division.

[82] Most municipalities have similar ordinances. See also Los Angeles Municipal Code section 11.00(m), Norwalk Municipal Code section 1-3.2, Pasadena Municipal Code section 1.24.040, Redondo Beach Municipal Code section 6, Fontana Municipal Code section 18-2, Los Angeles County Code section 11.02.050, Inglewood Municipal Code section 1-19, Long Beach Municipal Code section 1.32.010(B), San Bernardino Municipal Code section 8.30.010, San Marcos Municipal Code section 1.12.090, Compton Municipal Code section 7-1.4, San Diego Municipal Code section 12.0204.

[83] The influence of the series of articles about the Langdon Street Gang on the decision to pursue an injunction is not clear. While the supervisor of the LACA Hardcore Gang Unit indicated that the series triggered the injunction initiative, the lead prosecutor stated the series had no effect on the decision. According to the lead prosecutor, he was asked to look at the entire North Hills narcotics area, which consisted of the Langdon Street target area and a similar size area east of Sepulveda Boulevard, to develop on overall plan to deal with the narcotics sales and other gang issues. Because the Langdon Street target area was controlled by one gang while the east side of Sepulveda Boulevard, which is literally across the street from the target area, was muddled with 43 separate gangs, the Langdon Street gang was chosen as the target for an injunction. It is possible that the *Los Angeles Times* series brought the LACA's attention to the entire area, from which Langdon Street was chosen as the most appropriate target. A similar situation existed in Pacoima, where the LACA was asked to look into an injunction against one gang due to a series of drive-by shootings in which innocent persons were shot. However, the LACA sought an injunction against another gang that represented the real problem in the Pacoima area.

[84] Throughout this research, the principal investigator scanned the *Los Angeles Times* on a daily basis and was surprised to read about so many gang-related homicides in the City of Los Angeles. Particularly disturbing was the prevalence of stories about innocent bystanders, many of them children, being seriously injured or killed by stray bullets.

[85] For the purpose of this study, elected officials do not include elected city and district attorneys, which are included in the self-initiated category.

[86] Included in this category are town-hall type meeting, in which residents meet with prosecutorial agencies to voice their complaints and suggest intervention methods.

[87] Although it is recognized that an elected official is part of the local governing authority, the categories local governing authority and elected official are distinguished to account for cases in which the local governing authority had to take some official action to embark on an injunction initiative, such as approving funding. This is the case in all of the LADA injunctions outside the City of Los Angeles, in which the local governing authority must sign a contract with the LADA and fund the salary of a deputy district attorney. In these cases, the prosecutors may not have knowledge about the entity that initiated the request by the local governing authority. In contrast, elected

official can directly call for an injunction from the prosecutor's office without any official action by the local governing authority.

88 Vertical prosecution refers to the assignment of each case to the same prosecutorial team from the time a complaint is reviewed until final disposition of the case. The advantage is that all interested parties deal with the same representatives of the prosecutor's office from the inception of a case to its conclusion.

89 One prosecutor explained that a Hispanic prosecutor and a Hispanic investigator 'dressed down' as gang members to solicit information and declarations within the target areas. Other prosecutors stated that, because of the fear of retaliation, citizens did not want to be seen talking to attorneys/investigators in the neighborhood, but were willing to speak to them outside the target area.

90 Operational security refers to an attempt by prosecutors to conduct an injunction initiative in a covert manner, so that gang members are not aware of the initiative. This low profile is often necessary to allow prosecutors to gather evidence of a continuing public nuisance and to serve notice of the action on named defendants, which is required before a defendant can be subjected to the provisions of an injunction. If word of the injunction initiative got out to gang members, they may go underground for a period of time to decrease their street presence, thereby decreasing the evidence of a continuing public nuisance, and to avoid the serving of notice.

91 The Mexican Mafia, also known as 'La Eme', is a Mexican prison gang that allegedly controls many of the Hispanic gangs from inside the state penitentiaries. La Eme selects gang leaders based on their loyalty and ability to take care of street business. In return, La Eme gets the majority of the 'rent' money collected by the gangs.

92 Caucasian gangs account for 7% of the gangs in the West.

93 For extremely large gangs, such as the 18th St. Gang, which is alleged to have a membership in the tens of thousands, the size of the specific cliques targeted by the injunction initiatives are used.

94 The number of defendants enjoined is not considered because named defendants must be served before being subject to the terms of the injunction Service is one of the difficulties facing prosecutors and the police. Gang members often go underground or leave the area when word gets out that named defendants are getting served with court papers. Therefore, the number of named defendants often does not coincide with the number of defendants enjoined. Even though some gang members are not served, the injunction may be effective against them if they have permanently left the area, which has been reported by prosecutors in a number of initiatives.

95 If charged with criminal contempt proceedings for the violation of an injunction, indigent defendants have the same Sixth Amendment right to counsel as for any other criminal violation.

96 The latest injunction initiative in the study, *People v. Eastside/Westside Wilmas* (2001) was delayed for almost one year by an attorney representing six

of the thirty named defendants ((Los Angeles Assistant City Attorney Martin Vranicar, Jr., personal communication, March 18, 2001).

[97] The Afro-American groups are the Nation of Islam in *People v. Venice Shoreline Crips* (1999) (Ehrenreich 1999b) and the National Association for the Advancement of Colored People (NAACP) in *City of Pasadena v. Pasadena Denver Lanes* (1995). The opposition to these cases is discussed in Chapter VI.

[98] The LADA has denied a request by the ACLU for notification of impending filings for temporary restraining orders so an opposing brief could be prepared.

[99] Prosecutors were requested to designate the single characteristic that they believed exerted the greatest influence on the potential effectiveness of the initiative.

[100] One initiative used target locations instead of a target area within certain boundaries. The twelve target locations ranged from a single address to several city blocks. When asked why target areas were used, the prosecutor stated that the entire area was about three square miles, causing the prosecutors to be uncomfortable with seeking an injunction throughout the entire area. Therefore, they picked the hot spots in the gang's turf. This injunction initiative was included in the over two square mile category because there is no other way to measure the area other than the estimate of three miles by the prosecutor. This initiative was also included in the one target area category in the following section because prosecutors could have drawn a boundary around the target location. Incidentally, the prosecutor reported no problems with displacement into the areas between the target locations.

[101] Incorporated municipalities in Los Angeles County are charged $95,000 per year for a dedicated SAGE deputy from the Los Angeles District Attorney's Office. In contrast, the San Diego District Attorney's Office does not charge municipalities for deputies to seek gang injunctions. City attorney's offices vary, as city attorneys who are elected may not be required to seek funding from a governing body, but may take the funds from their budget. Because the present staff is used in the initiatives, the expense factor may not be an issue, but they still might seek the blessing of the governing body, or they might merely advise the governing body of the action prior to filing so that the governing body does not learn about the initiative through the media.

[102] Prosecutors did not know who participated in the decision in two *high-drug* initiatives. These initiatives are not included in Table 5-31.

[103] The LACA and SBCA are elected officials, permitting a greater degree of independence from governing bodies than offices in which the city attorney is appointed. However, the SJCA is an appointed position.

[104] The target areas of two earlier injunctions have been brought into this program, which did not exist at the time of those initiatives.

[105] A humorous anecdote shared by one prosecutor involved an injunction provision prohibiting "possessing dogs, engaging in dog fights, or using dogs to intimidate, harass, annoy, challenge, assault, and/or batter any person" (*People v. Lincoln Park* 1998, Complaint for injunctive relief to abate a public nuisance). In the training session, the prosecutor told police officers "We've

got to be reasonable about this. If you see a gang member walking down the street with a poodle, don't cite him. Don't bring this case to me because I'm not going to bring it before the judge. But, if you got a pit bull, that's what I'm talking about, because I had someone who robbed a guy with a pit bull."

[106] The original formulation of the book is attributed to the police officers of the City of Redondo Beach, who were involved in the injunction against the North Side Redondo 13.

[107] In unincorporated areas of Los Angeles County, the District Attorney's Office prosecutes both misdemeanor and felony charges.

[108] One prosecutor spoke of a research proposal to sit at a specific location in a target area and count people in a pre/post-injunction experiment. Unfortunately, the study did not receive funding and, therefore, never took place.

[109] When served, defendants are given a packet of legal documents delineating the activities of the defendants and the relief being requested. This packet includes the complaint, the legal arguments, and evidence not sealed by the court, such as declarations of police officers and the criminal records of adult defendants. As a result, the defendants are notified of the pending legal action and the evidence against them prior to a ruling by the court.

[110] When asked why every prosecutor think they are effective, one prosecutor admitted that prosecutors get protective of gang injunctions because of the amount of work involved in the initiatives.

[111] 'Jumping in' is an initiation ritual common among gangs, in which gang members beat a prospective member for a certain period of time to test his bravado.

[112] Buerger (1994b) has identified four primary roles for community participation in community policing: (1) informant – acting as the eyes and ears of the police; (2) cheerleading – intervening on behalf of the police in the political arena; (3) resource provision – augmenting approval with monetary assistance; and (4) statement-making – which implies the threat of opposition and sanctions for continued misconduct, such as 'Take Back the Night Rallies' or posting drug-free school zones and neighborhood watch signs. The typology used in this study combined Brueger's categories of cheerleading, resource provision, and statement-making into the single category of supporter.

[113] Although attending church services is not specified as a 'carve-out', prosecutors agreed that the non-association provision would not be enforced during church services, but would be enforced against defendants going to and leaving church as a group.

[114] Civilian declarations might not be submitted as evidence for two reasons: the judge refused to seal the declaration, or there was ample evidence of the public nuisance without the declarations.

[115] This process is informally referred to in California as being STEPped or STEPping a gang, in reference to the STEP Act.

[116] The murder was connected with a violent cocaine ring that extended from the Venice Shoreline Crips to associates in Atlanta, St. Louis, Detroit, and

Baltimore. A federal indictment naming twenty-two suspects on drug conspiracy charges connected the murder to the cocaine ring. A third party, who is a prime suspect in the cocaine ring, has been charged with conspiracy in the murder. Both of the murder suspects from Venice had previously been named as defendants in gang injunctions against the Venice Shoreline Crips and Venice 13. The Venice Shoreline Crip member was killed in an unrelated shooting in April 2002 (Leovy 2002; Leovy and Kay 2002).

[117] The initiative was not included in this study because a complaint was never filed with the court.

[118] This is based on thirty-two initiatives for which data on gang longevity were available.

[119] For a more general review of the literature on community-based crime prevention, see Rosenbaum 1988.

[120] The information for this section was provided by the prosecutor for the Lennox 13 injunction and by the Director of School Programs for the Richstone Family Center, who is also the chairperson of the Lennox Gang Violence Suppression Council.

[121] Proposition 21 is a juvenile crime initiative statute approved by California voters on March 7, 2000 to amend the *Gang Violence and Juvenile Crime Prevention Act of 1998.* Among the provisions of the initiative is the enhancement of punishment for gang-related felonies, including witness intimidation, which subjects violators to an indeterminate life sentence (California Secretary of State 2000).

[122] City Attorney Gene Locke of Houston, Texas, has declined to use the strategy because of concerns about overall effectiveness, costs, and liability for violating individual civil liberties (Jacobius, 1996).

References

BOOKS AND ARTICLES

ACLU Foundation of Southern California. (1997, May). *False Premise / False Promise: The Blythe Street Gang Injunction and Its Aftermath.* Los Angeles, CA: American Civil Liberties Union Foundation of Southern California. [Online]. Available: http://www.aclu-sc.org/blythe.html.

Albuquerque Tribune. (1997, August 11). Campaign roundup. P. A3. [Online]. Available: http://www.lexis-nexis.com/universe.

Allen, R. (1998). Note: People ex rel. Gallo v. Acuna: (Ab)using California's nuisance law to control gangs. 25 *Western State University Law Review* 257.

Alonso, A. (1999). *Territoriality among African-American Street Gangs in Los Angeles.* Unpublished master's thesis. University of Southern California, Los Angeles.

American Prosecutors Research Institute. (1995). *Community Prosecution Implementation Manual.* Alexandria, VA: American Prosecutors Research Institute.

Associated Press. (1999, December 7). White House joins suit on gun cos. [Online]. Available: http://www.nytimes.com/aponline.

Associated Press. (2000a, January 20). D.C. sues gun industry. [Online]. Available: http://www.nytimes.com/aponline.

Associated Press. (2000b, March 12). Gangland violence on rise in Rampart. *San Diego Union Tribune.* [Online]. Available: http://www.uniontribune.com.

Associated Press State and Local Wire. (1999, August 26). War on street gangs resumes in Cicero. [Online]. Available: http://www.lexis-nexis.com/universe.

Banks, J. (2001, August 14). Court action targets gangs: San Bernardino. *Press-Enterprise.* [Online]. Available: http://www.lexis-nexis.com/universe.

Battin-Pearson, S.R., T.P. Thornberry, J.D. Hawkins, and M.D. Krohn. (1998, March). Gang membership, delinquent peers, and delinquent behavior. *Juvenile Justice Bulletin.* Washington, DC: U.S. Department of Justice, Office of Justice Programs, Office of Juvenile Justice and Delinquency Prevention.

Bayley, D.H. (1994). *Police For the Future.* New York: Oxford University Press.

Bazemore, G. and A.W. Cole. (1994). Police in the 'laboratory' of the neighborhood: Evaluating problem-oriented strategies in a medium-sized city. *American Journal of Police*, 13 (3), pp. 119-147.

Belluck, P. (1999, April 27). Illinois town hopes to exile its gang members to anywhere else, U.S.A. *New York Times*, p. A16.

Berry, S., S. Glover, and M. Lait. (2001, November 8). D.A. says no new charges expected in Rampart probe. *The Los Angeles Times.* [Online]. Available: http://www.latimes.com.

Boga, T.R. (1994). Turf wars: Street gangs, local governments, and the battle for public space. 29 *Harvard Civil Rights-Civil Liberties Law Review* 477.

Boland, B. (1998a). Community prosecution: Portland's Experience. In *Community Justice: An Emerging Field*, D.R. Karp (ed.). Lanham, MD: Rowman and Littlefield Publishers, Inc. Pp. 253-277.

Boland, B. (1998b). The Manhattan Experiment: Community Prosecution. In *Crime and Place: Plenary Papers of the 1997 Conference on Criminal Justice Research and Evaluation.* Washington, D.C.: U.S. Department of Justice, Office of Justice Programs, Bureau of Justice Assistance. Pp. 51-67.

Bratton, W.J. (1995). The New York City Police Department's civil enforcement of quality-of-life crimes. 3 *Journal of Law and Policy* 447.

Buerger, M.E. (1994a). The problems of problem-solving: resistance, interdependencies, and conflicting interests. *American Journal of Police*, 13 (3), pp. 1-36.

Buerger, M.E. (1994b). The limits of community. In *The Challenge of Community Policing: Testing the Promises*, D.P. Rosenbaum (Ed.). Thousand Oaks, CA: Sage Publications. Pp. 270-273.

Bureau of Justice Assistance. (1998, May). *Addressing Community Gang Problems: A Practical Guide.* Washington, D.C.: U.S. Department of Justice, Office of Justice Programs, Bureau of Justice Assistance.

Bureau of Justice Assistance. (1997, January). *Addressing Community Gang Problems: A Model for Problem Solving.* Washington, D.C.: U.S. Department of Justice, Office of Justice Programs, Bureau of Justice Assistance.

Bureau of Justice Assistance. (1993). *Problem-oriented drug enforcement: A community-based approach for effective policing.* Washington, D.C.: U.S. Department of Justice, Office of Justice Programs, Bureau of Justice Assistance.

California Secretary of State. (2000). *Juvenile Crime. Initiative Statute.* [Online]. http://www.primary2000.ss.ca.gov/VoterGuide/Proposition/21.htm.

Capital News Service. (1998, December 18). Lawyers spar over right to counsel in civil gang-abatement actions. [Online]. Available: http://www.lexis-nexis.com/universe.

Capowich, G.E. (1995). *Evaluating Problem-oriented Policing: Process and Outcomes in Tulsa and San Diego* (executive summary). Alexandria, VA: Institute for Social Analysis.

Capowich, G.E. and J.A. Roehl. (1994). Problem-oriented policing: Actions and effectiveness in San Diego. In *The Challenge of Community Policing: Testing the Promises*, Rosenbaum, D.P. (ed.). Thousand Oaks, CA: Sage Publications.

Castorena, D. (1998a, March 9). *SAGE Gang Injunction Cases.* Unpublished report by the Hardcore Gang Division, Office of the District Attorney, County of Los Angeles.

Castorena, D. (1998b, March 17). *The History of the Gang Injunction in California.* Unpublished report by the Hardcore Gang Division, Office of the District Attorney, County of Los Angeles.

Cheh, M.M. (1991). Constitutional limits on using civil remedies to achieve criminal law objectives: Understanding and transcending the criminal-civil law distinction. 42 *Hastings Law Journal* 1325.

Cheh, M.M. (1998). Civil remedies to control crime: Legal issues and constitutional challenges. In *Civil Remedies and Crime Prevention*, L.G. Mazerolle and J. Roehl (Eds.). Monsey, NY: Criminal Justice Press. Pp. 45-66.

City News Service. (2001, November 30). Permanent injunction issued against Long Beach gang. [Online]. Available: http://www.lexis-nexis.com/universe.

City News Service (2003, December 3). Gang injunctions. [Online]. Available: http://www.lexis-nexis.com/universe.

Clear, T.R. and D.R. Karp. (1998). The community justice movement. In *Community Justice: An Emerging Field*, D.R. Karp (ed.). Lanham, MD: Rowman and Littlefield Publishers, Inc. Pp. 3-28.

Coles, C. (1997, May/June). Street fighting man: In courts and D.A.'s offices, "Community Prosecution" is the new watchword. *The New Democrat*, p. 20. [Online]. Available: http://www.lexis-nexis.com/universe.

Cordner, G. (1998). Problem-oriented policing vs. zero tolerance. In *Problem-oriented Policing: Crime-specific Problems, Critical Issues, and Making POP Work*, T.O. Shelley and A.C. Grant (Eds.). Washington, DC: Police Executive Research Forum. Pp. 303-313.

Corwin, M. (2000, March 15). Commission hears calls for Rampart probe. *The Los Angeles Times*, Metro ed., p. B-1.

Curry, G. D. and R.W. Thomas. (1992). Community organization and gang policy response. *Journal of Quantitative Criminology*, 8 (4), pp. 357-374.

Daunt, T. (2001, July 24). N.Y. mob prosecutor to take on the LAPD. *The Los Angeles Times*. [Online]. Available: http://www.latimes.com.

DeLeon-Granados, W. (1999). *Travels through Crime and Place: Community Building as Crime Control*. Boston, MA: Northeastern University Press.

Destro, R.A. (1993). Gangs and civil rights. In *Gangs: The Origins and Impact of Contemporary Youth Gangs in the United States*, S.Cummings and D.J. Monti, (Eds.). Albany, NY: State University of New York Press. Pp. 277-304.

Destro, R.A. (1994). The hostages in the hood. 36 *Arizona Law Review* 785.

DiMaggio, P.J. and W.W. Powell. (1983). The iron cage revisited: Institutional isomorphism and collective rationality in organizational fields. *American Sociological Review*, 48 (2), pp. 147-160.

Do, A. (1993, August 31). City can't keep gang members apart, court rules. *The Orange County Register*, p. A01. [Online]. Available: http://www.lexis-nexis.com/universe.

Dolan, M. (1996, November 5). Court urged to approve anti-gang injunction. *The Los Angeles Times*. [Online]. Available: http://www.latimes.com.

Duffee, D. (1997). Working with communities. In *Community Policing in a Rural Setting*, Q.C. Thurman and E.F. McGarrell, (Eds.). Cincinnati, OH: Anderson. Pp. 85-96.

Duffee, D., R. Fluellin, and T. Roscoe. (1999). Constituency building and urban community policing. In *Measuring What Matters*, R. Langworthy (Ed.). Washington, DC: U.S. Department of Justice, Office of Justice Programs, National Institute of Justice.

Dunbar, W.H. (1898, February). Government by injunction. *Economic Studies*, 3 (1). Pp. 5-43.

Eck, J. and W. Spelman. (1987a). *Problem-solving: Problem-oriented Policing in Newport News.* Washington, D.C.: Police Executive Research Forum.

Eck, J. and W. Spelman. (1987b). Who ya gonna call? The police as problem-busters. *Crime and Delinquency*, 33 (1). Pp. 31-52.

Ehrenreich, B. (1999a, January 15). Chainedgang. *L.A. Weekly*, p. 26 [Online]. Available: http://www.lexis-nexis.com/universe.

Ehrenreich, B. (1999b, July 9). Crips and Bloods unite. *L.A. Weekly*. [Online]. Available: http://www.lexis-nexis.com/universe.

Eljera, B. (1993, October 28). Judge's ruling on gangs appealed. *Los Angeles Times, Orange County Edition.* [Online]. Available: http://www.lexis-nexis.com/universe.

Esbensen, F. and D. Huizinga. (1996). Gangs, drugs, and delinquency in a survey of urban youth. In *The Sociology of Juvenile Delinquency*, 2nd ed., R.J. Berger (Ed.). Chicago, IL: Nelson-Hall. Pp. 69 - 87.

Everitt, B.S. (1993). *Cluster Analysis.* 3rd Edition. London: Edward Arnold.

Feldman, P. (1987, December 12). Judge OK's modified measures to curb gang. *The Los Angeles Times*, Metro, part 2, p. 3. [Online]. Available: http://www.lexis-nexis.com/universe.

Finn, P. and K.M. Healey. (1996, November). *Preventing Gang- and Drug-Related Witness Intimidation.* Washington, DC: U.S. Department of Justice, Office of Justice Programs, National Institute of Justice.

Finn, P. and M.O. Hylton. (1994, October). *Using Civil Remedies for Criminal Behavior: Rationale, Case Studies, and Constitutional Issues.* Washington, DC: U.S. Department of Justice, Office of Justice Programs, National Institute of Justice.

Fiss, O.M. (1978). *The Civil Rights Injunction.* Bloomington, IL: Indiana University Press.

Fitzsimmons, E. and J. Dobner. (2001, July 13). Escondido gangs focus of injunction effort. *San Diego Union-Tribune.* [Online]. Available: http://www.lexis-nexis.com/universe.

Flynn, D. (1998, July). *Defining the "Community" in Community Policing.* Washington, D.C.: Police Executive Research Forum. [Online]. Available: http://www.policeforum.org/cp.pdf.

Flynn, K. (2000, February 9). Judge asked to bar gang from gathering. *The New York Times on the Web.* [Online]. Available: http://www.nytimes.com.

Frazier, J. (1999, August 6). Drug, gang evictions law takes effect. *Press-Enterprise*. [Online]. Available: http://www.lexis-nexis.com/universe.

Garafalo, J. and J. Laub. (1978). The fear of crime: Broadening our perspective. *Victimology* (3). Pp. 242-253.

Garcia, I. (1999a, June 24). Home Depot employees beautify Blythe Street park. *Los Angeles Times*, Valley Edition, P. 3. [Online]. Available: http://www.lexis-nexis.com/universe.

Garcia, I. (1999b, November 19). Community mourns death of activist Evelio Franco. *Los Angeles Times*, Valley Edition, P. 1. [Online]. Available: http://www.lexis-nexis.com/universe.

Garcia, I. (2001, April 21). Around the valley: A motor home full of hope. *Los Angeles Times*, Valley Edition, P. 1. [Online]. Available: http://www.lexis-nexis.com/universe.

Genelin, M. (1997, December 7). Injunctions against gangs. *Los Angeles Times*, Part M, P. 4. [Online]. Available: http://www.lexis-nexis.com/universe.

Gerstenzang, J. (2000, May 2). Gore steers to the center with anti-crime proposals. *The Los Angeles Times*. [Online]. Available: http://www.latimes.com.

Glover, S. and M. Lait. (2001a, August 30). Federal grand jury probing Rampart case. *The Los Angeles Times*. [Online]. Available: http://www.latimes.com.

Glover, S. and M. Lait. (2001b, November 16). Rampart officers claim malicious prosecution. *The Los Angeles Times*. [Online]. Available: http://www.latimes.com.

Glover, S. and M. Lait. (2001c, November 30). Perez to pay full restitution to victims. *The Los Angeles Times*. [Online]. Available: http://www.latimes.com.

Goldberg, L. (1996, September 13). City may sue street gangs: Winburn, Tillery seek to combat crime. *The Cincinnati Enquirer*, p. B01. [Online]. Available: http://www.lexis-nexis.com/universe.

Goldberg, O. (2001, October 6). Pacoima gang latest targeted for injunction. *The Daily News of Los Angeles*, p. N1. [Online]. Available: http://www.lexis-nexis.com/universe.

Goldstein, H. (1990). *Problem-oriented Policing*. New York: McGraw-Hill.

Gottlieb, J. (1999, January 28). Buena Park: Proposed law could force landlords to evict bases on arrest. *The Los Angeles Times*. [Online]. Available: http://www.latimes.com.

Graham, S. (1996, November 5). Court seems split over injunction aimed at gangs. *The Recorder*, p. 1. [Online]. Available: http://www.lexis-nexis.com/universe.

Green, L. (1996). *Policing Places with Drug Problems*. Thousand Oaks, CA: Sage Publications.

Green Mazerolle, L.and J. Roehl. (1998). Civil remedies and crime prevention: An introduction. In *Civil Remedies and Crime Prevention*, L.Green Mazerolle and J. Roehl (Eds.). Monsey, NY: Criminal Justice Press. Pp. 1-18.

Grinc, R.M. (1994). "Angels in Marble": Problems in stimulating community involvement in community policing. *Crime and Delinquency*, 40 (3), pp. 437-468.

Grogger, Jeffrey. (2000, July 21). *The Effects of the Los Angeles County Gang Injunctions on Reported Crime*. Los Angeles, CA: Department of Policy Studies, University of California, Los Angeles.

Harcourt, B.E. (2001) *Illusion of Order: The False Promise of Broken Windows Policing*. Cambridge, MA: Harvard University Press.

Harcourt, B.E. (1998, November). A critique of the social influence conception of deterrence, the broken windows theory, and order-maintenance policing New York style. 97 *Michigan Law Review* 91.

Harmon, D. (1998, July 2). County trying to ban gang from Austin turf. *The Austin American-Statesman*, p. A1. [Online]. Available: http://www.lexis-nexis.com/universe.

Harris, M.D. (1988, May 26). City attorney says novel injunction reduced gang crime. *United Press International*. [Online]. Available: http://www.lexis-nexis.com/universe.

Harris, S.A. (1996, February 29). High court rules on gang injunction. *United Press International*. [Online]. Available: http://www.lexis-nexis.com/universe.

Henning, P.J. (1998). Symposium: Individual liability for conduct by criminal organizations in the United States. 44 *Wayne Law Review* 1305.

Herd, B. (1998). Note: Injunctions as a tool to fight gang-related problems in California after *People ex rel. Gallo v. Acuna*: A suitable solution? 28 *Golden Gate University Law Review 629.*

Hernandez, R. and F. Butterfield. (1999, July 21). 2 gun makers and said to be negotiating to avoid a New York State lawsuit. *The New York Times on the Web*. [Online]. Available: http://www.nytimes.com.

Hong, R. (1999, February 10). Buena Park passes ordinance requiring eviction of arrestees. *The Los Angeles Times*, part B, p. 4. [Online]. Available: http://www.lexis-nexis.com/universe.

Hope, T.J. (1994). Problem-oriented policing and drug market locations: Three case studies. In *Crime Prevention Studies*, Volume 2, R.V. Clarke (Ed.). Monsey, NY: Criminal Justice Press. Pp. 5-32.

Horowitz, R. (1996). Community tolerance of gang violence. In *The Sociology of Juvenile Delinquency*, 2nd ed., Ronald J. Berger (Ed.). Chicago: Nelson-Hall. Pp. 355-370.

Howell, J.C. (1998, August). Youth gangs: an overview. *Juvenile Justice Bulletin.* Washington, DC. U.S. Department of Justice, Office of Justice Programs, Office of Juvenile Justice and Delinquency Prevention.

Howell, J.C. and S.H. Decker. (1999, January). The youth gangs, drugs, and violence connection. *Juvenile Justice Bulletin.* Washington, DC: U.S. Department of Justice, Office of Justice Programs, Office of Juvenile Justice and Delinquency Prevention.

Huff, C.R. (1998, October). Comparing the criminal behavior of gang members and at-risk youths. *Research in Brief.* Washington, DC: U.S. Department of Justice, Office of Justice Programs, National Institute of Justice.

Huffaker, D. (1999, May 23). Neighborhood enjoying area's rebirth: Scourge of gang removed from Burbank site. *The Daily News of Los Angeles*, p. N3. [Online]. Available: http://www.lexis-nexis.com/universe.

Hunger, K. (1999, June 8). Gang activity restricted in S.A. neighborhood. *San Antonio Express-News*, p. 1A. [Online]. Available: http://www.lexis-nexis.com/universe.

Jacobus, P. (1994, June 18). Judge throws out Oakland suit against street gang. *The San Francisco Chronicle*, p. A19. [Online]. Available: http://www.lexis-nexis.com/universe.

Jacobius, A. (1996). Going gangbusters: Prosecutors fight gangs with injunctions banning conduct such as using beepers and applying graffiti. 82 *American Bar Association Journal* 24.

Jackson, R.L. (1999, March 30). 'Community prosecution' wins fans, federal funds. *The Los Angeles Times*, Part A, p. 5. [Online]. Available: http://www.lexis-nexis.con/universe.

Johnson, D. (2000, February 22). Chicago council tries anew with anti-gang ordinance. *The New York Times*, p. A14.

Jones, M.B. and D.R. Jones. (2000). The contagious nature of antisocial behavior. *Criminology*, 38 (1), pp. 25-46.

Kahan, D.M. (1997, March). Social influence, social meaning, and deterrence. 83 *Virginia Law Review* 349.

Kandel, J. (2000, November 28). Shooting defies cleanup efforts. *Daily News of Los Angeles*. [Online]. Available: http://www.lexis-nexis.com/universe.

Kariak, P. (1995, November 3). Gang injunction protested. *Pasadena Star-News.* In *S.A.G.E. - Strategy Against Gang Environments: A Handbook for Community Prosecution,* Office of the District Attorney, County of Los Angeles, (1996, June), Appendix GG.

Karp, D.L. (Ed.). (1998). *Community Justice: An Emerging Field* Lanham, MD: Rowman and Littlefield Publishers, Inc.

Kaufman, L. and Rousseeuw, P.J. (1990). *Finding Groups in Data: An Introduction to Cluster Analysis*. Wiley Series in Probability and Mathematical Statistics. New York, NY: John Wiley and Sons, Inc.

Kelling, J.L. and C.M. Coles. (1996). *Fixing Broken Windows: Restoring Order and Reducing Crime in Our Communities.* New York, NY: The Free Press.

Kelly, D. (1999, April 12). Along baseline, a new approach to the oldest profession. *The Press-Enterprise*, p. B01. [Online]. Available: http://www.lexis-nexis.com/universe.

Kennedy, D.M. (1993). *Closing the market: controlling the drug trade in Tampa, Florida*. Washington, D.C.: U.S. Department of Justice, National Institute of Justice.

Klein, M.W. (1998). The problem of street gangs and problem-oriented policing. In *Problem-oriented Policing: Crime-specific Problems, Critical Issues, and Making POP Work*, T.O. Shelley and A.C. Grant (Eds.). Washington, DC: Police Executive Research Forum. Pp. 57-86.

Klein, M.W. (1996). Street gangs and deterrence legislation. In *Three Strikes and Your Out: Vengeance as Public Policy*, D. Shicher and D.K. Sechrest (Eds.) Thousand Oaks, CA: Sage Publications. Pp. 203-231.

Klein, M.W. (1995). *The American Street Gang: Its Nature, Prevalence, and Control*. New York, NY: Oxford University Press.

Kisliuk, B. (1995, July 11). Ganging up on crime. *The Recorder*, p. 1. [Online]. Available: http://www.lexis-nexis.com/universe.

Knoke, D. (1982). The spread of municipal reform: Temporal, spatial, and social dynamics. *American Journal of Sociology*, 87, pp. 1314-1339.

Krasnowski, M. (2001, May 23). Loved, hated and barely reviewed, gang injunctions become issue in L.A. mayor's race. *Copley news service*. [Online]. Available: http://www.lexis-nexis.com/universe.

Kurki, L. (2000). Restorative and community justice in the United States. In *Crime and Justice: A Review of the Research*, Volume 27, M. Tonry (Ed.). Chicago: The University of Chicago Press. Pp. 235-303.

Lacy, M. (1999, September 23). Tobacco industry accused of fraud in lawsuit by U.S. *The New York Times on the Web*. [Online]. Available: http://www.nytimes.com.

Lait, M. and S. Glover. (1999, September 16). Ex-officer says he shot unarmed man. *The Los Angeles Times*. [Online]. Available: http://www.latimes.com.

Lait, M. and S. Glover. (2000a, April 18). 71 more cases may be voided due to Rampart. *The Los Angeles Times*. Available: http://www.latimes.com.

Lait, M. and S. Glover. (2000b, April 24). First arrests of officers expected in Rampart probe. *The Los Angeles Times*. [Online]. Available: http://www.latimes.com.

Landsburg, M. (2000, April 20). D.A. defends crime prevention efforts. *The Los Angeles Times*. [Online]. Available: http://www.latimes.com.

Larrubia, E. (1999, May 21). Anti-gang injunction approved. *The Los Angeles Times*. [Online]. Available: http://www.latimes.com.

Law Enforcement News. (1999, April 30). Gang-bangers given 60 days to get out of town. P. 6.

Leovy, J. (2002, March 13). Crime: Two murder suspects now in custody are among those named in federal indictment. *The Los Angeles Times*. [Online]. Available: http://www.latimes.com.

Leovy, J. and L.F. Kay. (2002, March 14). Violence: James Richards was viewed as a snitch who was harming the lucrative drug trade, officials say. *The Los Angeles Times*. [Online]. Available: http://www.latimes.com.

Levin, M. (1999, October 8). Judge rejects Cincinnati's suit against gun makers. *The Los Angeles Times*. [Online]. Available: http://www.latimes.com.

Levitt, S.D. and S.A. Venkatesh. (1999). A look at the books. *Researching Law: An ABF Update* 10 (1): 1.

Lichtblau, E. and R. Alonso-Zaldivar. (2000, March 18). Smith and Wesson to settle suits with safety changes. *The Los Angeles Times*, Metro ed., p. A-7.

Livingston, D. (1997). Police discretion and the quality of life in public places: Courts, communities, and the new policing. 97 *Columbia Law Review* 551.

Loh, L (2002, April 18). City seeks new court order to suppress 18th Street Gang. *The Los Angeles Times*. [Online]. Available: http://www.latimes.com.

Lopez, R.J. and R. Connell. (1999a, September 21). Police probe forces suspension of Rampart anti-gang injunctions. *The Los Angeles Times*. [Online]. Available: http://www.latimes.com.

Lopez, R.J. and R. Connell. (1999b, September 23). Targets of gang injunctions were named by officers in police probe. *The Los Angeles Times*. [Online]. Available: http://www.latimes.com.

Lorr, M. (1983). *Cluster Analysis for Social Scientists*. San Francisco, CA: Jossey-Bass Publishers.

Los Angeles City Attorney Gang Prosecution Section. (1995). Civil gang abatement: a community based policing tool of the Office of the Los Angeles City Attorney. In *The Modern Gang Reader*, M.W. Klein, C.L. Maxson, and J. Miller (Eds.). Los Angeles: Roxbury.

Los Angeles Times. (1999a, November 4). Four gang-related slayings unsolved after a year. [Online]. Available: http://www.latimes.com.

Los Angeles Times. (1999b, December 25). Life after the injunction was lifted. [Online]. Available: http://www.latimes.com.

Los Angeles Times. (1999c, March 6). Teen fatally shot in his driveway. [Online]. Available: http://www.latimes.com.

Los Angeles Times. (1999d, March 7). New future, new reputation. [Online]. Available: http://www.latimes.com.

Los Angeles Times. (2000a, May 5). Six convictions are voided in scandal. [Online]. Available: http://www.latimes.com.

Los Angeles Times. (2000b, May 18). Tow more cases overturned in Rampart scandal. [Online]. Available: http://www.latimes.com.

Los Angeles Times. (2000c, October 9). Bystander, 10, dies in gang killing. [Online]. Available: http://www.latimes.com.

Los Angeles Times. (2000d, February 17). Tree-planting, trash cleanup planned. Valley Edition, P. 7. [Online]. Available: http://www.lexis-nexis.com/universe.

Los Angeles Times. (2001, December 3). Editorial: A scandal's proper revival. [Online]. Available: http://www.latimes.com.

Los Angeles Times. (2002, February 21). Judge lifts injunction against gang members. [Online]. Available: http://www.latimes.com.

Lyons, L. (1987). *The Community in Urban Society*. Philadelphia, PA: Temple University Press.

MacDonald, J. (1997, February 16). Anti-gang plan may get new life. *The Orange County Register*. [Online]. Available: http://www.lexis-nexis.com/universe.

Maloney, J.A. (1991). Constitutional problems surrounding the implementation of "anti-gang" regulations in the public schools. 75 *Marquette Law Review* 179.

Marosi, R. (1999, July 3). Gang membership up, crime down. *The Los Angeles Times* [Online]. Available: http://www.latimes.com.

Martinez, D. (1994, June 18). Oakland can't ban suspected thugs. *The San Francisco Examiner*, p. A-2. [Online]. Available: http://www.lexis-nexis.com/universe.

Maxfield, M.G. and E. Babbie. (1998). *Research Methods for Criminal Justice and Criminology*. 2nd ed. Belmont, CA: Wadsworth Publishing.

Maxson, C.L. (1998, October). Gang members on the move. *Juvenile Justice Bulletin*. Washington, DC: U.S. Department of Justice, Office of Justice Programs, Office of Juvenile Justice and Delinquency Prevention.

Maxson, C.L. (1995, September). Street gangs and drug sales in two suburban cities. *Research in Brief*. Washington. DC: U.S. Department of Justice, Office of Justice Programs, National Institute of Justice.

Maxson, C.L. and T. Allen. (1997, October). *An Evaluation of the City of Inglewood's Youth Firearms Violence Initiative*. Los Angeles, CA: Social Science Research Institute, University of Southern California.

Maxson, C.L., K. Hennigan, and D. Sloane. (1997, December 16). *An Assessment of the Community Impact of Civil Gang Injunctions*. Unpublished proposal to the National Institute of Justice, Investigator-Initiated Research Program.

Maxson, C.L., K. Hennigan, and D. Sloane. (2003). For the sakes of the neighborhood: Civil gang injunctions as a gang intervention tool in Southern California. In *Policing Gangs and Youth Violence*, S. Decker (ed.). Belmont, CA: Wadsworth Publishing.

Maxson, C.L. and M.W. Klein. (2001). Play groups no longer: Urban Street gangs in the Los Angeles Region. In *From Chicago to L.A.: Making Sense of Urban Theory*, M. Dear (ed.). Newbury Park, CA: Sage Publications.

McClellan, E. (1998). *People ex rel. Gallo v. Acuna*: Pulling in the nets on criminal street gangs. 35 *San Diego Law Review* 343.

McGabey, R. M. (1986). Economic conditions, neighborhood organizations, and urban crime. In *Communities and Crime*, A.J. Reiss, Jr. and M. Tonry (Eds.). Chicago: University of Chicago Press. Pp. 231-270.

McGreevy, P. (2001, September 20). Delgadillo sets ambitious goals. *The Los Angeles Times*. [Online]. Available: http://www.latimes.com.

Meares, T.L. and D.M. Kahan. (1998). Laws and (norms of) order in the inner city. 32 *Law and Society Review* 805.

Meier, B. (1999, July 22). Local governments attack gun industry with civil lawsuits. *The New York Times on the Web*. [Online]. Available: http://www.nytimes.com.

Meier, B. and D. Johnston. (1999, September 26). How inquiry into tobacco lost its steam. *The New York Times on the Web*. [Online]. Available: http://www.nytimes.com.

Melendi, D. (1999, July 27). Supervisors OK anti-gang law ACLU calls "blatantly unconstitutional. *City News Service*. [Online]. Available: http://www.lexis-nexis.com/universe.

Meyer, J. (1999, July 23). Project prosecutes crime a neighborhood at a time. *The Los Angeles Times*. [Online]. Available: http://www.latimes.com.

Miles, M.B. and A.M. Huberman. (1994). *Qualitative Data Analysis: An Expanded Sourcebook*. 2nd ed. Thousand Oaks, CA: Sage Publications.

Moore, J. (1993). Gangs, drugs, and violence. In *Gangs: The Origins and Impact of Contemporary Youth Gangs in the United States*, S. Cummings and D.J. Monti (Eds.). Albany, NY: State University of New York Press. Pp. 27-46.

Moran, G. (1997, December 15). Fighting criminal activity with civil law: Use of injunctions as policing tactic on rise. *The San Diego Union-Tribune*, p. A-1. [Online]. Available: http://www.union-tribune.com.

Morrison, P. (2000, October 20). Slaying of Venice activist proves danger of truth-telling. *Los Angeles Times*. [Online]. Available: http://www.latimes.com.

New York Times. (2000, January 28). Bill on legal aid for gang defendants is rejected. P. A33.

Norusis, M.J. (1994). *SPSS Professional Statistics 6.1*. Chicago, IL: SPSS, Inc.

Norusis, M.J. (1993). *SPSS for Windows Base System User's Guide, Release 6.0*. Chicago, IL: SPSS, Inc.

Office of Criminal Justice Programs. (2001, September 10)). *Gang Violence Suppression Program (Multi-component)*. [Online]. Available: http://www.ocip.ca.gov/programs/pro_gv_gvsupmlti.htm.

Office of the District Attorney. (1996, June). *S.A.G.E. - Strategy Against Gang Environments: A Handbook for Community Prosecution.* Office of the District Attorney, County of Los Angeles.

Office of Juvenile Justice and Delinquency Prevention. (1997, August). *1995 National Youth Gang Survey.* Washington, DC: Office of Juvenile Justice and Delinquency Prevention, Office of Justice Programs, U.S. Department of Justice.

Office of Juvenile Justice and Delinquency Prevention. (1999). *Promising Strategies to Reduce Gun Violence: Profile No. 27.* Washington, DC: Office of Juvenile Justice and Delinquency Prevention, Office of Justice Programs, U.S. Department of Justice. [Online]. http://ojjdp.ncjrs.org/pubs/gun_violence/profile27.html.

Office of Juvenile Justice and Delinquency Prevention. (2000, November). *1998 National Youth Gang Survey.* Washington, DC: Office of Juvenile Justice and Delinquency Prevention, Office of Justice Programs, U.S. Department of Justice.

Packer, H.L. (1968). *The Limits of the Criminal Sanction.* Stanford, CA: Stanford University Press.

Padilla, F.M. (1992). *The Gang as an American Enterprise.* New Brunswick, NJ: Rutgers University Press.

Pasadena Weekly. (1995, November 24). It's time to decide. In *S.A.G.E. - Strategy Against Gang Environments: A Handbook for Community Prosecution.* Office of the District Attorney, County of Los Angeles. (1996, June). Appendix GG.

Piccalo, G. (1999a, September 24). Nation of Islam says Crips have denounced gang ties. *Los Angeles Times.* [Online]. Available: http://www.latimes.com.

Piccalo, G. (1999b, September 26). Gang shooting trial to begin this week. *Los Angeles Times.* [Online]. Available: http://www.latimes.com.

Piccalo, G. (2000, October 24). Anti-crime activist mourned as police urge cautious vigilance. *Los Angeles Times.* [Online]. Available: http://www.latimes.com.

Piccalo, G. and K. Streeter. (2000, October 19). Venice anti-gang activist killed in his driveway. *Los Angeles Times.* [Online]. Available: http://www.latimes.com.

Pinsky, M.I. (1993, August 31). Judge lifts ban on gang gatherings. *The Los Angeles Times*, part A, p. 6. [Online]. Available: http://www.lexis-nexis.com/universe.

Pogrebin, M.R. and E.D. Poole. (1989). South Korean immigrants and crime: a case study. *Journal of Ethnic Studies*, 17 (3). Pp. 47-80.

Powell, T.R. (1928, June). The Supreme Court's control over the issue of injunctions in labor disputes. *Proceedings of the Academy of Political Science: Fact-Finding in Labor Disputes*, 13 (1). Pp. 37-77.

Puig, C. (1988, April 15). Couple told to crack down on gang visitors at home. *The Los Angeles Times*, part 2, p. 8. [Online]. Available: http://www.lexis-nexis.com/universe.

Raack, D.W. (1986). A history of injunctions in England before 1700. 61 *Indiana Law Journal* 539.

Reuters. (2000, March 28). Browning rejects gun settlement with U.S. *The Los Angeles Times*. [Online]. Available: http://latimes.com.

Riccardi, N. (2000, May 11). Rampart scandal's cost to county rising fast. *The Los Angeles Times*. [Online]. Available: http://latimes.com.

Robinson, M. (1999, May 12). Cicero launches $11 million lawsuit against street gangs. *The Associated Press State and Local Wire*. [Online]. Available: http://www.lexis-nexis.com/universe.

Rodrigues, G. (2001, August 5). Rocky Delgadillo: Latino new democrat. *The Los Angeles Times*. [Online]. Available: http://www.latimes.com.

Rojas, M. (2000, February 10). City seeks injunction against Venice 13. *Los Angeles Times*. [Online]. Available: http://www.latimes.com.

Romesburg, H.C. (1984). *Cluster Analysis for Researchers.* Belmont, CA: Lifetime Learning Publications.

Rosen, M.D. (1999). Our nonuniform constitution: Geographic variations of constitutional requirements in the aid of community. 77 *Texas Law Review* 1129.

Rosenbaum, D.P. (1988). Community crime prevention: a review and synthesis of the literature. *Justice Quarterly*, 5 (3). Pp. 323-395.

Rosenzweig, D. (2000, July 19). Indictment targets 18th Street Gang in racketeering case. *Los Angeles Times*. [Online]. Available: http://www.latimes.com.

Sadovi, C. (1999, July 29). Cicero's car seizure law is unfair, ACLU suit charges. *Chicago Sun-Times*, p. 12. [Online]. Available: http://www.lexis-nexis.com/universe .

Sampson, R.J. and S.W. Raudenbush. (1999, November). Systematic social observation of public spaces: A new look at disorder in urban neighborhoods. *American Journal of Sociology* 105 (3). Pp. 603-651.

San Diego Union-Tribune. (1997, December 18). Novel crime control: Activity ban will dilute gang's power. P. B-12. [Online]. Available: http://www.union-tribune.com.

San Diego Union-Tribune. (2001a, July 19). Escondido using injunction to squash gang problem. P. B-9. [Online]. Available: http://www.lexis-nexis.com/universe.

San Diego Union-Tribune. (2001b, May 12). Concert, games set for Libby Lake Park. P. NC-2. [Online]. Available: http://www.union-tribune.com.

Sanders, W. B. (1994). *Gangbangs and Drive-bys: Grounded Culture and Juvenile Gang Violence*. Hawthorne, NY: Aldine De Gruyter.

Schweizer, K. (1999, October 21). 2nd Avenue Market ends '99 run. *The Los Angeles Times*. [Online]. Available: http://www.latimes.com.

Shah, A. (1998a, July 11). Judge limits acts of seven alleged gang members. *The Austin American-Statesman*, p. B5. [Online]. Available: http://www.lexis-nexis.com/universe.

Shah, A. (1998b, July 29). Area called 'open air market' for drug sales. *The Austin American-Statesman*, p. B1. [Online]. Available: http://www.lexis-nexis.com/universe.

Shah, A. (1998c, August 1). Judge issues injunction to curb crime. *The Austin American-Statesman*, p. A1. [Online]. Available: http://www.lexis-nexis.com/universe.

Sherman, L. (2001a, April 5). Oceanside OK's Coast Highway condo plan. *The San Diego Union-Tribune*, p. NC-2. [Online]. Available: http://www.union-tribune.com.

Sherman, L. (2001b, February 28). Oceanside commission backs builder to low-income housing. *The San Diego Union-Tribune*, p. NC-2. [Online]. Available: http://www.union-tribune.com.

Shuster, B. (1999, September 26). Prepares for fallout from police probe. *The Los Angeles Times*. [Online]. Available: http://www.latimes.com.

Short, J.F. and F.L. Strodtbeck. (1965). *Group Process and Gang Delinquency*. Chicago, IL: The University of Chicago Press.

Skipitares. (2000, July 29). Court restricts gang's activity. *San Jose Mercury News*. [Online]. Available: http://www.newslibrary.com.

Skogan, W.G. (1988). Community organizations and crime. In *Crime and Justice: A Review of Research*, Vol. 10, Tonry, M. and Morris, N. (eds.). Chicago, IL: The University of Chicago Press. Pp. 39-78.

Skogan, W.G. (1990). *Disorder and Decline: Crime and the Spiral Decay in American Neighborhoods*. NY: The Free Press.

Skogan, W.G. and M.G. Maxfield. (1981). *Coping with Crime: Individual and Neighborhood Reactions*. Beverly Hills, CA: Sage Publications.

Skogan, W.G., S.M. Hartnett, J. DuBois, J.T. Comey, J.H. Lovig, and M. Kaiser. (1999). *On the Beat: Police and Community Problem Solving*. Boulder, CO: Westview Press.

Skogan, W.G., S.M. Hartnett, J. DuBois, J.T. Comey, K. Twedt-Ball, and J.E. Gudell (2000). *Public Involvement: Community Policing in Chicago*. Washington. DC: U.S. Department of Justice, Office of Justice Programs, National Institute of Justice.

Skolnik, S. (1999). Taking it to the streets: The Department of Justice puts big money behind community prosecution. 155 *New Jersey Law Journal* 739.

Slater, E. (1999, April 29). Crime: Cicero says gangs are personae non gratae. *The Los Angeles Times*. [Online]. Available: http://www.latimes.com.

Soto, O.R. (2001a, May 12). Appeals court raises bar for anti-gang injunction. *San Diego Union-Tribune*. [Online]. Available: http://www.union-tribune.com.

Soto, O.R. (2001b, July 14). Judge imposed restrictions on gang members. *San Diego Union-Tribune*. [Online]. Available: http://www.lexis-nexis.com/universe.

Spector, M.B. (1999). Crossing the threshold: Examining the abatement of public nuisances within the home. 31 *Connecticut Law Review* 547.

Spencer, J.R. (1989). Public nuisance - A critical examination. 48 *Cambridge Law Journal* 55.

Spergel, Irving A. (1995). *The Youth Gang Problem: A Community Approach*. New York: Oxford University Press.

Steiker, Carol S. (1998). Forward: The limits of the preventive state. 88 *Journal of Criminal Law and Criminology* 771.

Stewart, G. (1998). Black codes and broken windows: The legacy of racial hegemony in gang civil injunctions. 107 *Yale Law Journal* 2249.

Streeter, K. (2000, October 21). A conflicted portrait of slain activist. *Los Angeles Times*. [Online]. Available: http://www.latimes.com.

Tamaki, J. (1995, April 11). Preemptive strike on crime stirs debate. *The Los Angeles Times*, part A; p. 3. [Online]. Available: http://www.lexis-nexis.com/universe.

Tamaki, J. (1997, May 29). Blythe St. injunction assailed in report. *The Los Angeles Times*, part B, p. 1. [Online]. Available: http://www.lexis-nexis.com/universe.

Tanamachi, C. (1998, November 25). Disputed gang injunction dropped. *The Austin American-Statesman*, p. B1. [Online]. Available: http://www.lexis-nexis.com/universe.

Taylor, R.B. (2001). *Breaking Away from Broken Windows: Baltimore Neighborhoods and the Nationwide Fight Against Crime, Grime, and Decline*. Boulder, CO: Westview Press.

Taylor, R.B. (1999, July). Crime, grime, fear, and decline: A longitudinal look. *Research in Brief.* Washington. DC: U.S. Department of Justice, Office of Justice Programs, National Institute of Justice.

Thornberry, T.P. and J. H. Burch. (1997, June). Gang members and delinquent behavior. *Juvenile Justice Bulletin*. Washington, DC: U.S. Department of Justice, Office of Justice Programs, Office of Juvenile Justice and Delinquency Prevention.

Toch, H. and J. D. Grant. (1991). *Police as Problem Solvers*. New York: Plenum Press.

Thrasher, F.M. (1927/1963). *The Gang: A Study of 1,313 Gangs in Chicago*. Chicago, IL: University of Chicago Press.

Treviot, J. (2001, May 25). Politics in the street. *LA Weekly*, p. 14. [Online]. Available: http://www.lexis-nexis.com/universe.

Uranga, R. (2002, January 4). City attorney hoping to boost quality of life in neighborhoods. *Copley News Service*. [Online]. Available: http://www.lexis-nexis.com/universe.

Vigil D. (1993). The established gang. In *Gangs: The Origins and Impact of Contemporary Youth Gangs in the United States*, S. Cummings and D.J. Monti (Eds.). Albany, NY: State University of New York Press. Pp. 95-112.

Villa, J. (2000, June 6). Injunction against gang denied: Phoenix sought ban on activities. *The Arizona Republic*, p. A1. [Online]. Available: http://www.lexis-nexis.com/universe.

Warren, R.L. (1972). *The Community in America*, 2nd ed. Chicago: Rand McNally and Co.

Wasby, S.L. (1980, March). *Political Science Contributions to the Interdisciplinary Study of Criminal Justice.* Paper presented at the meetings of the Academy of Criminal Justice Sciences, Oklahoma City, OK, March 13-15.

Weisel, D.L. (1998). The problem of street gangs and problem-oriented policing: Comments from Deborah Lamm Weisel, PERF. In *Problem-oriented Policing: Crime-specific Problems, Critical Issues, and Making POP Work*, T.O. Shelley and A.C. Grant (Eds.). Washington, DC: Police Executive Research Forum. Pp. 86-88.

Weisel, D.M. (1990). Playing the home field: A problem-oriented approach to drug control. *American Journal of Police*, 9 (1). Pp. 75-95.

Werdegar, M.M. (1999). Note: Enjoining the Constitution: The use of public nuisance abatement injunctions against urban street gangs. 51 *Stanford Law Review* 409.

Werner, E. (2001, July 25). Officer in police corruption freed. *The Los Angeles Times*. [Online]. Available: http://www.latimes.com.

Westside Weekly. (1999, September 19). Community briefs: Malibu. [Online]. Available: http://www.latimes.com.

Wides, L. (2000, March 19). Judge grants injunction on Venice 13. *The Los Angeles Times*. [Online]. Available: http://www.lexis-nexis.com/universe.

Wilson, J.Q. (1975). *Thinking About Crime*. New York, NY: Basic Books.

Wilson, J.Q. and G.L. Kelling. (1982, March). Broken windows: The police and neighborhood safety. *The Atlantic Monthly*. Pp. 29-38.

Witmer, J. and D. Anker. (1996, June). The history of the gang injunction in California. Appendix M in *S.A.G.E.: Strategy Against Gang Environments: A Handbook for Community Prosecution.* Office of the District Attorney, County of Los Angeles.

Wolcott, H.J. (1999, August 23). History of fights at fair makes gang fair game. *The Los Angeles Times*. [Online]. Available: http://www.latimes.com.

Yeager, M. (1998). *People ex rel. Gallo v. Acuna*: Cities allowed a new weapon in their arsenal for the crackdown on gangs. 19 *Whittier Law Review* 595.

Yoo, C.S. (1994). The constitutionality of enjoining criminal street gangs as public nuisances. 89 *Northwestern University Law Review* 212.

Zahniser, D. (2003, February 11). Mayor, police chief seeks law aimed at gang intimidation. *Copley News Service*, [Online]. Available: http://web.lexis-nexis.com/universe.

CASES, CODES, AND SECONDARY LEGAL SOURCES:

American Jurisprudence 2d, S.v. Nuisance, sections 35-42 (Lawyers Co-operative, 1997).

Barr v. United Methodist Church, 90 Cal. App. 3d 259 (Cal. App. 1979).

Bennis v. Michigan, 116 S. Ct. 994 (1996).

Black's Law Dictionary, 6th Ed. (West 1990).

California Code of Civil Procedure, section 369.5 (Deering 2000).

California Code of Civil Procedure, section 731 (West 1997).

California Civil Code, sections 3479 - 80 (West 1997).

California Civil Code, section 3491 (West 1997).

California Code of Civil Procedure, section 369.5 (Deering 2001).

California Code of Civil Procedure, sections 525-527 (Deering 1999).

California Code of Civil Procedure, section1209 (Deering 2001).

California Code of Civil Procedure, section 1218 (Deering 1999).

California Code of Civil Procedure, section 1222 (Deering 1999).

California Government Code, section 26507 (Deering 1999).

California Government Code, section 26528 (Deering 1999).

California Penal Code, section 166 (Deering 1999).

California Penal Code, section 186.20 et seq. (*Street Terrorism Enforcement and Prevention Act*) (West 1997).

City of Chicago v. Morales, 687 N.E.2d 53 (1997).

City of Chicago v. Morales, 119 S.Ct. 1849 (1999).

City of Erie v. Pap's A.M., 120 S.Ct. 1382 (2000).

Cohen v. California, 403 U.S. 15 (1971).

Commonwealth v. Guilfoyle, 521 N.E. 2d 984 (Mass 1988).

Corpus Juris Secundum, S.v. "nuisances", section 110 (West 1997).

Department of Housing and Urban Development v. Rucker, _ U.S. _ (2002).

Farmy v. College Housing, Inc., 48 Cal. App. 3d 166 (Cal. App. 1975).

Gonzalez v. Gallo, 117 S.Ct. 2513 (1997).

Gooding v. Wilson, 405 U.S. 519 (1972).

Harvard, Ill. v. Gaut, 660 N.E.2d 259 (Ill. App. 1996).

In re Debs, 158 U.S. 564 (1895).

In re Englebrecht, 67 Cal. App. 486 (Cal. App. 1998).

Iraheta v. Superior Court of Los Angeles, 70 Cal.App.4th 1500 (Cal.App.1999).

Kansas v. Hendricks, 117 S.Ct. 2072 (1997).

Kolender v. Lawson, 461 U.S. 352 (1983).

Madsen v. Women's Health Center, 114 S.Ct. 2516 (1994).

Milk Wagon Drivers Union of Chicago, Local 753 v. Meadowmoor, 312 U.S. 287 (1941).

Papachristou v. Jacksonville, Fla., 405 U.S. 156 (1972).

People v. Acosta, No. EC010205 (Cal. Super. Ct. Los Angeles County, 1992).

People v. Acuna, No. 729322 (Cal. Super. Ct. Santa Clara County, 1993).

People v. Acuna, 40 Cal. Rptr.2d 589 (Cal. App. 1995).

People v. Acuna, 929 P.2d 596 (Cal. 1997), cert. denied sub nom. *Gonzalez v. Gallo*, 117 S.Ct. 2513 (1997).

People v. Amaya, No. 713223 (Cal. Super. Ct. Orange County, 1993).

People v. Blythe Street Gang, No. LC20525 (Cal. Super. Ct. Los Angeles County, 1993).

People v. Canoga Park Alabama, No. BC 267153 (Cal. Super. Ct. Los Angeles County, 2002).

People v. 18th Street Gang, Declarations in Support of the Plaintiff's Motion for Injunctive Relief to Abate a Public Nuisance, No. BC175684 (Cal. Super. Ct. Los Angeles County 1997).

People v. Englebrecht, 88 Cal. App. 4th 1236 (Cal. App. 2001).

People v. Gonzalez, 910 P.2d 1366 (Cal. 1996).

People v. Green, 278 Cal. Rptr. 140 (Cal. App. 1991).

People v. Kevorkian, 534 N.W.2d 172 (Mich. App. 1995).

People v. Playboy Gangster Crips, Statement of Decision, No. WEC118860 (Cal. Super. Ct. Los Angeles County, 1987).

People v. Varrio Pesole Locos, No. NO 76652 (Cal. Super. Ct. San Diego County, 1997).

People v. Venice 13 Gang, No. SC 060375 (Cal. Super. Ct. Los Angeles County, 2000).

People v. Venice Shoreline Crips Gang, No. SC 057282 (Cal. Super. Ct. Los Angeles County 1999).

Restatement of the Law 2d, Torts 2d, sections 821A -821C (American Law Institute, 1979).

Qutb v. Strauss, 11 F.3d 488 (5th Cir. 1993).

R.A.V. v. City of St. Paul, 505 U.S. 377 (1992).

State v. United-Buckingham Freight Lines, Inc., 211 N.W.2d 288 (Iowa 1973).

United States v. Original Knights of the Ku Klux Klan, 250 F. Supp. 330 (E.D. La.).

Index

Breinigsville, PA USA
03 October 2010

246550BV00002B/4/P